A LA

The Mowats o

MW00720877

A LAIRDSHIP LOST

The Mowats of Balquholly, 1309 – 1736

Diane Baptie

TUCKWELL PRESS

For my mother, Ethel,
who would have been proud

First published in Great Britain in 2000 by
Tuckwell Press
The Mill House
Phantassie
East Linton
East Lothian EH40 3DG
Scotland

Copyright © Diane Baptie, 2000

ISBN 1 86232 052 7

British Library Cataloguing in Publication Data

A Catalogue record for this book is available
on request from the British Library

The right of Diane Baptie to be identified as the author
of this work has been asserted by her in accordance with
the Copyright, Design and Patent Act 1988

Typeset by Hewer Text Ltd, Edinburgh
Printed and bound by Cromwell Press, Trowbridge, Wiltshire

Contents

Maps

Family tree

Acknowledgements

If Tess Campbell in Canada had not employed me to find out why a forebear of hers had spent many hundreds of pounds trying to prove that he had a claim to the lands of Mergie in Kincardineshire, this book would never have been written. It was this initial research which spurred me on to find out more about the Mowats and why J. Malcolm Bulloch had called the Mowats of Balquholly 'a forgotten family'. She has continued to show a keen interest in my research and to help in tracking down much genealogical material. I am also indebted to two of my fellow researchers. John Ballantyne has unfailingly passed on all Mowat references he came across both in the Scottish Record Office (now the National Archives of Scotland) and in the Shetland Archives. Alison Mowat gave me several sheets of Mowat references, some of which proved to be invaluable. Towards the later stages, Professor Robin Adam passed on many early references and Ian B. D. Bryce shared his knowledge of castles with me. I would never have uncovered so much without their help. I would also like to thank my husband, Rob, for introducing me to the mysteries of the computer.

I would like to thank Sir John Clerk of Penicuik, Mr John Scott of Gardie, Mr D.R.M. James Duff of Hatton, the Earl of Seafield and Sir Archibald Grant of Monymusk for very kindly giving me permission to make use of and quote from their family papers. I would like to thank the Keeper of the Records of Scotland and his staff and also Brian Smith, archivist at Shetland Archives.

Diane Baptie

Introduction

During the seventeenth century, many landed families in Scotland disappeared, some having owned their lands for centuries. The causes were
manifold, but one of the most common was debt. The end of the sixteenth
century brought increased taxation and devaluation of the currency. There
were poor harvests, due to the vagaries of the weather which resulted in
years of dearth and disease, a state of affairs which was to pepper the
ensuing century, culminating in the great famine at its end. Once in debt, a
family found it almost impossible to prevent the debt from growing and
finally were forced either to sell their lands or resign them to a creditor.
This is the story of one of those families. They were a family of ancient
descent, their ancestor having come over from Normandy. Of this they
were extremely proud, and made mention of it in many of the deeds they
drew up. Tombstones which have survived are emblazoned with their
arms. Their pride almost certainly contributed to their downfall, but it also
meant that they did not give in easily. The result was that they struggled
for over a century to hold onto their lands, a remarkable length of time
considering the size of the debts they contracted and that they continued to
maintain their place in society and to sustain a standard of living they could
ill afford. They were relatively small, insignificant landowners who played
no part in the making of Scotland's history, and yet their history is part of
that history.

Very little has been written about the family, and what has been contains
many omissions and much erroneous information. What has made it possible
to reconstruct the history of their decline is the fact that they did get into
debt and were involved in a considerable amount of litigation. Several
members of the cadet branches were lawyers and one, in particular, was
employed by one of the Clerks of Session, resulting in a large number of
deeds and actions being recorded. In addition, a considerable number of
their papers have survived in several collections of private muniments.

Denominations given in the text are in pounds Scots unless otherwise
specified. There were 12 pennies in a shilling and 20 shillings in a pound. A

merk was worth 13/4d. From 1600 onwards, £1 Scots was worth 1/12th of
£1 sterling.

Sources of a genealogical nature, such as dates of marriages and deaths, are
not given in the text, but can be found in the genealogical tables in the
Appendices. It has not been possible to confirm certain relationships using
original sources, although other evidence suggests their correctness. This
uncertainty is indicated in the genealogical tables but not, for the most part,
in the text.

The spelling of place-names has been modernised, as far as possible. Some
places have long since disappeared.

In transcriptions from original documents, the missing letters of contrac-
tions have been inserted. The old letters 'yoch' and 'thorn' have been
written as 'y' and 'th' respectively, and '&' has been written as 'and'.

Since I completed my researches, the Scottish Record Office (SRO) has
been renamed the National Archives of Scotland. My references, however,
are still to the 'SRO'.

CHAPTER ONE

Financial Troubles

In September 1602, Patrick Mowat, second laird of Balquholly, sounded the alarm. He admitted that

> the haill lardschipe and leving of Bolquhollie is not onlie appeirand to fall in gret danger, Bot also the said Patrik licklie to be trublit with horningis and divers utheris inconvenientis now in his auld aige gif spedie remeid be not put thereto.[1]

He had come to accept that his attempts to solve the family's financial difficulties had failed and that they were in danger of losing lands which had been in the family for almost 300 years. What he could not have foreseen was that the ensuing century would be taken up with a sometimes desperate struggle by the main line and cadet branches to prevent those lands from falling into other hands.

The Mowat lands lay in Aberdeenshire and the county of Caithness. They had also owned lands in Ross but had disposed of these by the mid-sixteenth century.[2] Their main lands were the fertile farmlands of Loscraigie, a few miles south and east of the town of Turriff. These had been granted to Patrick de Monte Alto by King Robert the Bruce in 1309, following his defeat of the Earl of Buchan at Inverurie the previous year.[3] The lands consisted of several holdings, each with a different name. The whole extent was known as Loscraigie, but it was also the name of a part (later known as Lescraigie) and was where, in 1517, the family are recorded as having their 'house'.[4] All that remains of it are the bases of four corner towers which were incorporated into Hatton Castle in the early part of the nineteenth century. Its layout, however, can be seen on a plan made in 1769.[5] This suggests that over time alterations and additions may have been made to a much older 'strong' castle. Following the Reformation, the freeing of church lands led to an upsurge in castle building and it seems possible that it was at this period that parts of Balquholly castle may have been altered. Nearby Delgatie and Towie Barclay castles, built in the abundant red sandstone of the Turriff area, date from that time, as does Gight and several others further to the south.

Their other lands of Freswick lay in the parish of Canisbay in the north-east corner of Caithness. The ruins of their ancient courtyard castle of Buchollie can still be seen today, standing on a high rock, joined to the shore by a narrow strip of land. It was also known as Freswick castle and is reputed to have been Lambabourg, the stronghold of Sweyn Asliefson, a Norse pirate of the twelfth century. A later house may have been built at Burnside, beneath the site of present-day Freswick House, close to the shore at Freswick Bay. The lands of Freswick had also been granted to them during the fourteenth century and were confirmed to them in a charter by Robert, Duke of Albany in 1405.[6]

The Mowats had originally hailed from Normandy, their Norman name being Monhault or Montealt. Monte Alto was the Latinised form. During the reign of David I (1124–53), when Sweyn Asliefson and his fellow Norsemen were dominating the Northern and Western Isles, Norman knights who had settled in England and Wales were invited to take up estates in Scotland. One of these knights was a Montealt. The family settled in Angus, as Lords of Fern, where they remained until the early fifteenth century.[7] In time, descendants spread to other parts of the country, among whom were the Monte Altos who were granted Loscraigie and Freswick. By the fifteenth century, this family was known as Mowat, a corruption of their Norman name. During the next century, they changed the name of their lands from Loscraigie to Balquholly. Magnus Mowat of Loscraigie who succeeded to the lands in June 1516 was the last member of the family to use both the old and the new designations.[8] He almost caused the family to lose their lands at that time. They were forfeited after he, Alexander Hay of Ardendraught and David Lyon were implicated in the murder of Alexander Bannerman of Waterton. Magnus and Alexander Hay fled to Denmark. In October 1517, the Danish King wrote to Scotland expressing both men's wish to be restored to favour. The Council which had been appointed to rule by the Regent, Albany, during his absence in France, were reluctant to comply, fearing that the men's return might encourage Alexander Bannerman's kin to seek vengeance and the malefactors themselves to commit further acts of aggression. But, not more than a year later, in June 1518, through the intercession of Andrew Forman, Archbishop of St Andrews, both men were granted a pardon and their lands, castles and goods were restored to them.[9] Magnus Mowat died eight years later, possibly not from natural causes, and two years after that Alexander Hay of Ardendraught was murdered.

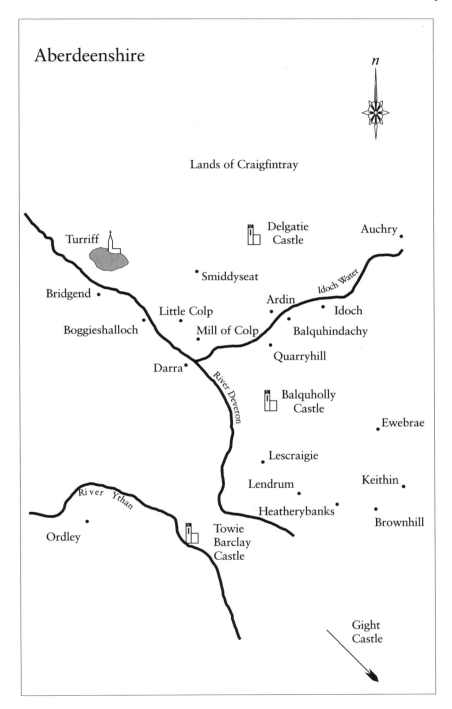

Aberdeenshire

n

Lands of Craigfintray

Turriff

Delgatie
Castle

Auchry

Smiddyseat

Idoch Water

Bridgend

Ardin

Idoch

Little Colp

Boggieshalloch

Mill of Colp

Balquhindachy

Darra

Quarryhill

River Deveron

Balquholly
Castle

Ewebrae

Lescraigie

River Ythan

Lendrum

Keithin

Heatherybanks

Brownhill

Ordley

Towie
Barclay
Castle

Gight
Castle

Magnus Mowat's heir was his son, Patrick, who was a minor at the time, and so Mr Alexander Seton of Meldrum was given the gift of the ward.[10] When Patrick succeeded to the lands in 1532, he dropped the title of Loscraigie and so became the first laird to style himself 'of Balquholly'. His father had been an ally of the Earl of Erroll and he continued the alliance. Until their suppression by James VI in 1594, the two most powerful and rebellious lords in the North-East had been the Earl of Erroll and the Marquis of Huntly. Both had remained true to the Roman Catholic faith and had continued to plot for its restoration. Lesser lairds had found it convenient to shelter under the wings of either lord. Patrick signed a bond of manrent for 11 years with George, Earl of Erroll in December 1544 and three years later accompanied him to the battle of Pinkie.[11] Following his death in 1564, his son, also Patrick, succeeded him as second laird of Balquholly. He carried on the family's alliance with the Earl, witnessing in 1577 the marriage contract drawn up between Andrew Hay of Erroll and his second wife, Agnes Sinclair, and the Earl's Testamentary Declaration in 1585.[12] After the Earl's death, his widow stayed for a short time at Balquholly, but in November 1591/2 Patrick broke with tradition, putting an end to further alliances with the new Earl, by signing a bond with the King to keep the peace and apprehend rebels.[13]

By then, Patrick was getting on in years and had pressing financial troubles. He had lived through momentous times. He had been a young man when James V, following his defeat at Solway Moss, died at Falkland. The King's unexpected death had thrown the country into confusion, for his heiress had been an infant. When Mary Queen of Scots returned from France to reign in 1561, Patrick was married with a young family. Three years after his father's death, Mary had been forcibly deposed and the Earl of Moray had become the regent. In 1572, following the Earl of Moray's death, James, Earl of Morton had been appointed regent and remained so until James VI came of age. While changing monarchs and regents may not have had any immediate influence on the life of a laird in the North-East, the Reformation in 1560 had affected everyone. Both Patrick and his father would have experienced the corruption which was rife in the Church of Rome. Lairds were required to pay a tax in the form of teind silver to the church of the parish in which their lands lay. The money should have been used to maintain the fabric of the church and to help the poor of the parish, but instead had found its way into lay hands. In 1545, for example, the parson of Turriff, John Erskine, let the teinds to the Earl of Erroll. Patrick's father withheld his teind silver from 1557 to 1562, amounting to £120. It transpired that had he paid the money, it would have been used to offset a debt owed by Mr William Hay, parson of Turriff at that time.[14] 1557 was the year in which several leading Protestant nobles, desirous of church reform, signed a Common Band to that effect. In August 1560, the Reformation Parliament met. The authority of the Pope was abolished, celebration of the Mass forbidden and a Confession of Faith approved. Scotland had become a Protestant country. Three years after that, Mr William Hay was replaced by Mr Andrew Mowat who had previously been the parish clerk. He acted as exhorter at Turriff between 1563 and 1567.[15] He appears to have been a member of the Balquholly family, witnessing documents drawn up by them, and was often to be found at the Earl of Erroll's castle at Slains along with other Mowats. His appointment as exhorter suggests that the Mowats may not have been strongly Roman Catholic, but he does not appear to have been a godly man. He was guilty of various misdemeanours, suggesting that he may have been one of the 'manie popishe preistis, unabill and of wicked life' who were initially admitted to charges after the Reformation.[16]

At that time when descent and kinship were all-important for establishing a family's position in society, the Mowats could proudly claim to be one of the oldest families in their neighbourhood. Relations with their neighbours and the manner in which they lived would therefore have been governed by the fact that they were descendants of such an ancient line. Their ancient castles at Balquholly and Freswick, although providing them with security, would also have been tangible evidence of their sense of importance in the area. A list of goods stolen from their castle at Freswick in 1603 gives a glimpse of their standard of living. They lost 24 feather beds, quantities of sheets, blankets, pillows and coverings, table covers, serviettes, 10 dozen plates, 6 quart stoups, 4 flagons, 16 dozen trenchers, 4 locked coffers within one of which was a bonnet case, containing 2 gold chains, a pair of gold bracelets, 10 gold rings, 1,770 merks in gold coins and quantities of satin, velvet, cambric and fine wool.[17]

Altering or adding to the castle at Balquholly would have been an expensive undertaking, given the many other expenses a landed family had at that time. In addition to Balquholly, the Mowats also had their castle at Freswick which would have needed to be kept in good repair. Servants would have been required whose wages would have had to be met. A great lord, such as William Keith, 4th Earl Marischal, who died in 1581, employed 100 servants, his annual wage bill amounting to £1,045/13/4d. The

Inventory of his estate gives an indication of the variety of servants employed by landowners at that time. There were the gentlemen of the household, the lord's personal servants, ordinary household servants, such as the pantryman and steward. In the kitchen were the cook, intaker, fireman, vesselman and boys. Outside were gardeners, the 'grintalman', the peat man, the man in charge of the horses, watchmen, the keeper of the park, overseers of the woods, grieves, the storer and barrowmen. The Earl Marischal had several estates and these were managed by chamberlains and their staff. Those estates which were part of baronies had bailies and other officers to administer local justice in the baron courts. All were men, apart from three 'unnamed' laundresses.[18] The Mowats were not in the same league as the noble earl and so would not have employed such a wide range of servants, but they would still have employed a fair number.

A laird's family would be an extended one and included unmarried sisters, widowed mothers and often natural children. The household would frequently be augmented by a steady stream of relatives and other visitors who would have to be fed and entertained. Accounts written at the time describe this hospitality as extremely generous. Money would have to be set aside for payment of daughters' dowries. Patrick Mowat's sister, Beatrix, for example, had married Alexander Mortimer of Auchinbady and, in a deed made in 1565, it was recorded that her husband had 'ressavit grete soumes of money in tocher with hir'.[19] When the laird died, his widow, in addition to her agreed liferent of part of the lands, would sometimes be left an additional sum, and sons and daughters, if they had not received settlements during their father's lifetime, would also have to be provided for. Fortunately for them, landowners were not required to pay annual taxes to the Crown at that time. In the past, taxes had always been levied in times of war. James VI, however, was forced to impose several large taxes in time of peace to stave off the financial crisis which threatened the earlier part of his reign. For example, a tax was imposed for his marriage in 1588, a tax for £10,000 was levied in 1593 and one for £20,000 in 1597.[20]

All these expenses had to be met out of the rents and taxes paid by the tenants on the Mowat lands. What Balquholly tenants paid at the end of the sixteenth century is difficult to ascertain. In 1636, the incoming tenant of the lands of Over and Nether Smiddyseat agreed to pay 36 bolls of meal, 4 bolls of bear, a wedder, a lamb, a dozen capons and a dozen hens.[21] The everyday needs of the laird's household were met out of the produce of the mains or home farm. It adjoined the castle and was seldom, if ever, rented out.

In 1584, Patrick Mowat had raised the rents and brought actions of removing against some of his tenants who had defaulted, indicating that it had been necessary for the family to increase its income.[22] Two years later, the harvest had failed and in 1595 the crops had been destroyed by heavy rains in the autumn, resulting in a scarcity of food for several years. In 1598, the wheat had been blasted, and in 1600 there had been a famine, resulting in many deaths throughout the country. These unforeseen circumstances had upset the economic balance, causing a steady drop in the family's income as the sixteenth century drew to a close.

When times are hard, a solution has always been to borrow. At the end of the sixteenth century, people in need of money had various options open to them. They could borrow in the short term, the date of repayment and interest being set and the arrangement being recorded in a Bond and Obligation. Sometimes, the granter of the loan would require the borrower to name someone as cautioner or surety. If the borrower defaulted, then the cautioner would be liable to repay the debt on his behalf. If the borrower required a larger sum of money, then he could wadset part of his lands. By doing so, he would pledge those lands as security, the written arrangement containing a clause of redemption and reversion, so that once the loan was repaid, the lands would revert to him. The wadsetter would be the virtual owner, drawing the rents from those lands, until such time as the loan was repaid. Another method of repaying a large loan involved the borrower granting the lender an annualrent out of his lands. In this way, the borrower could retain his lands, while the lender would receive rent off those lands annually.

All these arrangements were transferable. A Bond and Obligation, for example, could be sold to a third party or used to repay a loan, as long as the initial granter was informed. When the term of repayment arrived, the loan had to be repaid. There were four terms in the year – Candlemas, Whitsunday, Lammas and Martinmas (2nd February; 15th May; 1st August and 11th November). In the case of a Bond and Obligation, the amount repaid would include interest (by law not more than ten per cent). Some lenders would allow a borrower a certain amount of leeway and very occasionally agree to the arrangement being renewed, in the form of a Bond of Corroboration, but in general, once they found that there was no prospect of the loan being repaid, would take the borrower to court.

Long before 1602, Patrick Mowat had been forced to borrow money. He had granted bonds and obligations and wadset a considerable part of his lands. In September 1602, he had feared that 'in caice the saidis soumes be not payit at the termes to cum appointit for payment', he would have had to face legal action. This would have taken the form of 'horningis and utheris inconvenientis'. His creditor would have obtained royal letters under the signet, ordering him to repay the debt within six days. If he failed to do so, then he would have been put to the horn. The messenger who had delivered the letters to him would then have gone to the mercat cross in Aberdeen, head burgh of the Sheriffdom in which he lived. There he would have publicly read the letters, blown three blasts on his horn and denounced him a rebel of the Crown. Thereafter, all his movable goods would have been confiscated. The escheat, as it was called, would then have been gifted to his creditor for his lifetime use only. An earlier form of horning had been letters of four forms where a debtor had to endure being charged four times within 48 hours. The other 'inconvenientis', Patrick Mowat being a land-owner, would have included Letters of Inhibition being raised by his creditors against him, preventing him from alienating or selling any part of his lands. A creditor could also obtain actual ownership of part or all of his lands by apprising them. Letters of Apprising under the signet could be obtained, instructing a messenger-at-arms to summon a court of apprising in order that lands to the value of the debts could be made over to the creditor. There was also the threat of imprisonment for debt. All these 'inconve-nientis' were to affect the ensuing generations.

Patrick Mowat's timing had been unfortunate but had been necessary because of unforeseen circumstances. The loans he had contracted were affected by stringent fiscal measures introduced by James VI after his accession. At that time, the royal coffers were found to be virtually empty, and between 1583 and 1596 the coinage was devalued on various occasions. Devaluation was necessary, there being a shortage of bullion which pre-vented the minting of new coins. When new coins were minted, they were produced from old coinage which had been handed in to be melted down. Sometimes these old coins were merely over-stamped. Coins in common use were not restricted to Scottish ones, but included those from many European countries. As Scottish coins became debased with each new minting, foreign coins, having a greater gold and silver content, became more valuable. Bad money drove out good as a result, the good-quality coins finding their way into hoards. This would explain the presence of 1,770 merks in 'fyne cunzeit gold' and the gold jewellery in the bonnet case taken from Freswick in 1603.

When deeds involving financial arrangements were drawn up, the amount was always given in merks or pounds, shillings and pence. These were the currencies used for accounting purposes. The amount was sometimes qualified with 'in silver and gold'. Each coin, whether minted in Scotland or abroad, had a value in merks or pounds, the value changing with great frequency during the latter part of the sixteenth century. Patrick Mowat would therefore have found that he would have had to pay out far more in terms of actual money than the original accounting money agreed between him and his creditors, when the terms of repayment came round.

Ten years before Patrick Mowat sounded the alarm, he had possessed a somewhat unusual 'financial asset'. He had an unmarried son and heir, Magnus. A solution to their difficulties in 1592 had been to find a bride for him who would bring in a sufficiently large dowry. Elizabeth Cheyne (later called Isobel), Lady Kermucks, daughter of William Cheyne of Arnage, was chosen. She had been recently widowed. Her first husband, John Kennedy of Kermucks, had died the previous year.[23] The marriage contract was drawn up on 3rd November 1592. Patrick, for his part of the bargain, agreed to grant Magnus and Elizabeth Lescraigie and to make Magnus his universal successor. They were to be given 16 chalders of oats, but would have to buy the oxen and seed corn themselves. Elizabeth was to receive the liferent of the lands of Lescraigie, Broadfoord and Broadgreens, Darra and Balmellie and the mill of Colp. She was also to receive the teind sheaves (one-tenth of the annual produce of the lands), and should she survive Magnus was to get a reasonable terce as well as Magnus's mother's terce after her death – in all a very generous settlement. However, it soon became apparent why this was to be so. Magnus and Elizabeth, for their part, were to pay Patrick 6,000 merks (£4,000) in instalments over two years. The money was to be used to pay Patrick's debts and to redeem the wadset lands. In addition, part of it was to be used for settlements on his two unmarried daughters and his second son, James, then living at Smiddyseat.[24] The 6,000 merks was to be given by Elizabeth Cheyne's father who was well aware that it was to be used for Patrick and Magnus's relief.[25] The marriage contract also listed Patrick's debts which amounted to more than 6,000 merks, the largest amount being owed to the Gardins of Blackford and appearing to have been part of the tocher for Patrick's daughter, Christine, who had married James Gardin, fiar of Blackford, in 1591.[26] Elizabeth Cheyne's dowry money was therefore insufficient to cover Patrick's debts and proposed settlements. It also meant that she and Magnus would receive no part of it, but Elizabeth had additional income from her previous marriage in the form of the liferent of 32 oxgates of the Kermucks lands in Ellon and was due to receive 54 bolls of meal from the lands of Kirkhill annually.[27]

Having temporarily alleviated the situation, there is little evidence that Patrick Mowat took steps to economise. In 1595, he arranged to lend 4,200 merks (£2,800) to the Meldrums of Fyvie. In exchange, he was to have received the wadset of the lands of Ordley in the neighbouring parish of Auchterless. In November 1596, they met at Turriff where he made a down-payment of just 200 merks (£133/6/8d). Not surprisingly, the Meldrums refused to formalise the agreement.[28] It would have taken great strength of character, on Patrick's part, to accept that he and his family were living beyond their means and had a somewhat inflated opinion of their place in society. His son, Magnus, had been forced through circumstances to sign away his wife's dowry. After their marriage, he and his wife received none of the income due from her previous marriage.[29] The income from Lescraigie appears to have been insufficient for their needs. In 1598, Magnus approached his cousin, James Mowat, a solicitor or writer in Edinburgh, for a loan. James Mowat agreed to lend him 5,000 merks (£3,333/6/8d) 'for the luif I haif and beiris to the said Magnus and for the weill and standing of his hous' and further agreed not to pursue him in the courts, should the money not be repaid at the agreed term.[30] Magnus must have given James particularly strong assurances that the money would be repaid in time, although the inclusion of the 'weill and standing of his hous' suggests that he also appealed to their shared pride in their family name. The Bond and Obligation was drawn up at Edinburgh on the last day of July 1598. It was to play a central role in later events.

In November 1600, Patrick journeyed to Aberdeen to have a Bond and Obligation drawn up in order to honour his promise made in the marriage contract to name Magnus and his heirs his universal successors. He was careful on this occasion to include the word 'lawful', missing in the marriage contract with regard to Magnus's heirs, as Magnus had an illegitimate son, Thomas. He also had a clause inserted in which he named four overseers – Alexander Calder of Asloun, Mr John Cheyne of Pitfichie, Patrick Copland of Idoch and Patrick Cheyne of Ferryhill, to make sure that, after his death, Magnus behaved himself 'as becumis ane loveing sone in homage humilitie and reverence towardis his fatheris 'tome' in all tyme cuming'. Before that, however, they were to ensure that Magnus did not make 'defectioun in his honesty dewtie and behaviour' towards him. If he did, then Patrick would 'be in his awin place as I wes befoir'.[31] The inclusion of these clauses suggests that all was not well between father and son. This became more apparent when Magnus brought an action against his father in January 1601, claiming that although his father had made a bond and obligation in his favour, there was evidence that he planned to dispose of some of the Balquholly property without his consent, thereby defrauding him of his heritable right and succession.[32]

Further pressure from Magnus resulted in a Contract being drawn up between them in September 1602 in which Patrick made the admission about the family's plight. The dowry money and James Mowat's loan had temporarily alleviated the earlier financial crisis, but the old debts had been replaced by new ones. Patrick admitted that he owed 4,530 merks (£3,020) in bonds and obligations and wadsets which he personally had contracted and further debts of 9,200 merks (£6,133/6/8d) incurred with the consent of Magnus. He had therefore decided to yield to Magnus and hand over the reins. He was an old man and the strain of trying to keep the family solvent had become too much for him. Magnus was to receive all the lands and the two castles with their contents. He was also to receive a Decreet of the Court of Session for the removing of James Sinclair of Murkle who was illegally occupying a part of their Caithness lands. Magnus's mother Christine Ogilvy's liferent of the teind sheaves and her terce were reserved. Magnus was to repay all the debts. He was also to

> susteine the said Patrik his father and Cristiane Ogilvie his mother in
> houshald in meit, claythes and utheris necesser with ane man servand to
> serve his said father and ane woman servand to serve his said mother
> during the lyftyme of the said Patrik as also the said Elizabethe Mowat
> his sister ay and quhill sho be mareit.

When Elizabeth did marry, she was to receive 3,000 merks (£2,000) in tocher. Once again, Patrick included overseers to make sure that Magnus observed the terms of the contract and behaved as 'ane godlie and loving sone' towards his father and mother. If the overseers found that he had failed to do so, they were at liberty to deal with him as they thought fit. There was an air of weariness and resignation in Patrick's statement that he wished to 'haif na farder ail bot to serve god and leive at his awin eis'.[33] He died shortly afterwards, leaving Magnus facing a daunting task.

SOURCES:
1. RD1/91 f.71
2. Mey papers (SRO) – GD96/8; Cromartie muniments (SRO) – GD305/1/19/1–3; 5, 6, 8–10
3. *RMS* i, App 2, 36
4. *ADCP*, 94
5. RHP 2529 – Photostat copy of plan of Park and Policy of Hatton Lodge, 1769 (Duff of Hatton muniments)
6. *RMS* i, 929
7. A J Warden – *Angus or Forfarshire*, iii, 268
8. *RSS* i, no.2781
9. *ER* xiv, 346; D Hay (ed.) – *Letters of James V*, 53, 61; T Riis – *Should Auld Acquaintance Be Forgot*, i, 139
10. *RSS* i, no.3561
11. Inventory of Erroll Charters (NRAS – 0925), nos. 438, 456
12. Ibid, nos. 862; 1097; 1149
13. *RPC* iv, 814 (first series)
14. RD1/6 f.151
15. Charles H Haws – *Scottish Parish Clergy at the Reformation, 1540–1574* (Scottish Record Society), 241; Inventory of Erroll Charters (NRAS – 0925), no. 516
16. F D Bardgett – *Scotland Reformed*, 91
17. CS15/89 – 5 Jan 1604
18. Edinburgh Commissary Testaments, CC8/8/11f.56 – 15 June 1582 – Testament of William Keith, Earl Marischal
19. RD1/8 f.365; CS7/85 f.365
20. A and H Tayler – *The Valuation Roll of the County of Aberdeen for the Year 1667* (TSC), xii
21. RD1/541 f.281
22. *Records of the Sheriff Court of Aberdeenshire* (NSC), i, 307
23. *SN&Q*, 2nd series, iii, 174
24. Mey papers (SRO) – GD96/240
25. RD1/478 – 11 Nov 1634
26. CS7/409 – 22 Dec 1627; 28 Mar 1628
27. CS7/226 – 19 Feb 1607; DI 21/10 f.57
28. CS7/453 – 18 Jul 1632
29. DI 21/10 f.57
30. Mey papers (SRO) – GD96/279
31. RD1/75 f.456
32. DI 21/10 f.244
33. RD1/91 f.71

CHAPTER TWO

Conflicts

Not only had James VI to contend with a lack of money, but he had also inherited a kingdom wracked with blood feuds. In his *Basilikon Doron*, written in 1597, he listed three iniquities the nobles were guilty of, the third being:

> For any displeasure that they apprehend to be done against them by their neighbour, to take up a plaine feide against him and without respect for God, King or Commonweale to bang it out bravelie, he and all his kin against him and all his.[1]

This third iniquity was particularly appropriate with regard to the lairds in the North-East. Most were fairly modest landowners and jealousies existed among them, usually involving land. Land meant wealth and power. Disputes arose over the ownership and boundaries of lands. The parties seldom settled their quarrel in court, but instead indulged in the 'wrangus, violent and universall spoliation, awaytaking, resetting, intrometting, detenying and withhalding' of each other's goods and gear. This involved the stealing of cattle, horses and sheep. Corn growing in the ground would be trampled down and tenants and servants intimidated. If a victim did seek retribution in the courts, the outcome generally resulted in the aggressor being put to the horn and his goods being confiscated. In 1545, Patrick Mowat, first laird, and his brother-in-law, John Pantoun of Pitmedden, had had their goods confiscated for fire-raising and committing 'certane poyntes of oppressioun' against John Cheyne of Arnage and his servants, for example.[2]

For many years, the Mowats had been in dispute with their neighbours, the Craigs of Craigfintray. Relations had become strained after Margaret Mowat, one of the first laird's daughters, had divorced John Craig of Craigfintray in November 1562 and had then run off with his uncle.[3] Out of this grew a quarrel over the 6 oxengate lands of Balmellie, just outside Turriff. In 1574, Patrick Mowat, second laird, and two of his servants together with Gilbert Mowat and Mr Andrew Mowat in Turriff were accused by four tenants of the Craigs of stealing 30 oxen, 14 work horses, 39 milk cows with their 'following' and 40 milk ewes at harvest time in September 1573. The raid had been the outcome of a quarrel between Gilbert Mowat and William Craig of Craigfintray over the lands of Balmellie. Gilbert Mowat and William Adaill, one of Patrick's servants, had actually stolen the animals, but the fact that Patrick Mowat was among those accused indicates that he had condoned the raid.[4] There was no mention of Balmellie being part of the lands of Balquholly when the King granted the Gift of the non-entry to Magnus in 1589. During James VI's minority, Patrick Mowat had applied for the two separate baronies of Freswick and Balquholly to be united into one. He had omitted to pay for the alteration to be made and had also failed to 'enter' or record the change, hence the Gift of his non-entry to his son.[5] The Mowats and Craigs were still disputing the ownership of Balmellie 20 years after the stock had been stolen from the tenants. In February 1594/5, Patrick Mowat had to find someone to stand as surety or cautioner to ensure that he would not harm Lewis Craig, son and heir of Mr Thomas Craig, advocate, by then heritable proprietor of Balmellie.[6] Later in that year, however, money changed hands, ending the long-running dispute between them, and thereafter Balmellie featured in Mowat charters.[7]

In the seventh year of her reign, Mary Queen of Scots' governor, the Earl of Arran, issued Letters in her name requiring the landowners in Aberdeen-shire to convene at Aberdeen to attend an Inquest for Taxation because 'our auld enemies of Ingland intendis the Spring of this yeir to invaid our Realme with all thair force and power'. At a court held on 5th January 1548/9, the return of 33 barons who attended was completed. The annual income of each laird whose lands gave four pounds to twenty shillings of 'auld extent' was recorded. This income bore no relation to the actual income from their lands in 1548/9, it being of 'auld extent'. Whether the 'auld extent' went back to the valuation made in the thirteenth century during the reign of Alexander III (1249–86) or to the 'new extent' of 1366, during the reign of David II (1329–71), is not certain. What is of value was the ranking in the return. Heading the list was the Marquis of Huntly whose valued rent was £306/13/8d. In the vicinity of Balquholly, the laird of Fyvie's valued rent was £40, the lairds of Delgatie and Towie Barclay £20, the laird of Gight £12 and the laird of Balquholly £8. Below the Mowats were the Coplands of Idoch at £6 and the laird of Craigfintray at 40 shillings. In these terms, the Mowats were small, insignificant lairds.[8] What is significant, however, is that later feuds in which the Mowats were involved were with those neighbours just above or below them in the return and with some who did not qualify to be included. Apart from the dispute with the Craigs, Patrick Mowat, second laird, appears to have lived on relatively peaceable terms with his neighbours and, by signing the bond with the King to keep the peace in 1591/2, stayed out of the conflict between the King and the Earl of Erroll and Marquis of Huntly, thereby saving Balquholly from the fate which befell nearby Delgatie castle which had to withstand a siege of six weeks by the King's men and suffered considerable damage as a result. The Marquis of Huntly's castle was severely damaged and the King personally supervised the blowing up of the Earl of Erroll's castle at Slains in 1594.

The man who stood surety for Patrick Mowat in the bond with the King was an immediate neighbour, Patrick Copland of Idoch. He was also one of the cautioners in February 1594/5, one of the overseers named in the Bond and Obligation made between Patrick and Magnus and, in the Contract which followed in 1602, being also a witness to the latter. He was the eldest son of Thomas Copland of Idoch (d.1574). Thomas Copland's second wife was Janet Mowat who probably belonged to the Balquholly family. So Patrick Copland and Patrick Mowat were bound to one another in friendship and by marriage. The amity which existed between them did not extend to Magnus, however. A month after the Contract was signed in 1602, Patrick Copland raided Balquholly, taking away 'guidis, geir, cornis, cattell, hors, nolt, meiris, oxen, ky, scheip and utheris'.[9] His action may have been prompted by the fact that the Mowats owed him and his brother 900 merks (£600), but his third brother Alexander's invasion of Freswick and 'keeping it a house of war' later in that year suggests there was more to it.[10] Perhaps the debts owed to the Coplands had had some connection with building work at Balquholly or Freswick. In 1590, Patrick Copland had been appointed warden of all the masons in the North-East by the King, his father and grandfather also having held the office.[11] His brother, Alexander, appears to have been a freebooter. In January 1604, he was lodging with widow Ramsay in Edinburgh, 'he not haiffing ony uther dwelling place formerlie . . . within this realme thir twa yeiris bygone'.[12] Not only did Alexander steal the household goods already listed from Freswick castle, but he also took away 24 drawing oxen, 12 cows and their calves, 6 mares and their foals, 8 work horses, 60 four-year-old wedders, 100 milk ewes and 40 young sheep. The milk ewes alone were valued at £3 each, so that the spoils taken by the brothers from both castles far exceeded the money owed to them.

The Coplands owned less land than the Mowats. Their father, Thomas Copland, had been a portioner of Idoch, owning only half the lands.[13] It is possible that Patrick Copland, being privy to Mowat affairs, saw an opportunity of taking advantage of them, knowing them to be in a weak position financially. By robbing both castles and their mains, he and his brothers could have forced the Mowats to quit their lands. Patrick Copland's raid, having taken place after Patrick Mowat had handed over control to his son, could also have been 'justified' in his role as one of the overseers.

Patrick Copland had had troubles of his own following the death of his father. He had been a minor at the time and the Regent, James, Earl of Morton, had gifted the Ward and Marriage to his confidant, George Auchinleck of Balmanno, who had, in turn, assigned the gift to his cousin, William Auchinleck of Shethin.[14] This meant that during Patrick's minority, the income from Idoch went into Auchinleck purses and they had the right to marry him to a woman of their choosing. As an Elizabeth Auchinleck became his wife, it would appear that this is exactly what they did.[15] However, the Auchinlecks found Patrick's stepmother, Janet Mowat, a lady to be reckoned with. Although she had no liferent agreement, she stubbornly stayed put at Idoch, despite a prolonged action by William Auchinleck to force her to remove.[16] Even her stepson was forced to bring an action against her when he came of age. She finally left after she married John Roy Grant of Carron.[17] Her relationship to the Balquholly family may also have contributed towards the Coplands' later aggression towards Magnus.

What was not mentioned in the Contract of 1602 was that further losses had been incurred by the Mowats in 1601 when they had had to endure several raids by the notorious Gordons of Gight. The raids appear to have stemmed from the Mowats' recent acquisition of the lands of Balmellie, although the Gordons hardly needed an excuse to go pillaging. In May of that year, the trouble began when George Gordon of Bridgend, nephew of William Gordon of Gight and occupier of the lands adjacent to Balmellie, began to build a fold dyke on Mowat land. One of Magnus's servants tried to stop him and was wounded. The next month, Gordon of Bridgend and William Gordon of Gight, with twenty men armed with hagbuts, pistolets, swords and lances, rode through the fields of Balquholly, trampling down the corn. In this raid, they attacked three more of Magnus's servants. Robert Catto was shot in the face, Andrew Jaffray cut with a sword on his shoulder and Thomas Cheyne threatened with a pistol. This raid was followed by yet another one, this time by 300 men wearing steel bonnets, gauntlets and jacks and armed with hagbuts and spears who once again trampled down the corn. These 'evill disposed personis' then went on to break the doors and windows of the houses of Mowat tenants at Lescraigie, Jackston and Brownhill. One of the tenants, William Smith, was 'violentlie dang' within his own house and then taken off to Gight. The rest of the raiders rounded off the day by pillaging the town of Turriff. The outcome of an action brought against them by Magnus was that the Lords ordered the Gordons to be summoned to Edinburgh to answer the charge. A messenger was dispatched to deliver the Summons at Gight castle. On his way back to Aberdeen, he was pursued by the Gordons who took him back to Gight where the summons was boiled up in a soup and the messenger forced to eat it.[18] No wonder John Gordon of Ardlogie, second son of the laird of Gight, could later plead that he had never been summoned![19]

Magnus had conceived a deadly hatred for John Gordon of Ardlogie. He alleged that John Gordon was attempting to drive him and his tenants off Balquholly lands, so that he could 'appropriat the samen to himself'.[20] John Gordon appears to have been a particularly aggressive and violent character. He was the founder of a gang of thugs known as the 'Society of Boys'. While the raids on Balquholly had been against property and the tenants, John Gordon had singled out Magnus as his target. He had shot in through the windows of the castle at Balquholly, fired at Magnus when he was on his way to the kirk at Turriff, hidden in the fields of Balquholly, intending to ambush him 'to bereave him of his life', and had even followed him to the port of Brechin where he had once again attempted to kill him.[21] Magnus was no match for the seven sons of Gordon of Gight. Nor did he get anywhere with his action against Alexander Copland, who even tried to intimidate Magnus's cousin, Alexander Mowat, a writer in Edinburgh, who had been dealing with Magnus's action against him. His action against Patrick Copland of Idoch was cut short by Patrick's death at the beginning of 1606.[22]

In 1607, Magnus had to find caution for 2,000 merks (£1,333/6/8d) not to harm another neighbour, Patrick Con of Auchry, by then the heritable proprietor of half the lands of Idoch, and Elizabeth Auchinleck, Patrick Copland's widow. Conflict had broken out amongst them over Elizabeth Auchinleck's liferent possession of Balquhindachy. This time the aggression appears to have been started by Magnus who with his servants pastured cattle on Idoch land, made paths through the fields and broke down the fold dykes. They also took peats from the mosses of Idoch daily between January

and July 1607, arming themselves with 'hagbuts and pistoletes'. In retaliation, Patrick Con enlisted the services of Magnus's old enemy, John Gordon
of Ardlogie, as well as Alexander Copland of Idoch, William Seton of
Mounie and Mr Robert Udny of Tillycorthie who arrived at Glenhill on
Balquholly lands where tenants were cutting peats and loading them onto
carts. They forced the tenants to drive their laden carts to Idoch and Auchry,
breaking up those not loaded and casting what they had destroyed back into
the peat bogs. Later in the day, John Gordon and his men, egged on by Con
of Auchry and Copland of Idoch, went to Balquholly castle 'and thair rankit
thame selffes' between it and the moss, hoping to kill Magnus when he
emerged from the castle, but fortunately he stayed inside.[23] The following
January, Magnus requested the amount of caution to be reduced, saying that
he could only find caution for 1,000 merks (£666/13/4d), he being but 'ane
mean gentilman'.[24]

He certainly was 'ane mean gentilman'. He had inherited an estate heavily
burdened with debts. Apart from the poor harvests suffered in the closing
years of the sixteenth century, he had also had to endure his crops being
trampled down and both castles being robbed and the home farms denuded
of stock. He had spent money raising actions in the Court of Session and
presented Petitions to the Privy Council against his aggressors which had had
little effect.

A curious action was brought by Magnus against his two young daughters,
Elspeth and Christian, in June 1603. Two years before, he had granted them
the lands of Lescraigie and Darra in the form of a wadset. The redemption
involved his paying each of them a gold sun crown, a nominal amount. In
May 1603, he summoned them to appear at Turriff with their tutors or
curators 'gif thay ony have' to receive the coin and grant him a renunciation of
the lands. Given that the elder daughter would have been at best 10 years old,
it is not surprising that they did not appear. What is surprising is that in the
following month, Magnus brought an action against them in the Court of
Session in Edinburgh for their delaying.[25] He needed the lands urgently as he
intended wadsetting them to William Gordon and his wife, Janet Con.[26] It is
interesting to speculate as to why he had granted the lands to his daughters in
the first place. Had he alienated them to prevent his father disposing of them,
had he done so to prevent them falling into the hands of creditors or had
Elizabeth Cheyne's family forced him to do so, fearing that Elizabeth would
lose her liferent of them and her daughters have no settlements made on
them? What is even more curious is that the children were initially summoned

to Turriff, which was a stone's throw from Balquholly castle. This action suggests that his daughters may not have been living at the castle and also that a rift may have arisen between him and his wife.

If he and his wife were estranged, this would certainly explain later conflict with Con of Auchry whose son, Alexander Con, had married Margaret Kennedy, Elizabeth Cheyne's daughter by her first marriage. Relations between Magnus and Alexander Con and his wife were strained. In July 1603, Magnus had agreed to grant them the old mill of Arnage, known as the Doupmylne, part of the Cheyne lands.[27] He himself had obtained a charter of the mill from his brother-in-law, Walter Cheyne of Arnage, on 27th April 1597, but appears to have deliberately delayed granting Alexander Con and his wife a charter of his own.[28]

Many of those with whom Magnus clashed had remained and continued to remain firm adherents of the Roman Catholic church. Patrick Con of Auchry, out of the country by 1631, was excommunicated, nonetheless. Those left in charge of his estate appropriated it and threw him into destitution.[29] William Gordon of Gight had been excommunicated in 1595, his eldest son being ordered by the Privy Council to conform to the true religion in 1612.[30] Another son, John Gordon of Ardlogie, formed his 'Society of Boys', using Rome as a front for their nefarious deeds. (Magnus had on one occasion accused the Gordons of not behaving 'as it becomis Christianis'.) Elizabeth Cheyne's first husband was buried in St Nicholas churchyard, Aberdeen, being heritable constable of that burgh, but had been a staunch Catholic. Their son, James Kennedy of Kermucks, was excommunicated in 1604.[31] Even her own family still adhered to the Roman Catholic faith. Patrick Mowat of Balquholly died a Roman Catholic. His younger son, James Mowat of Smiddyseat, almost certainly remained one, but Magnus appears to have espoused the Reformed Church and in so doing would have aroused further animosity in those who had not.

The feuds appear to have abated as time wore on. Some of Magnus's aggressors, such as the Gordons of Gight, turned their attention to new targets, some like the Cons and Coplands moved away, while others died. It was fortunate for Magnus that the feuds did not persist, as he had many other problems to contend with.

SOURCES

1. James I – *Basilikon Doron*, ed. James Craigie (Scottish Text Society), 83.
2. *RSS* iii, no.1376.

3. R Pitcairn – *Criminal Trials*, i, part ii,*459
4. CS7/60 f.87
5. PS1/60 f.20 – Patrick Mowat appears to have resigned his lands into the King's hands during the King's minority; Seafield muniments (SRO) – GD248/408/2
6. *RPC* v, 644 (first series)
7. RD1/97 f.389
8. SC1/2/2 – inserted at end of volume dated 1573
9. CS7/205 – 5 Jan 1603
10. *RPC* vi, 804 (first series); RD1/91 f.71
11. D Stevenson – *The Origins of Freemasonry*, 32
12. CS15/89 – 5 Jan 1604
13. *Records of the Sheriff Court of Aberdeenshire* (NSC), i, 193
14. *Ibid*, 225
15. *RMS* vii, 121
16. SC1/2/2 – 20 June, 5 July, 30 July 1575; 10 May, 23 June, 3 Oct, 9 Oct 1576
17. RD1/20/1 f.351
18. DI 21/11 f.402
19. *RPC* viii, 657 (first series)
20. DI 21/11 f.402
21. *RPC* v, 657 (first series)
22. *Records of the Sheriff Court of Aberdeenshire* (NSC), ii, 60
23. *RPC* xiv, 495, 508, 537 (first series)
24. *RPC* viii, Addenda, 42 (first series)
25. CS7/206 – 23 June 1603
26. *Records of the Sheriff Court of Aberdeenshire* (NSC), ii, 99
27. DI 21/14 – 20 June 1608
28. Mey papers (SRO) – GD96/265; DI 21/15 f.17
29. R Chambers – *Domestic Annals of Scotland*, ii, 59
30. J Malcolm Bulloch – *House of Gordon*, i, 38; *RPC* viii, 50 (first series)
31. *SN&Q*, 2nd series, iii, 174

CHAPTER THREE

The Lawyer Sons

Patrick Mowat, second laird, had two brothers, James and Magnus, who, as young men, left Balquholly and settled in the parish of Fetteresso in Kincardineshire. Magnus appears to have been the first to move. In 1568, he and his wife, Isobel Hay, were granted a charter of the small property of Coupar's croft by the Hays of Ury.[1] It therefore seems likely that Isobel Hay was a member of that family. The property appears to have been in the burgh of Cowie, a thriving burgh at the end of the sixteenth century, as Magnus is recorded as 'in Cowie'. The Hays of Ury were a cadet branch of the house of Erroll and Magnus's father's and grandfather's alliances with the Earls of Erroll must have occasioned the initial contact. James married Agnes Auchinleck who belonged to the Balmanno family. The Auchinlecks had connections with Idoch after 1574, as has already been noted, and it seems likely that James and his wife met at Balquholly. One of their grandsons claimed in 1661 that the family had been in possession of their farm in Kincardineshire for over 80 years, which puts their arrival there in the 1580s.[2] James became the well-to-do tenant of Redcloak and Over Auquorties, also Hay properties, although the latter was acquired by the Earl Marischal at the beginning of the seventeenth century. George, 5th Earl Marischal, granted them a lease at that time.[3] Their house was at Redcloak about a mile away from Cowie where Magnus and his wife lived. Agnes Auchinleck also had a married sister living at Annamuick in the neighbouring parish of Glenbervie.[4] While the brothers may have escaped the heavy burdens which the main line was saddled with, being scions of an ancient house, they would have had some standing in the community. When James's son, George, was appointed Great Bailie of the baron court of Ury in March 1620, he was described as 'ane discreit gentilmane'.[5] Magnus's son, John, a student of grammar, was granted the Gifts of the chaplainries of the Rude in Elgin and of Navity belonging to the Cathedral Church of Ross in 1587. The Gift of the chaplainry of the Rude had actually been made on 13th May 1583 'for the support of the said John at the school' for seven years, but when his father, as his lawful administrator, had attempted to uplift the rents for that year, he had met with opposition and the tenants had been ordered to be warded in the castle of Blackness.[6] The subsequent Gift appears to have been confirmation of the earlier one. Their social standing would, therefore, have required both families to maintain a certain standard of living. Income would have come from the produce of the lands and the animals they reared. They would also have drawn rents from their sub-tenants. Outgoings would have included servants' wages. James would have had to pay rent and customs and to have given his services or those of his servants to the Hays and the Earl Marischal when required. Both he and his brother would have had to pay teind silver annually, although this would not have amounted to much. He would also have had to pay multure meal to the miller of the mill to which he was thirled. In 1604, the money value of the rent of Redcloak was £108 a year.[7] By 1634, James's son, George, was paying £20 money rent at the terms of Whitsunday and Martinmas, 4 bolls of malt, 3 bolls of horse corn, 4 wedders, 18 capons and 18 poultry.[8] This rent had been set in August 1617. Both James and Magnus would have had to lay out money for their daughters' dowries, although Magnus had only one daughter and James two. When Agnes Auchinleck, by then a widow, died in 1622, an inventory was taken of her goods and gear. She had 22 drawing oxen, 9 cows and their calves, 7 young beasts, 4 horses, 2 mares, 60 ewes, 60 hogs (young sheep), 40 wedders, 40 bolls of infield oats, 40 bolls of bear and 240 bolls of outfield oats. The 'insicht plenishings' of the house were valued at £266/13/4d. When her son, George, died in July 1645, the inventory taken then was almost the same.[9] They were wealthy farmers.

The brothers did not escape the feuds. Both their names and those of their sons appear in the records of the Privy Council, although the quarrels in which they were involved were petty compared to those their nephew, Magnus Mowat of Balquholly, was caught up in. In 1604, an act was ratified by the baron court of Ury in an attempt to put an end to

> the mennifauld trublis and molestationis that accuris amangis nychtbouris and tennentis in the grund, the one oppressing the wther be violence.

The fine was set at £10 and included compensation being paid to the victim.[10]

James Mowat had five sons, three of whom became lawyers in Edinburgh, as did the eldest son of his brother, Magnus. James VI did much to organise the legal profession. The records of the time reflect the upsurge in matters of the law, containing deeds recorded and actions brought by people from all walks of life wishing to settle disputes or record arrangements and transactions which would stand 'the strenth of time'. It followed therefore that to be a lawyer could be very lucrative, especially if chosen to be the 'doer' for a powerful lord. Recompense could take the form of a pension for life, guaranteeing an annual income. Income could be used to lend out at interest, and property both movable and immovable could be acquired through legal channels, if clients did not settle their bills.

A young man would start his legal career by becoming apprenticed to an established lawyer. He would act as his servitor while learning and would be engaged in writing documents in his 'buith'. After serving his apprenticeship, he would become a solicitor or writer. He could also became a Writer to the Signet. The Society of Writers to the Signet was formed in 1594, being an exclusive society, having the right to sign documents passed by the Court of Session. He could also become an advocate, a member of the Scottish Bar, and thereby plead cases in the superior courts. The Faculty of Advocates was formed in 1619, prospective members being required to sit an entrance examination.

James Mowat, eldest son of Magnus, was the first member of the family to move to Edinburgh where he became servitor to the Commissary Clerk, Mr John Nicolson, advocate.[11] In 1587, he was made solicitor for the ministers of the kirk, the King

> understanding the great skaith and hinder that the ministrie within this realme hes sustenit thir mony yeiris bygone throw the want of ane diligent sollicitare to await and attend upoun thair effairis persewit and defendit befoir the lordis of counsall and sessionis.

He was to receive a fee of £100 to be paid out of the income of the abbey of Fearn and the priory of Beauly.[12] James Mowat's first wife was Isobel Strang, who was dead by 1593. He then married Jonet Hay, daughter of the leading reformer, Mr George Hay, minister of Rathven. She too did not live long, leaving him with two infant daughters. He abandoned his career in Edinburgh and returned initially to Kincardineshire where his mother was still living. She accompanied him to Aberdeen where they set up house in the Castle Gate.[13] There, he started his own legal practice and became solicitor for the burgh, having already been made a burgesss *ex gratia* in 1596 for serving them while he had been in Edinburgh. During his time in Edinburgh he had acted as the Earl of Caithness's 'doer' and had been promised a yearly pension of £20. The Earl had been slow in honouring the agreement, and when James moved to Aberdeen he brought an action against him for non-payment of the pension. The Earl's lawyer, well-versed in the niceties of the law, argued that the original agreement had only applied to the time James had been in Edinburgh – between 1580 and 1599.[14] There was no shortage of work or people to lend money to up north, however. Before the death of his first wife, James had acquired the wadset of Pathbeth (Powbair?), part of the mains of Ury in his native parish of Fetteresso.[15] In 1603, he became the wadsetter of Logie (also recorded as Logieterre) there, and shortly afterwards the lands of Crackenhill.[16] His brother, William, took charge of managing the properties. James married, for the third time, to Katherine Forbes and by her had seven children, not all of them surviving. In 1619, by which time he had become an established advocate in Aberdeen, he purchased the estate of Ardo in the parish of Banchory Devenick and thereafter designed himself 'of Ardo'.[17] His tombstone in St Nicholas church, Aberdeen recorded him as having been a singular man both in private and in public. It was this James Mowat, while a writer in Edinburgh in 1598, who lent Magnus Mowat of Balquholly 5,000 merks in silver and gold.

The three sons of James Mowat in Redcloak who entered the legal profession were Alexander, Mr Roger and Mr Hugh. Mr Hugh, a graduate of King's College, Aberdeen in 1606, appears briefly as a writer in Edinburgh and as a witness to various family documents and then disappears. He may have become solicitor-martial to Spynie's regiment in the Danish service and thereafter solicitor-martial general to Mackay's regiment after the former was disbanded in February 1629.[18]

Alexander appears to have been the first of the brothers to move to Edinburgh. He started out as servitor to his uncle, George Auchinleck of Balmanno, signing himself as 'Saunders' Mowat, when witnessing an obligation.[19] He was obviously very young at the time. Following his uncle's death, he began his legal training as servitor to Mr John Hay, but by 1601 his new master was Mr Alexander Gibson, one of the Clerks of Session. His signature, in a clear and pleasing secretary hand, appears in the margin of one of Gibson's Registers of Deeds in June 1614. His first wife was Katherine Nisbet, widow of George French, a merchant and burgess of the burgh. At the end of 1612 he married his second wife, Margaret Barclay. She was the daughter of John Barclay, indweller in Edinburgh, a member of the Barclay of Mathers family. Her father was a wealthy man, but left nothing to her in his will. Her stepmother was left 10,000 merks. Alexander made sure she received her bairn's part.[20] By her he had two children, neither of whom appears to have survived. He seems to have been a diligent man. Apart from serving Mr Alexander Gibson, he also acted for several lairds, among whom was Crichton of Frendraught. He acquired an annualrent out of a fourth part of the lands of Broughton in Edinburgh, income from the chaplainry of Meigle and various gifts of escheats (a part or the whole of those estates forfeited to the Crown by defaulters). He owned property in Edinburgh in Blackfriars Wynd and the Templeland beneath the castle wall. His contribution to the Mowat story was as their 'doer', their deeds and actions being found almost exclusively in Gibson's registers until his death in 1636. It was his younger brother, Roger, who was to play a central role in the struggle by the main line to retain their lands.

If James Mowat of Ardo was singular in private and public, then his cousin, Mr Roger Mowat, was exceptional. While the main line were busy accumulating debts, he was busy amassing wealth. He was most likely a graduate of King's College, Aberdeen, where he was later a civilist.[21] He appears to have gone to Edinburgh, as a replacement for his cousin, James Mowat, beginning his career as servitor to Mr John Nicolson, advocate. By 1607, he was acting as solicitor for the ministers of the kirk, as James had done. By then he was already an advocate in his own right. In that year he was granted the Gift of the escheat of John Pattoun in Farrochie, a neighbour of the Mowats at Redcloak with whom his family, including his uncle, Magnus, had been in conflict.[22] Ten years later he received the more substantial Gift of the escheat of Andrew Mowat of Swenzie (now Swiney), a Caithness laird, but had great difficulty in acquiring it. He had to institute several actions against him. In 1619 he acquired the wadset of the lands of Logie in Kincardineshire which had formerly belonged to his cousin, James.[23] Thereafter, he became known as 'of Logie'. His income came from his legal fees and interest on money he loaned out. In 1620, for example, he was able to lend out over 16,000 merks (over £11,000) to various people. By 1648 he was able to make a single loan of 20,000 merks (£13,333/6/8d) to Patrick Ogilvy of Inchmartin and his son.[24] In addition, he was also granted pensions by grateful clients, such as one granted to him by Alexander Wisheart of Phesdo 'for giving faithfull counsall and advyce in my effairis'.[25] Not all pensions were forthcoming, however. In 1630, he had to prosecute Sir John McDougall of Duonolich for non-payment of an annual pension for five years, during which time he had continued to serve him.[26] Campbell of Cawdor granted him a pension of £26/13/4d ('for the pryce of twa ky') for his assistance, although most of Lord Cawdor's business was done by James Mowat, W.S., a colleague and friend of his but who was no relation.[27] (See Appendix 2.) Roger acted as James Mowat's factor whenever James had to go to England on Lord Cawdor's business.

In 1638 he acquired the wadset of Dumbreck and Newseat in the parish of Udny from Alexander Keith of Balmoor, son of William Keith of Ludquharn.[28] Alexander Keith was unable to redeem the wadset and so Roger became owner of the property, as well as of the lands of Balmoor in the parish of Peterhead and Northfield, part of the lands of Troup which he had apprised from Alexander's father.[29] After being granted a charter of the lands, he changed his designation to Dumbreck. He may have called himself the laird of Dumbreck and been the owner of several other properties in various parts of the country, but as an advocate it was necessary for him to live in Edinburgh. Moreover, his wife, Margaret Marjoribanks, was a native of the burgh. Her father was a wealthy merchant and bailie. Roger's country estates were merely investments which brought in additional annual income. He also owned various properties in Edinburgh. In 1625 he purchased some lands beyond the Netherbow, on the south side of the High Street, and in March 1642 a tenement of land on the same side at the head of Aikman's Close. It was possibly in the latter tenement that he and his family lived. It remained in the family after his death, eventually being sold by his grandson, Sir William Mowat of Inglishton, in December 1684.[30]

Most of his income came from civil business. He had many important clients. By the 1640s, for example, he was dealing with such men as Lord Angus, the Earl of Crawford, the Earl of Mar, Sir William Dick of Braid and the Earl of Traquair. One of his letters on legal business to Lord Ogilvy has survived. It is written with clarity and precision.[31] On his death, in the first half of 1653, he left unredeemed bonds for large amounts which had been granted to him by the Duke of Hamilton, the Marquis of Argyll and Campbell of Kintyre. He was also involved in criminal prosecutions. In 1627 he successfully defended Alexander Hervie in Inverurie who had been accused of laming a servant of George Leslie in New Leslie in 1613. Roger pointed out that the apparently crippled man had managed to walk the 80 miles to Edinburgh to appear in court. He was not so successful in 1643 when he and Mr Thomas Nicolson defended Mr James Mowat of Ollaberry and Ninian Nevin of Windhouse and his brother, accused of mutilating Mr Patrick Cheyne of Vaila and his brother in a skirmish outside Scalloway castle in Shetland. They were found guilty, although, through a legal technicality, they had been unable to present their own witnesses. This case was to have an indirect bearing on later events.[32]

Magnus Mowat of Balquholly benefited from having cousins who were lawyers and, in particular, one who was an advocate. In 1624, for instance, he employed Roger to institute an action against Sinclair of Murkle who was still occupying a part of his Caithness lands.[33] However, while Magnus may have given Roger much business, it is doubtful whether he was ever as generous with his payment. A more reliable client was another relative, James Mowat of Ardo's son, a tailor in Paris. He appointed Roger as his factor in 1641 to deal with his affairs in Scotland.[34] But it was Roger's immediate family who benefited most from his assistance.

He belonged to a close-knit family whose nucleus was the farm of Redcloak, just outside Stonehaven. In 1612 his father, James Mowat, 'guidman of Reidcloak', died in his 80th year, having survived both his brothers at Balquholly and Cowie. Roger too was the longest-lived of his generation and it therefore fell to him to act as the family's head. His longevity explains his involvement in so much of the family's business. His brother, George, took over the farm after their father's death, in addition leasing the Waulkmill of Ury and purchasing a tenement in Stonehaven.[35] George died in July 1645, leaving a widow much younger than himself and no children. He had died a wealthy man, leaving a well-stocked farm and 900 merks (£600) in ready money.[36] Roger took over the settling of his estate, granting an Obligation to his brother's widow, Isobel Orchardtoune, whereby she was to receive the annual interest on his brother's money, part of which he invested. A wealthy widow soon attracted suitors and it was not long before Isobel Orchardtoune married again. Her second husband did not live long and she subsequently married for a third time. When a widow remarried, she often forfeited any income she was entitled to from her previous marriage. A clause was generally inserted to that effect in the marriage contract. George Mowat and Isobel Orchardtoune appear not to have drawn up such a document, but nonetheless, shortly after Isobel married her second husband, Roger instituted an action against her to reclaim some of his brother's money which she had retained, including £66/13/4d which had been realised from the sale of his brother's 'abulzie-ments' (clothes). He also wished to prevent her having the liferent of his brother's tenement in Stonehaven, although she had been infeft in it along with her husband in 1633.[37] Isobel survived all her husbands, living to a great age. Her third husband, Alexander Barclay, was dead by 1675 and she found that all his movable goods had been gifted to John Scot of Canterland who was his creditor and that she had been left with nothing. She appears to have been unsuccessful with an action she brought in order to reclaim her portion.[38] By then she was 'a poor aged woman'. William Rait of Hallgreen took pity on her and supported her financially for the rest of her life. In gratitude she assigned to him the Obligation which Roger had granted to her just after his brother George's death in 1645. But Isobel Orchardtoune's goods themselves had been forfeited as a result of the action Roger had subsequently brought against her, and the Obligation was no longer of any value. After her death, in desperation, William Rait petitioned the Treasury for repayment of all the money he had expended on her.[39] Had she not remarried, Roger's treatment of her would have been very different.

He was most supportive towards his nephews and nieces, in particular to several of the sons of his eldest brother, John, who died in 1633. His brother's eldest son was Mr James Mowat, a graduate of King's College in 1619. Mr James had inherited his father's movable estate as well as an equal half of the mill of Tillihelt from his maternal grandfather. After his grandfather's death the Gordons of Tillihelt had refused to fulfill the contract they had made with him, and James's complaint to the Privy Council led to their being warded in Blackness castle.[40] He wisely disposed of the property shortly after that. He chose, as a career, to become governor to young lairds, accompanying them on the Continent, among them being Lord Maitland, John, Earl of Loudon and Alexander Forbes, eldest son of Alexander Forbes of Boyndlie.[41] He was among the Scots in London listed in the Wardlaw MS, being described as having 'been twice over the Alps as governour to the gentry' and as 'a discreet gentleman, who as governor to young noblemen had attended sundrie in France, Germanie and Italie' by John Row, Principal of King's College.[42] At a later date, he acquired the wadset of Logie and so became Mr James Mowat of Logie. Roger arranged for Alexander, another of John's sons, to carry on the farm at Redcloak after George's death in 1645. He took his brother's youngest son, Roger, to Edinburgh with him to train him as a lawyer. It was fortunate for those young people that they had such a capable, energetic and caring uncle who had found time to break off from his affairs in Edinburgh to attend to theirs.

Having become head of the family, Roger found it necessary to be present on nearly every occasion when a legal document involving the family was drawn up, whether at Redcloak or elsewhere. He also acted for nearly all their causes. The family appear to have relied on him, which is understandable given his sphere of influence, and for his part he appears to have acted with their interests at heart. If, at times, he may have been somewhat overbearing, they almost certainly would have hesitated to show any resentment. He must have been a formidable man.

Perhaps he had inherited his strength of will peppered with a dash of arrogance from his mother's side. In his hey-day his uncle, George Auchinleck of Balmanno, had been the powerful and influential confidant of the Regent, James, Earl of Morton. His official title had been 'collectour and ressaver of his majesteis patrimony and propertie for furnessing and provisioun of my lord Regentis hous'.[43] He had also been the parson of Kilbucho in Peeblesshire, although he does not seem to have ministered to the parishioners, but merely to have enjoyed the revenue of that parish.[44] He had survived an attempt on his life by William Bickarton of Casch and four others who had set upon him in a passage near St Giles Cathedral in Edinburgh, shooting him through the body and leaving him for dead. He had also been tortured by the Earl of Arran, following his part in the Ruthven Raid in 1582, when the young James VI had been detained at Ruthven castle for ten months by a group of extreme Protestants.[45] To have survived both indicates that he must have been a man with a strong will and constitution.

At the time Roger lived, family connections and influence coupled with the achievements of earlier members played an important part in a man's success and advancement in his career. George Auchinleck of Balmanno's son, for instance, became a Lord of Session. By the time Roger began his career in Edinburgh, George Auchinleck was dead. None of his immediate Mowat forebears had been involved in affairs of state. They had been too embroiled in local politics and so had restricted their horizons. He did, however, owe much to his cousin, James Mowat, who had led the way and smoothed his path to begin with. His ensuing success was entirely due to his own abilities. He seems to have been a remarkably clever, able and conscientious man and, above all, to have had boundless energy. His descendants stood in his shadow.

SOURCES

1. *RMS* iv, 2191
2. CS15/305 – Earl Marischal v Mowat
3. *RMS* v, 1435; Rait of Hallgreen papers (SRO) – RH15/37/48
4. Edinburgh Commissary Court, CC8/8/26 – Testament of John Orchartoun in Annamuk, 23 July 1594

5. *The Court Book of the Barony of Urie* (SHS (first series), vol 12), 29

6. PS1/56 f.84; CS7/96 – 11 June 1583

7. *The Court Book of the Barony of Urie*, Introduction, liv

8. *Ibid*, 75; RD1/343 f.21

9. Rait of Hallgreen papers (SRO) – RH15/37/95

10. *The Court Book of the Barony of Urie*, 7

11. RD1/51 – 22 Nov 1595

12. PS1/60 f.84

13. CS7/240 – 14 Mar 1609

14. CS7/226 – 16 June 1607

15. RS6/1 – 1 Jan 1600

16. RS6/1 – 10 Nov 1603; RS6/2 f.254

17. RS1/3 f.156

18. T. Riis – *Should Auld Acquaintance Be Forgot*, ii, 119, 136

19. RD1/29 – 25 May 1594

20. CC8/8/49 – 21 Dec 1616; RD1/259 – 17 Mar 1617

21. *Officers and Graduates of King's College* (NSC), 32; John Spalding – *Memorialls of The Trubles in Scotland and England, AD1624 – AD1645* (SPC), i, 261

22. CS7/226 – 22 May 1607

23. RS7/1 – 24 May 1619

24. Seafield muniments (SRO) – GD248/572/3

25. RD1/295 – 25 April 1620

26. CS7/436 – 4 June 1630

27. *The book of the thanes of Cawdor* (SPC), 295

28. RD1/515 – 15 Sept 1638

29. RD1/528 – 22 Feb 1641; *RMS* xi, 512

30. Moses Index (Edinburgh City Archives), i, p.24; ii, no.940; iv, no.3577

31. Airlie Muniments (SRO) – GD16/41/286

32. *Selected Justiciary Cases, 1624–1650* (Stair Society), i, 67; ii, 466

33. CS7/386 – 10 Sept 1624

34. RD1/536 – 9 Mar 1642

35. *The Court Book of the Barony of Urie*, 75; RS7/2 – 30 June 1624; RS7/3 – 2 Nov 1633

36. Rait of Hallgreen papers (SRO) – RH15/37/95

37. CS22/39 – 22 Nov 1672; RS7/3 – 17 Mar 1633

38. Rait of Hallgreen papers (SRO) – RH15/37/152

39. *Ibid* – RH15/37/174

40. RS5/10 f.349; *RPC* vi, 295 (second series)

41. RD1/573 – 22 Nov 1652; CS138/3529 – Roger Mowat v debtors; A and H Tayler – *The House of Forbes* (TSC), 317

42. *Wardlaw MS* (SHS (first series), vol 47), 427; *SN&Q*, second series, vii, 52

43. *RSS* vi, 2262

44. RD1/20/2 f.267

45. R Chambers – *Domestic Annals of Scotland* (Abridged Edition), 89

CHAPTER FOUR

Magnus Mowat's Struggle

When James Mowat lent the 5,000 merks to Magnus Mowat of Balquholly in 1598, Magnus agreed in the Obligation drawn up to repay the sum by 1600. By Whitsunday 1599 he had only managed to repay 500 merks (£333/6/8d), and James, seeing no doubt that there was little likelihood of the rest being forthcoming, brought an action against him, thereby forcing Magnus to give him some form of security. Magnus offered him the contentious lands of Balmellie, possibly because most of his other lands were in the hands of wadsetters. An Obligation to that effect was drawn up in November 1603.[1] Soon after that James, by then resident in Aberdeen and closer to Balquholly, heard that Magnus was planning to sell or wadset Balmellie. While James had promised that he would never pursue Magnus during his (Magnus's) lifetime, he now saw the prospect of losing the 5,000 merks altogether. He decided, as a result, to raise an action to inhibit Magnus alienating his lands.[2] James's thoughts about the honour of the house appear to have been forgotten. Magnus's subsequent decision, in August 1608, to grant James, his wife and two sons, Alexander and Robert, the lands of Lendrum and Brownhill was obviously an attempt to appease James.[3]

Meanwhile Magnus had other problems to contend with. There were the debts listed in the Contract of 1602 to be repaid, chief among them one owed to his brother-in-law, William Bruce of Stanstill, who was wadsetter of Auckingill and Midtown of Freswick, part of the family's lands in Caithness. His other sister, Elizabeth, was planning to marry George Crawford of Annochie, and her settlement would have to be paid. His father was nearing the end of his life, and his mother would have to receive her terce and liferent settlement and his brother, James, would have to be paid 1,000 merks (£666/13/4d). The conflict with the Gordons of Gight had destroyed his crops and most of his land was in the hands of wadsetters. In 1603 he approached William Gray, burgess of Aberdeen, and his wife for a loan of 4,000 merks (£2,666/13/4d) 'for outredding of his affeiris'.[4] The Grays required security for the loan and Magnus persuaded his wife (now called Isobel) to pledge her liferent lands of Kermucks. To do this they had to get permission from James Kennedy of Kermucks, her son. James Kennedy, in turn, required some form of security from Magnus, and so Magnus agreed to infeft his wife, Isobel, in the liferent of the castle and mains of Balquholly and James Kennedy in fee. In addition he included the lands of Woodend and part of Brownhill and agreed to redeem all for 10,000 merks (£6,666/13/4d). He must have been in desperate straits to have promised so much. In 1605 he was, therefore, able to repay William Bruce of Stanstill 2,000 merks (£1,333/6/8d) and so redeem the lands in Caithness.[5] In June the following year he went to Aberdeen to pay 4,000 merks (£2,666/13/4d) to James Kennedy and to hand him a charter of the lands of Woodend and Brownhill which he promised to redeem for 3,000 merks (£2,000). According to Magnus, James Kennedy refused both and he was forced to leave the money and the charter in the care of Mr John Cheyne of Pitfichie. The outcome of an action brought by Magnus against James was that the Lords of Session decerned James to reassign Isobel's liferent lands and the Balquholly lands to Magnus.[6] A month later it was James Kennedy's turn to bring an action against Magnus in which he stated that he had been 'ovir mair' ready to accept the money and the charter and had offered Magnus and his wife his renunciation and grant of redemption of the lands, on condition that they gave him a discharge. This they had not done. As regards the money in Mr John Cheyne's hands, he had often asked for it, but Mr John Cheyne had refused to hand it over to him. He alleged that Magnus was the delayer and not he.[7] Any further disagreements between stepfather and stepson were put an end to by the death of James Kennedy in 1608.[8]

The previous year had been the year in which the conflict with Con of Auchry and Elizabeth Auchinleck had taken place. Thereafter Magnus struggled on. In 1606 he persuaded his wife to ratify his wadsetting of the Mill of Colp, part of her liferent lands, for 3,000 merks (£2,000). He also induced his sister, Elspet Mowat, to renounce 3,000 merks, given to her by her father, due out of the lands of Jackston and Ewebrae. At the beginning of the next year another sister, Jean, Lady Asloun, agreed to renounce hers out of the lands of Woodend of Balquholly and parts of the lands in Caithness.[9] In the following years he redeemed and then wadset parts of his lands over and over again. In 1620 the sheriff depute and procurator fiscal of Aberdeenshire brought an action against him for breaking 'ane arrestment maid upone his guidis and cornis', indicating that there had been no let-up in his financial troubles.[10] A shadow from the past arose in November 1623, when the Earl of Erroll's son raised an action against him as heir to his father,

Patrick. Patrick Mowat had acted as cautioner to Henry, Lord Sinclair, and his son when the marriage contract between Andrew Hay and Agnes Sinclair had been drawn up. The sum involved had been 9,000 merks (£6,000). Soon after her husband's death Agnes Sinclair had obtained letters of four forms against them, but in 1588 the three men had obtained a Decree of Suspension, thereby delaying further action.[11] Thirty-five years later that further action was taken. In 1624 Magnus attempted to have the Decreet against James Sinclair of Murkle, which his father had given him, implemented. James Sinclair had illegally occupied the 18 penny lands of Harpsdale, part of the Freswick lands, for over 35 years.[12] The case dragged on into 1627. In that year he brought an action against his brother-in-law, George Crawford of Annochie, who owed him 4,380 merks (£2,920).[13] Further action ended with the death of George Crawford.

At no time had he attempted to repay his cousin, James Mowat. In 1628 James once again brought an action against him, but once again nothing was forthcoming from Magnus.[14] Finally, in September 1633, James sold the Obligation drawn up between them in 1598 to their cousin, Mr Roger Mowat, advocate.[15] Roger, however, was after an even greater prize.

By January 1634 it was apparent that Magnus had not long to live. On the 21st of that month he made his will at Balquholly, naming his son-in-law, Sir John Sinclair of Dunbeath, his sole executor. (His signature betrays how close to death he was.) In it, he made a final attempt to placate James Mowat of Ardo. He left 2,000 merks (£1,333/6/8d) to James's eldest son, Thomas Mowat, provided James discharged Magnus's heirs of the Obligation and all actions and decreets involving it.[16] It appears to have been the one loan he could not forget. He obviously did not know that the Obligation was already in the hands of Mr Roger Mowat. Shortly after Magnus made his will, his brother, James Mowat of Smiddyseat, described him as 'being now heavilie diseasit and lyk to depart furth this mortall lyff'.[17] No sympathy was felt for him by his creditors. James Annand, son of Henry Annand in Old Aberdeen, raised an action against him over a debt of 300 merks (£200). Magnus complained from his sick bed that this had been 'to take advantage aganes him be ressoun of his sickness'.[18] Meanwhile, the forces were gathering as Magnus lingered on. He had no sons and so his brother, James, was to be his heir. Any differences the brothers may have had were put aside, for once more the house was in danger. James was deeply aware of the 'integritie to the name of Mowat' and that any actions he might take would have to be 'for the weill and standing of the hous'. James decided to name as his heir his grandson, Magnus, son of his own son, Patrick. No reason was given for his passing over Patrick.[19] By March, Magnus was dead. James, now of Balquholly, executed a deed in which he declared that he was in no way responsible for his brother's debts.[20] This was a vain hope as, being Magnus's heir, he would inherit all the burdens on the estate. In May, Sir John Sinclair of Dunbeath, Magnus's son-in-law and executor, fearing that James Mowat might alienate the lands and thus prevent the legacies in Magnus's will from being paid, raised Letters to inhibit his doing so.[21] He also claimed that James had appropriated a writs coffer belonging to Magnus within which was an Obligation in his and his wife's favour for 10,000 merks (£6,666/13/4d).[22] They complained that James Mowat would

> not fullfill the samene tochair nor yitt will he compeare befoir the Lordis of Counsall and consent to the registrateing thairof in thair buikes of counsall.[23]

Waiting on the sidelines was Mr Roger Mowat, advocate. On 8th July, James Mowat of Balquholly drew up a Bond and Obligation in which he recorded that Mr Roger Mowat, his 'loving cousigne', had advanced him

> certaine great sowmes of money to certaine persounes my creditoris lykas I stand obleist to him in certaine utheris great sowmes of money pairtlie at the desyre of Umqhill Magnus Mowate of Balquhollie my brother and pairtlie borrowit and ressavit be me . . . sen the deceist of my said Umqhill brother haillie convertit to my awine use utilitie and profeitt.

The amount Roger advanced was 14,072 merks (£9,381/6/8d), the date of repayment being set for 1st August, a ridiculously short term.[24] There was no way James Mowat could find such a large sum of money in so short a time. The 1st of August came and went. Four days later Roger applied for Letters of Apprising to be issued against James. It was arranged that the court of Apprising would meet in Edinburgh where, Roger predicted, 'thair will mony difficultis, argumentis and questiones arryse upon deductioun of the said apprysing'.[25] The outcome was predictable. The new owner of Balquholly was Mr Roger Mowat, advocate. Having acquired all the burdens on the estate, he held the trump card. His action appears to have been prompted by his being a member of such an ancient family, but his ultimate satisfaction must have been to have become one of the actual lairds.

That Magnus was able to die at Balquholly in his old age was remarkable, considering the attempts made on his life and the debts he had inherited.

These had amounted to 13,730 merks in 1602. Mr Roger Mowat had paid his brother, James Mowat of Balquholly, 14,072 merks which did not include James Mowat of Ardo's loan of 5,000 merks. Magnus had never, therefore, been able to reduce the size of the debts. What he had been able to do was to employ considerable ingenuity in keeping his creditors at bay. By borrowing further amounts, he had been able to pay those pressing for payment and so defer the 'inconvenientis' his father had been so concerned about. He must have been a persuasive man, possessed of a certain amount of charm, to have induced his cousin, James Mowat, 'never to persew craif or suit executioun' against him during his lifetime. Even his own sisters were persuaded to renounce what had been given to them by their father. To obtain money, he promised anything. His stepdaughter was promised a mill but he never gave her the rightful titles to it, his stepson Balquholly castle after Isobel Cheyne's death, his daughter and her husband 5,000 merks out of his lands or, if they are to be believed, 10,000 merks. What they must all have realised afterwards was that they had been beguiled by him. It was probably his success in always obtaining a loan when he needed one that caused him to live for so long. It is true that Magnus always had land to offer in security to prospective creditors and, should he have failed to redeem them, the lands would ultimately have been theirs, but no creditor was ever granted enough of the lands to make it possible for him to acquire the whole estate.

What of Isobel Cheyne who had been promised so much in her marriage contract in 1592? Magnus, in his will, left her the contents of Balquholly and the corn and cattle on the mains. On 11th November 1634, not long after her husband's death, she and members of her family took the new laird, James Mowat of Balquholly, to court over his refusal to register a contract which Magnus had made on 9th April 1603 with William Cheyne of Arnage. It transpired that, by that date, Magnus had wadset

> not onlie the maist pairt of the conjunct fie and lyfrent landis quhilkis
> schoe gatt be occasioune of the mariage betwixt hir and the said Magnus
> bot farder hes thralled hir remanent landis and leveing quhilkis schoe had
> abefoir to hir great disadvantage and that hir saides twa daughteris yit
> remaines unprovydit to ony lyveliehood.

William Cheyne had obviously stepped in to ensure that after having lent great sums of money to Magnus 'to the weill of the said Magnus and releiffe of his landis', his daughter would have some form of liferent agreement.

Magnus appears to have been forced to promise to infeft Isobel in the liferent of the mains of Balquholly and in the lands in Caithness. He had also been induced to provide his daughters, Elspeth and Christian, with annualrents of 700 merks and 500 merks respectively out of the Balquholly and Freswick lands and further that, if he had no lawful male heir, to increase the amounts to 5,000 merks and 3,000 merks. However, in November 1634, when the contract was finally recorded in the Books of Council and Session, it was stated that Magnus had 'at na tyme preceiding his deceis fulfillit' the contract.[26] Once again, Magnus had promised something he could not or did not intend to fulfill. After acquiring the lands, Roger Mowat appears to have allowed Isobel Cheyne to remain at Balquholly. She was still there in 1642, old and sick. After Magnus's death she had employed her grand-daughter, Elspet Kennedy, as her companion for four years. She had promised her £100 for her services and £50 for any merchandise she might purchase, apart from clothes.[27] The agreement had been verbal but had evidently been made in the presence of Mr Roger Mowat and his wife. In 1642 Elspet brought an action against her grandmother, claiming that she had not honoured their agreement. It is extraordinary that she should have chosen to do so against someone who was so old and isolated. In the event, Isobel Cheyne had allies. Mr Thomas Mitchell, minister at Turriff, wrote to the court to say that she was unable to travel to Aberdeen 'be reasoune of her sicknes'. Undaunted, the court decided that she should be examined at Balquholly, but when the court officials arrived, they were prevented from entering the castle by Isobel's loyal servant, William Con.[28]

In her widowhood she was denied the comfort and companionship of her elder daughter, Isobel, who had predeceased Magnus. Her second daughter, Christian, lived far away in Caithness at Dunbeath and appears to have been delicate, dying 'prematurely in the bloom of her life'. Had Christian lived closer to Balquholly, perhaps her mother might not have been so neglected in her old age.

SOURCES
1. RD1/472 – 1 Feb 1634
2. DI 21/12 – 5 April 1604
3. RS4/7 f.226
4. CS7/226 – 19 Feb 1607
5. RD1/110 f.124
6. CS7/226 – 19 Feb 1607
7. CS7/231 – 21 July 1607

8. *SN&Q,* 2nd series, iii, 174
9. *Records of the Sheriff Court of Aberdeenshire* (NSC), ii, 90; 98; 99
10. CS7/333 – 16 June 1620
11. DI 21/22 – 7 Nov 1623; Inventory of Erroll charters (NRAS – 0925), no 1228; Rosslyn muniments (SRO) – GD164/204
12. CS7/386 – 10 Sept 1624; CS7/392 – 19 Jul 1625; CS7/397 – 17 Feb 1627; 22 Mar 1627
13. CS7/397 – 13 Feb 1627
14. Seafield muniments (SRO) – GD248/218; DI 21/32 – 22 Mar 1631
15. RD1/472 – 1 Feb 1634
16. Mey papers (SRO) – GD96/683/1
17. Mey papers (SRO) – GD96/527
18. *Ibid.*
19. *Ibid.*
20. *Ibid.*
21. DI 21/25 f.34
22. Mey papers (SRO) – GD96/527
23. RD1/478 – 11 Nov 1634
24. Seafield muniments (SRO) – GD248/218; RD1/478 – 2 Aug 1634
25. Seafield muniments (SRO) – GD248/218
26. RD1/478 – 11 Nov 1634
27. *Records of the Sheriff Court of Aberdeenshire* (NSC), iii, 6, 39.
28. SC1/7/8 – 15 July 1642

CHAPTER FIVE

The Covenanter and the Tailor

Four members of the Mowat family died in the 1630s – Magnus Mowat of Balquholly and his three cousins, Alexander Mowat, writer in Edinburgh, and John Mowat in Auquorties (two of the sons of James Mowat in Redcloak) and James Mowat of Ardo (son of Magnus Mowat in Cowie). James Mowat of Ardo had been staying at Redcloak in September 1633, when he had assigned the Bond and Obligation which Magnus Mowat had granted to him in 1598 to Mr Roger Mowat. He was probably conscious that his end was near and anxious to put his affairs in order. His eldest son, Thomas, was also there and wrote the Assignation. James Mowat had three other sons, two of whom, Alexander and Robert, died not long after he did. His youngest son, James, went to Paris, shortly after his father's death.

Thomas Mowat, his eldest son, was baptised on 17th October 1602 at St Nicholas kirk, Aberdeen. He became a notary and assistant to his father with legal business. He was also responsible for writing many of the family's documents. At the age of 18, he was made a burgess of Aberdeen and throughout his life appears to have played an active part in civic affairs. In 1628, he was given the Gift of the income from the ministry of Trinity Friars in the burgh, although the money was not readily forthcoming.[1] On the death of his father, in 1636, he inherited the lands of Ardo.[2] He also fell heir to the wadset of half the lands of Lendrum and Brownhill which had belonged to his brother, Alexander.[3] He had also been left 2,000 merks by Magnus Mowat of Balquholly in 1634, although it is doubtful whether he would ever have received the money. The lands he inherited would have given him a reasonable annual income and yet, in August of that year, he borrowed £1,233/6/8d from Mr Roger Mowat. As security, he pledged the wadset of the half lands of Lendrum and Brownhill which he had recently inherited. They, being part of the lands of Balquholly, would have been more acceptable to Mr Roger Mowat than Ardo.[4] Thomas Mowat was never able to repay the loan during his lifetime and his two surviving daughters had to face litigation brought both by Mr Roger Mowat and his heirs after his death. The reason for the loan is not apparent. There is no evidence that his father had contracted large debts during his lifetime. He owned the property of Ardo and had recently disposed of the Obligation he had granted to Magnus Mowat. Thomas, himself, must have been in need of the money.

Perhaps he proposed to make a contribution to the Covenanters, for he was an ardent supporter of their cause. In May 1639, following their success at Turriff, the Royalists threatened to advance on Aberdeen. The burgh had previously been occupied by the Earl Marischal during which time anti-Covenanters had been forced to flee, but by that May the Earl Marischal had left for Dunnottar, followed by his army. The people of Aberdeen were relieved to be no longer occupied, but the Covenanters in the burgh once again found themselves in the situation they had been in before the Earl Marischal had arrived, when 'no covenanter dare be seen in the toun'. The Provost, bailies and several members of the town council, including Thomas Mowat, all of whom were Covenanters, 'took all the flight from the toune, ilk man for his awin saiftie, efter they had first put thair goodis and best geir out of the way'.[5] Thomas and his family headed south to Auquorties. By the middle of June the conflict was over, a peace treaty having been signed at Berwick on the 18th. Unaware of this, the Royalists and Covenanters in Aberdeenshire had continued to fight on the outskirts of Aberdeen until the following day. In November Thomas sold his lands of Ardo, with the consent of his wife and mother who both had the liferent. The new owner was Gilbert Menzies, son of Gilbert Menzies of Pitfodels.[6] What was extraordinary was that the elder Gilbert Menzies had been strongly opposed to the Covenanting cause.[7] Thomas and his family appear to have decided to remain in Auquorties, and in September 1640 he arranged for his wife, Jonet Ogilvy, to be infeft in the liferent of the other half of the wadset of the lands of Lendrum and Brownhill which he had since inherited, following the death of his other brother, Robert.[8] By 1643 Aberdeen was once again controlled by the Covenanters and Thomas felt it safe to return. He was appointed town clerk depute and in the same year represented the Presbytery of Aberdeen as one of the ruling elders at the General Assembly. But by March 1644 Aberdeen was once again threatened. On the 9th of that month the laird of Drum and his brother, John Gordon of Haddo, and several other young lairds, galloped into Aberdeen, taking the Provost hostage and plundering his house and those of the bailies. Again, Thomas was forced to flee.[9] Peace was finally restored when Charles I surrendered at Newark in May 1646, and in the following January, Thomas, back in

Aberdeen, was appointed principal clerk of the burgh.[10] His first wife, Jonet
Ogilvy, had died in the interim, and shortly before he married his second
wife, Margaret Forbes, he arranged for her to be infeft in place of his first
wife in the half lands of Lendrum and Brownhill.[11] He appears to have
resigned as town clerk shortly after he had been appointed, because he had
also been one of those chosen to sit on the town council by Parliament, it
having decided that the previous election in the burgh had not been carried
out with sufficient freedom.[12] Then, following the death of Patrick
Chalmer, town clerk, he was appointed conjunct clerk with John Chalmer.[13] His protocol book covering the period 26th February to 28th
November 1648 is still extant.[14] He died at the end of December. His
second wife, Margaret Forbes, lived until 1662, being buried in Turriff
churchyard. She, no doubt, lived off the income from her liferent of half the
lands of Lendrum and Brownhill. Thomas's daughter, Margaret, by his first
marriage, did not mention her father on the Ardo tombstone in Aberdeen.
Out of the seven children born to Thomas and his first wife, she and her
sister, Elizabeth, were the only ones who survived. As there were no male
heirs, Thomas's line died out, but his daughters, in particular Margaret,
inherited some of their grandfather's doggedness and in that way the family
lived on. Margaret's story is yet to be told. She and her sister appear to have
met their respective husbands through their youngest uncle, James Mowat,
who was enterprising enough to leave Scotland and set up business in Paris.

In contrast to his brother, James Mowat, although baptised in the
Protestant faith, later became a Catholic. As a young man he went to Paris
where he set up trade as a tailor in the Rue St Denis. Already there was John
Clerk (later of Penicuik) who had been sent there by John Smyth, merchant
and burgess of Edinburgh, to attend to his business in the city. The two
young men struck up a friendship, and when John Clerk returned to
Edinburgh at the beginning of 1647 they continued to correspond with each
other. It is through this correspondence that much about James Mowat's
personal and business life can be gleaned.[15]

In a letter to John Clerk, written in September 1649, James Mowat
describes himself as 'yor litill merchant that sells laice in the Rue St Denis'.
This was a somewhat self-deprecatory description, as he did more than that.
He was a successful tailor. In 1647, for example, he made clothes for Angus
(Aeneas) McDonald of Glengarry costing £770. In the Bond drawn up
between them, James Mowat was described as tailor to the Most Christian
Queen (the Regent, Ann of Austria).[16] He was also recorded as a banker,

lending money to Scots who visited Paris. In October 1638 he lent 450 francs (£600) to Mr Gilbert Mowat, son of James Mowat of Ure, a Shetland laird, 'for his utrikment and uthyr necessir affaires'. Three bonds were drawn up – one in French and two in 'Scottische'.[17] In 1641 he appointed Mr Roger Mowat, advocate, as his factor in Scotland, being described in the document as a merchant and banker in Paris.[18] He did for a time become involved in importing salmon from Aberdeen and was made a burgess of that burgh on 6th August 1652.

By 1644 James had married his 'litill wyff'. She was French, and with her came a mother-in-law. His wife had a brother, George, who was in Rouen in 1647 and then appears to have gone to 'Dangland'. The family had given him up for lost, when he passed through Paris in 1654, having 'growen a greatt talle handsome fellow, butt nothing within him'. He had become gentleman to the Duke of Savoy, and in a letter to John Clerk, James Mowat playfully chastised him, by saying with regard to the empty-headed George – 'god forgive his late mother and you that learned him to drink and liberty which hath spoyled him'. There was also James's sister-in-law, Marotte, of whom John Clerk was very fond, always remembering to send his good wishes to her. Marotte had married a baker and 'is as round as shoe is longe, I dare say hir hips is french ell[s] broad betymes with siting setting hir loaves'. Her husband had a rich brother and sister whose 'money will come to the baikyer his children be all appearance'.

After John Clerk returned to Edinburgh, James missed his company and frequently suggested that he return there and set up his own business. Their relationship was chiefly as friends, although they did a small amount of business together. James sent him hats, hatbands and perukes in 1650, made by Madame Selon, Monsieur Peronet and Monsieur Sequin respectively. All merchandise and packets of letters were sent via London. There, James had a business associate, Alexander Blair, originally from Aberdeen, who was a merchant and tailor in the city. He forwarded everything to Edinburgh. A packet of letters sent in November 1649 cost 3/6d to London and 2/8d from there to Edinburgh.

In January 1650 James announced to John Clerk, 'Blessed be god, Mr Kinloch is become soe riche'. The Kinloch cousins, banker and tailor, were also associates of theirs in Paris. Francis Kinloch, younger, was involved with Mr Alexander Charteris and Mr Crawford in the business of 'fournishing of moneys to gentlemen that comes out of Scotland'. Mr Francis Kinloch elder had started undercutting them by lending money at 2/- in the franc less, thus

forcing Mr Charteris, the leading partner in the other concern, to lend
money at times at a loss. James suggested that he was trying to force Mr
Charteris to leave Paris as Mr Kinloch had boasted he had done to John
Clerk in a similar manner. James had a very high opinion of Mr Charteris. In
1655 he described him as marrying 'a werry werry pretty Mademoiselle from
Picardy', but the following July wrote to Clerk saying that 'sweet Alexander
Charteris' had died and that he had lost a good friend. Francis Kinloch
younger lost even more – an able business partner.

By 1654 James Mowat's financial affairs were in a bad state. He had fallen
behind with his correspondence with John Clerk who had evidently written
him a long letter in which he had been very firm with him and had given
him advice on how to manage his affairs. James had been long in replying to
the letter because he had had to go to London to settle his affairs there. The
outcome had been that his creditors had given him six years in which to
repay his debts. He seems not to have been a very good businessman, saying
that he could not really understand the state of his affairs, that he had debts
owed to him by the Marquis of Montrose, Marquis of Douglas, Lord
Kinstone, Glengarry, James Robertson in Aberdeen and several others 'too
tedyouse to sett downe'. The Marquis of Montrose owed him and
Alexander Blair £4,603/10/-.[19] (In 1656, James heard that the Marquis
had married Lady Roxburgh and was hopeful that at last he would be paid.
The bill was finally settled more than ten years after that.) In his reply to John
Clerk's long letter, he wrote saying that he was determined to honour all his
debts, and that 'I haif not nor shall not god willing maik any men loose a
farthing with me'.

He was at odds what to do next. He had some rather ineffectual ideas,
such as some small commissions for merchants in Flanders or to employ a
man to peddle goods for him in Scotland, but lacked the finance for both.
He did not want to return to Scotland where he felt he and his wife would
be troublesome to their friends. He had let his shop in the Rue St Denis to a
surgeon and toyed with the idea of selling ribbons, buttons and hats 'if the
entre be not forbidden since the incorporation'. Five years before, he and his
family had moved in with his mother-in-law. She had a large house and
there were two or three apartments to spare which they had let out to Scots
visiting Paris, James declaring 'I will haiv no Frenches for they ar insolent in a
house'.

His business affairs in Scotland had been looked after by William Downy,
writer in Edinburgh, but he seems to have been too busy with his own affairs

to oversee those of James. John Clerk, his concerned friend, had written suggesting his brother-in-law, Mr John Anderson, advocate, would be a better man to assist him, and in April 1656 James signed a factory appointing Mr Anderson and arranged for William Downy to tranfer all his papers to him.

In that year John Clerk had requested James to arrange for some books to be bound for him in Paris. Monsieur Compein was engaged to do so, and when they were ready James dispatched them to Alexander Blair in London together with an account for £81, both being duly sent to John Clerk in Edinburgh. When John Clerk received the enclosed bill, he was extremely displeased by the large amount James had asked for and equally annoyed by James's 'rich comment at the tail of it', it being over-effusive. John Clerk wrote of the enclosed account that 'it is a mistak bot a great one, only to my disadvantage' and 'it seems ye had done it be gess'. He further pointed out that he had done business for friends himself, but never for profit.

In August 1659 a rather strained letter arrived from James, devoid of his usual effusiveness, in which he referred to the account for the books being overdue and complained about Mr Anderson's handling of his affairs in Edinburgh. His last letter to John Clerk was dated 15th November 1659 and was very brief. He told John Clerk that he had charged on him his only bill of exchange for £72 to be paid to Alexander Blair. It was signed 'your loving friend', which suggests that John Clerk may have replied to James's strained letter written in August. The whole incident, however, had had a souring effect upon their relationship, and as no further letters have survived, it would seem to have ended at that time.

In 1654, when James had been in such dire financial straits, several friends had suggested that he take a large lodging where he could accommodate the sons of gentlemen and other visitors to Paris. This he had done, establishing his students' hostel in the Rue de Vieux. He had recounted to John Clerk how he had had good guests since then. Francis Kinloch, younger, had become involved in arranging the finances and affairs of the sons of the nobility and lairds sent to France for their education, and James had been drawn into a similar venture. William Ord, factor in Paris for James Sinclair of Roslin (at a later date also involved in supplying money to these young men), wrote in a letter to Sinclair dated 17th September 1677 that it was necessary for these young men to have someone in charge of their affairs as they had a tendency to fall into great inconveniences either by staying her[e] alone or in travelling, there are a great abundance of Scots and Inglish about them that pray upon thir folly and ignorance.[20]

On 14th April 1665, John Lauder, son of the laird of Fountainhall, arrived in Paris. The following day, he went to introduce himself to Francis Kinloch, carrying his father's letter and bill of exchange. His father required him to study French and the Law at Poitiers, and had chosen Mr Kinloch instead of 'our Mr Mowat' whom several people had recommended. From there, John Lauder went on to visit two other establishments where other young Scots were studying. These were at Orléans, which was run by John Ogilvy, and Saumur which was run by Mr Doul.[21]

At Orléans he met David Ogilvy, son of the Earl of Airlie, whom he described as speaking 'wery fat nonesense whiles'.[22] Francis Kinloch had been initially involved with arranging David Ogilvy's affairs, but thereafter James Mowat had taken over. David Ogilvy had arrived in France at the end of 1664 and by the following September had written home to his father complaining that he had been abandoned by Mr Mowat. He complained that 'I am ashamed to come in companie for want of sufficient cloathes'. The masters at Orléans who taught him French, Latin, the violin, Dancing and Fencing had not been paid. James Mowat's action in abandoning the young man had been because he had advanced him a considerable amount of money and had been reluctant to lay out more. In April 1665 James had heard from his factor, John Brown, who had taken over the managing of his affairs in Edinburgh, that none of the bills of exchange had been paid by the Earl of Airlie. He wrote in person to the Earl, voicing his 'astonishment' at this state of affairs. Further letters followed. A year later he calculated that he was owed £3,182. £440 was all that John Brown was able to get from the Earl. When Mr James Sinclair of Roslin was dispatched to Orléans to fetch David Ogilvy, preparatory to his returning home, John Ogilvy and his wife would not let the boy leave because of unpaid bills. James Mowat had to go down personally and pay the bills, despite the fact that he was 'werry scarce'. The boy left Paris for Scotland on 29th June.[23] Three years later, the Earl of Airlie finally settled the bill.[24]

Another of James Mowat's clients was George Gordon, 4th Marquis of Huntly, who had lived with his mother, Marie Grant, in Elgin during the time when the estate had been forfeited and under the management of Argyll. Their standard of living had been 'very mean', but after his mother became the second wife of James, Earl of Airlie, the young Marquis was sent to Paris to be under the care of James Mowat.[25] In July 1668, a month after George Gordon's arrival, James wrote to the Earl to say that the boy was in good health and learning the language very well and that he was going to see Fountainebleau, and 'efter that he is to close himself upe in the academy to ply himself to his exercise'.[26] In that same year, William Mowat, great-grandson of James Mowat of Balquholly, arrived. Much has to be told before his sad life can be recounted.

James Mowat also continued his occupation as tailor. Gilbert Blackhall, who had been a Roman Catholic missionary in the North-East of Scotland, was in Paris in the mid-1660s. He records having 'bought from Mr Muat a new sut and cloack of gray serge de Berie, the which stud me to eight pistolles; and I gave for a new hatte and an pair of new bouttes, twenty francs'. Altogether his new outfit had cost him 400 francs. James Mowat also hired a horse 'of retour, as they call him, for fyve crownes, to make usse of him fyve days' when Gilbert Blackhall left Paris. It turned out to be a stubborn beast.[27]

James's association with Mr Kinloch also involved their 'fournishing of moneys' to visitors to France. Gilbert Blackhall records that 'Mr Muat or Mr Kinloch' would have given him money 'at the very first word'.[28] When Francis Kinloch visited Scotland on various occasions, he assisted James with some of his affairs there. Most of James's business, however, was conducted by Mr William Sydserfe, writer in Edinburgh, until his death, and then by John Brown, merchant in the burgh. In 1667, for instance, John Brown and his son arranged on James's behalf to make ready two ships to transport the Royal Scots regiment from the Firth of Forth to Dieppe.[29]

James Mowat's banking affairs caused him the most headaches. In his letters to John Clerk he often complained about their effect upon his 'cranium'. He appears to have lacked good business judgement. In February 1664 Francis Kinloch wrote to his wife from London complaining that 'James Mowat doeth harme to us and no good to himselfe by gewin moneys at 22 shillings per Frank at this time when no exchanges can be had in Edinburgh upon London under 5 or 6 per cent loss'. In addition, provisions and carriage of letters and a bond of exchange had to be taken into account. He suggested that a more realistic figure of 24 shillings per franc 'might be better for him and us'.[30] James Mowat appears to have dealt with an extraordinary number of Scots visiting Paris, in addition to the sons of noblemen. He also lent money to Scots in London, with the assistance of

Alexander Blair, his factor there. Recouping his money proved difficult. Being at such a great distance from Scotland, he had to rely on the services of factors and others in Edinburgh to collect his debts. Periodically he would send back bundles of bills of exchange for that purpose. In August 1658 he signed a contract of co-partnery with Alexander Brand, merchant in Edinburgh (later of Baberton). Alexander Brand was to receive all sums of money, goods and other commodities by bills of exchange, bonds and others from whatever country and 'to putt the samen to the accompt of the credit of the said James Mowat, And punctwally (without delay) give adwyse of the receat thairoff to the said James Mowat'. He was also to render 'perfect accompts of all my intromitiones'. James, in turn, was to grant him a discharge and pay him 10% commission.[31] One of the bills of exchange is still extant. It was written at Paris on 15th March 1664 and was addressed to the Right Worshipful Alderman Backwell in London. It reads:

> Sr At eight dayis sight please pay by this my first of Exchange to the order of Mr Alexander Blaire Two Hundred pounds Stirling and place the same to the accompte of the Earl of Tiviot.

It was signed with his distinctive signature – Ja: Mowat, underlined several times in the shape of a converse spiralled pyramid. On the back was Alexander Blair's signature. With it was a Discharge granted to Alderman Backwell by James Mowat.[32] These bills of exchange were the means by which merchants settled their debts. They were, as can be seen above, written by the creditor, addressed to the debtor requiring him either on demand or at a determined time to pay a certain sum to a specific person or to the bearer. The creditor was then required to grant a discharge to the debtor once the bill had been settled. They were also negotiable so that debts in another country could be settled through bills which the creditor had received in the currency of that country. Alderman Backwell's debt was to be used by Alexander Blair to make a loan or possibly to offset a debt to the Earl of Teviot on James Mowat's behalf. Less than a decade later the partnership with Alexander Brand had failed. In August 1667 James appointed Mr William Sydserfe as his factor to pursue Alexander Brand in order to reclaim all his financial documents from him.[33] The resulting action contained a list of bills of exchange which seems almost endless, and included those in the names of young Pitarrow, Lord Carnegie, the Earl of Lothian, Mr Robert Baillie, Lord Gray, Lord Wemys, Lord Montrose and Lord Abercrombie, among many others.[34] James Mowat's task of keeping track of all his debtors must at times have seemed impossible, and his complaints about their effect upon his 'cranium' are understandable.

At the beginning of 1672 he returned to Scotland. His reason for returning was that his effects there had been arrested by Henry Rankine, factor in 'Rotchell'. James was heavily in debt to him and in March was forced to assign various documents to him, including a Decreet of Apprising and several bonds, one of which was the one granted to him so long ago by McDonald of Glengarry.[35] His wife had accompanied him as far as London where she remained 'not resolved to com to Scotland to goe to Franc[e] or stay in Ingland'. James had settled on her half of a bond, originally granted by William, Earl of Erroll, in 1631, 'for an annuitie during hir lyff'. This was a satisfactory arrangement, as it involved an annualrent out of the lands of Slains. The bond had belonged to John Forbes of Culloden and had only become the property of James Mowat in 1667.[36] In that same year James had also acquired lands in the North-East belonging to Alexander Irvine of Drum, having apprised them.[37]

The rest of James's family remained in Paris. Patrick Caune or Con, grand-nephew of Patrick Con of Artrochie, then living in Paris, voiced his concern for James Mowat's 'poore children' during his absence. James Mowat owed Patrick Con 7,000 livres and had had to consign his plate, a cross and some other items to him as surety for the last 1,000 livres he had borrowed. In November 1671 James Sinclair of Roslin, back in Edinburgh, had written to Con suggesting the Earl of Erroll's bond might be worth acquiring from James Mowat and Patrick Con had agreed, with certain reservations. In a letter to James Sinclair dated 23rd March 1672, he expressed concern that there might be 'former ingagments upon that debt for those brouke marchands some tymes dispose twyce or thryce the same thing to divers personns'. He had also learned from James Mowat that his wife's annuity was linked to the bond, and he had 'told him that I would take upon me to pay hir yearly rent but she should take hir haserd of my Lord as I did'. (The 'good old woman' was due to receive an annual payment of £20 Sterling.) The settling of the arrangement dragged on. In April 1677 Patrick Con informed James Sinclair that he had written twice to James Mowat who was in Rome for his consent to settle his acquisition of the Earl of Erroll's bond. James Mowat had replied that long ago he had put the Earl's bond in James Sinclair's name for Patrick Con's use. He enclosed a bond dated 29th May 1677, recording that the arrangement had been made in 1669. The Earl of Erroll's bond was not the only document Patrick Con acquired. In 1674 James Mowat, then in Edinburgh, wrote to Patrick saying that he had put 10,000 livres owed to him by the Laird of Balquholly in his name and that the 'lands ar decreeted for that summe', asking him to give his children something on account. In a letter dated 9th September 1674, Patrick asked James Sinclair for his opinion as to what he ought to do about this arrangement.[38] What he did do emerged later.

In Edinburgh, in July 1674, James Mowat brought an action against Robert, Lord Southesk, to whom he had supplied money both in France and England when he was travelling abroad with his governor, James Maitland. His account covered the period 20th July 1659 to Lammas 1667 and amounted to £2,859. He informed the court that 'factors abroad doe never give money nor states accompts with young noblemen, bot only with ther governoris' – a very wise practice, but it was always the young noblemen's fathers who delayed settling the bills.[39] In that same month he had James Cowpar, a fellow merchant in Paris, brother of the laird of Gogar, incarcerated in the Edinburgh Tolbooth over a debt of £1,512, owing to him since 1669. The debt had been incurred on behalf of James Cowpar's employer, Ninian Williamson in London, and it was for that reason that James Cowpar was able to effect his release from imprisonment.[40] In happier times he, Francis Kinloch and James Mowat had shared 'a cup of good claret of the werie best' and 'remembered Mr Williamsone'.[41] James continued to stay in Edinburgh for the next two years, bringing further actions against his debtors in an attempt to get his affairs in order. His loyal friend and factor in London, Alexander Blair, had died, but James's money and papers had not been returned by Isobell Bruce, the widow. James instituted an action against her for the return of his property.[42] His former apprentice, John Allan, cousin of Francis Kinloch, having left his service and moved to London, had become tailor to the King. He had ordered considerable quantities of rich materials from his former master. The itemised bill also included the information that James Mowat had outfitted Captain George Douglas for the French wars. John Allan owed James £1,283/9/-.[43] Some of the outstanding debts were long overdue. John Drummond fiar of Balloch had been supplied with £187 'for cloathes and that necesser for his utrikement and urgent affaires' as far back as July 1648, and James had to institute an action against Mr Henry Drummond, his heir.[44] Another action was brought against the grandson of Patrick, Earl of Brandford. In 1648 and 1649 James had made elaborate outfits for the Earl and his wife, Lady Jean. The three-paged itemised bill came to £763.[45]

While James was away from Paris, an action was raised against him there by Marie Crumelin, widow of John Randeau, a merchant in Paris, and her new husband, Peter Cadelain, also a merchant. When John Moreau, sergeant and macer of Paris, went to James's house to deliver the summons, the door was answered by his daughter who refused to give her name. She was probably Susane to whom James sent 40 crowns in April 1675, shortly before he returned to the Continent.[46] The previous February, Alexander Irvine of Drum had paid him just over £9,000 to redeem his wadset lands. James's return in April and the fact that he was able to send Susane 40 crowns suggests that he had emerged from all the litigation with some money in hand. But in July 1675 Patrick Con wrote that Mr Mowat 'is at Bruxelles in gret necessitie wronged and disapoynted be evrie bodie'. In the following year, in a bid to escape from it all, he applied to the Jesuits to become a lay brother, but was turned down because of 'his age and ignorance of the language'. One of the fathers also remarked that 'he would have found it verie hard in his old age being his lifetime accostomed to libertie and all good commodoties'.[47]

He was back in Paris in 1680, when Patrick Con described him as being 'noe more in condition, to cleare nor looke after bussines' and that he was 'in great neede'. In 1677 he had written that despite being owed so much by James Mowat, 'yet I helpe him and his children dayly to subsist and hav done more for them, then anie friend ever they had'. The following year, he wrote to Sinclair saying:

> You know poore man, his too much trust and honestrie is cause of his miserie, if others had been true to him, he had failled to noe bodie; this betwixt you and me; that know him particularly; others speak ill of him, but with small reasone.[48]

SOURCES

1. DI 21/34 f.127
2. RS1/43 f.84
3. RS5/9 f.450
4. Seafield muniments (SRO) — GD248/218
5. John Spalding — *Memorialls of The Trubles in Scotland and England AD1624 — AD1645* (SPC), i, 202–3
6. *RMS* ix, 1799
7. J Mackintosh — *History of the Valley of the Dee*, 28
8. RS5/11 ffs.458; 467
9. John Spalding — *Memorialls of the Trubles in Scotland and England AD1624 – AD1645* (SPC) ii, 254, 260, 326

10. P J Anderson (ed) – *Charters relating to the burgh of Aberdeen*, XLI, 412
11. RS5/13 f.288
12. L B Taylor – *Aberdeen Council Letters*, iii, 77
13. CR.LIII, 113 (Aberdeen City Archives)
14. *Ibid*, 200
15. Clerk of Penicuik muniments (SRO) – GD18/2454 and GD18/2505 contain the correspondence between them – information referred to hereafter is from these two classes, unless otherwise specified
16. RD1/592 f.48
17. RD1/528 f.508
18. RD1/536 – 9 Mar 1642
19. RD2/16 f.734
20. CS181/Misc 10/3
21. *Lauder of Fountainhall's Journal* (SHS (first series)) vol 36), 2
22. *Ibid*, 4
23. Airlie muniments (SRO) – GD16/34/120
24. *Ibid* – GD16/42/413
25. *Wardlaw MS* (SHS vol 47), 439
26. Airlie muniments (SRO) – GD16/34/194
27. G Blackhall – *A Breiffe Narration of the Services Done to Three Nobles Ladyes* (SPC), 139
28. *Ibid*, 143
29. Henderson of Fordell muniments (SRO) – GD172/1919; GD172/2400
30. RH15/87/2 – Letter Francis Kinloch and his wife – 25 Feb 1664
31. Miscellaneous papers (Edinburgh City Archives) – Bundle 58, no.2610
32. CS181/3787 – James Mowat v Lord Rutherford
33. Miscellaneous papers (Edinburgh City Archives) – Bundle 58, no.2615
34. CS7 181/3754 – Mowat and factor v Brand
35. RD4/33 f.107
36. RS3/76 f.5 – 2 Aug 1699
37. RS3/35 f.12 – 12 Mar 1675
38. CS181 Misc 10/3937; CS7/508 – Mowat v Robert, Earl of Southesk
40. CS15/484 – Cowpar v Mowat
41. RH15/87/2– Letter Francis Kinloch to his wife – Dec 1657
42. CS181/3813 – James Mowat v Isobell Bruce etc
43. CS181/3809 – James Mowat v Allan
44. CS181/3795 – James Mowat v Drummond
45. CS181/3781 – James Mowat v Ruthven
46. CS15/478 – Crumelin and her spouse v Mowat
47. M V Hay – *The Blairs Papers* 1603–1660, Appendix iii, 245
48. CS181 Misc 10/3

CHAPTER SIX

The Baronet of Nova Scotia

After the lands of Balquholly had been apprised by Mr Roger Mowat, an anomaly existed in that there were two men using the title of Balquholly. Mr Roger Mowat assumed the title, after being granted a charter of the lands, while James Mowat, brother and heir of Magnus, continued to design himself 'of Balquholly'. Actual possession of the lands would only come after Roger's death, so James Mowat and his son, Patrick, and family continued to live on the lands. Moreover, seven years were allowed after an Apprising for the debt to be repaid. Given what had gone before, however, it is hardly surprising that James Mowat was never able to repay the money Roger had lent him. Roger's action appears to have been prompted by his desire to keep the lands in the family and to save the main line from bankruptcy. Balquholly and Freswick became just part of his many assets and he appears to have had no desire to force his cousin to quit the lands. Magnus Mowat's widow also continued to live at Balquholly. James Mowat survived his brother by about eight years. Then, after their grandfather's death, his grandchildren moved north to the family's castle of Freswick.

James Mowat's life might have been very different. In November 1571 the King confirmed a charter in which it was recorded that Charles Mowat of Knokintebir had named as his heir, to his lands in the parish of Kilmaurs in Ayrshire, his grandson, James Mowat, son of his eldest son, also James, who had predeceased him. If his grandson had no heirs, then the lands were to pass to his second son, William, and his heirs and whom failing to his third son, Alexander and heirs. If all failed, then the property was to go to James Mowat, second son of Patrick Mowat of Balquholly.[1] There was no immediate relationship between the Mowats of Knokintebir and the Mowats of Balquholly at that time. Any relationship must have dated back to a much earlier period. Friendship between the families, however, made it possible for Charles Mowat to make absolutely sure that the lands continued to be owned by someone bearing the name of Mowat. In the event, his grandson did survive and did have heirs. In 1626 James Mowat of Busbie was served heir to his grandfather.[2] In that year the Mowat lands in the parish of

Kilmaurs passed out of the family, having been sold to Andrew, Earl of Eglinton.[3] Pride in the name of Mowat was obviously not so strongly felt by Charles Mowat's descendants.

Patrick Mowat, James Mowat of Balquholly's son, was at the castle when his uncle Magnus was dying and he witnessed the bond recording Mr Roger Mowat's large loan to his father. Some of his time was spent up in Caithness where he was caught up in a feud between his second cousins, the sons of John Sinclair of Ulbster, and the Doull family in Wick. When the Sinclair brothers had been 'of tender years', their natural brother, William, had murdered John Doull. Thereafter, several clashes between the two families ensued, 'in remembrance of the slaughter'.[4] In March 1643 he was in trouble with the church, being summoned by the Presbytery of Turriff to answer a charge of relapse in adultery with Janet Gordon. Later that year he was again summoned to appear before them, this time charged with scandalous behaviour with Margaret Reid. He was an elusive customer, however, the minister of Turriff having frequently to report that Patrick was away in the south.[5] He appears to have married a daughter of Captain Alexander Copland who was a soldier of fortune in Poland, and it is possible that Patrick himself may also have been one for a time. This might explain his having been passed over by his father. Many Scots were killed in the wars in Europe and some never returned, having decided to settle abroad. He had been out of Scotland in 1623, for James Mowat, W.S, when travelling back to Edinburgh from his estate in Berwickshire, 'met Patrick Mowat returnit from England at Sowtray'.[6] Thereafter he became embroiled in the growing conflict between the Royalists and Covenanters, siding with the former. Muskets, powder and ball had been stockpiled at Balquholly castle. These were stolen by the young laird of Cromarty and taken off to Towie Barclay castle, to the south of Balquholly. It was during a raid on 10th May 1639 by the laird of Gight and other Royalist lairds in order to recover the stolen weapons that the first fatality of the Bishops' War occurred. David Pratt, a servant of the laird of Gight, was killed by a shot fired from the house-head. Four days later the Trot of Turriff resulted in the small army of Covenanters being put to flight by the Royalists under the Marquis of Huntly. Patrick Mowat continued in the Royalist cause until his death during the battle of Alford in July 1645.[7] In 1665 his son, Magnus, was charged by Letters of Horning raised by Sir John Wemys of Bogie, collector of the cess, to pay land tax for most of 1645 and part of 1646. Magnus informed the court that his father being killed in the service that year, his hous takine and made ane garison, his wholl landis quartered and poynded for above two yeiris. [His house and lands] were plundered and spuilzied and much of his timber work and plenishing destroyed.

He therefore felt that he should not be troubled and distressed with having to pay the cess, 'his father having suffered both his lyffe and so great loss for his loyaltie'. He also argued that the lands at that time had belonged to Mr Roger Mowat. Sir John Wemys replied that Roger's ownership had not been 'cled with possession' then.[8] Magnus had certainly been short of money after his father's death. In January 1649 Captain William Neilson of Artrochie, briefly the wadsetter of the lands the Cons of Auchry had moved to, had advanced Magnus a sum of money 'for the doing and outreding of certaine of my necessar affaires and bussiness'. Magnus had promised to deliver three chalders of oatmeal on his own horse to any place Captain Neilson named within six miles of the house of Balquholly and to pay him £21. The Obligation had been drawn up at Turriff and witnessed by his maternal grandfather, Captain Alexander Copland, who had apparently been unable to help him financially at that time. Magnus was then only 19.[9]

Mr Roger Mowat's base was in Edinburgh where his livelihood was. He had married the daughter of an Edinburgh merchant and his children had all been brought up in the burgh. He was ever conscious of his rural roots and of his connection with such an ancient family, but being an advocate in Edinburgh made him one of the professional elite. In the burgh, he dealt with and socialised with some of the leading men of the time, and it would have been anathema for him to have given it all up. In his old age he was just as active as he had been all his life. There were no thoughts of retiring. Two years before he died, he was up in Aberdeen, bringing several actions in the Sheriff Court. On his arrival in the burgh he crossed swords with Thomas Cargill who debarred him from entering premises he had used in the past. Undaunted, Roger brought an action against him and thereby gained entry.[10] He was not a man to be opposed. His second cousin, Thomas Mowat sometime of Ardo, had not been long dead, but nonetheless Roger set about settling the problem of the debt owed to him, by bringing an action against Thomas's daughters, Margaret and Elizabeth.[11] The following January he lent money to Patrick Leslie of Whitehall, a former Provost of Aberdeen, and his son.[12] Back in Edinburgh, in August 1652, he apprised the lands of Ardross and Elie in Fife belonging to Sir William Scott. Roger had lent him 10,000 merks in 1643 which had never been repaid. Sir William Scott had been impoverished by the civil war. He had stood as cautioner to the Earl of Crawford who had levied troops for the King's service, and he had been taken prisoner at the battle of Worcester in 1651. Roger made his elder son, George, his cessioner and assignee, and in October George received a charter of the Ardross and Elie lands and was infeft in them in November.[13] Not many months after that Roger was dead. He had been too old to get caught up in events leading to Cromwell's occupation. Many of those to whom he had lent money lost everything. For example, he had lent substantial sums of money to Sir William Dick of Braid in 1641 and 1652. Sir William Dick had been Provost of Edinburgh from 1638 to 1639, during which time he had lent his entire fortune to the Covenanting army. He was reputed to have been the richest man of his time in Scotland. He died in a debtors' prison in London on 19th December 1655.[14]

George Mowat was served heir to his father on 8th June 1653.[15] He was made a burgess of Edinburgh, but apart from that appears to have lived off the money and lands which his father had given to him during his lifetime or which he had fallen heir to after his death. A considerable part of the movable property he had inherited had been in the form of unredeemed bonds for large amounts. Several of these had been granted by men such as the Duke of Hamilton and the Earl of Traquair who had had their estates forfeited or sequestrated. Roger had, for example, lent the Earl of Traquair 16,000 merks (£10,666/13/4d) for 'defraying of his debts' in 1650. The likelihood of these debts ever being honoured was extremely slim. In 1661 the Earl of Traquair, who had been Lord Treasurer in Charles I's Privy Council, was found begging in the streets of Edinburgh.[16] The unredeemed bonds could also be sold. George Mowat did just that with the Earl of Traquair's bond. He assigned it to his brother-in-law, David Wood tutor of Bonnyton, shortly after his father's death. The Earl of Traquair's cautioners listed in the bond were the Earl of Southesk; the Earl of Queensberry; the Earl of Ethie; Lord Linton; Sir Alexander Carnegie and Sir John Veitch, an unusually large number which possibly explains why David Wood agreed to the purchase.[17] He may have used his wife's money. She had received a dowry of 10,000 merks, had another 10,000 merks of her own and had been promised a further 2,000 merks on the death of her father.[18]

George Mowat and his wife appear to have spent their early married life in Fife. She came from a Fife family. She was Elizabeth Hope, daughter of Sir John Hope of Craighall, a judge and President of Cromwell's Committee of

Justice. In January 1656 George Mowat gained possession of lands belonging to the Earl of Annandale, following his apprising of them, indicating that he had taken steps to reclaim some of the money which had been owed to his deceased father. By 1659 he and his wife had left Fife and moved to Balquholly. He or his father had obviously had the castle repaired. Alterations also appear to have been made to turn the fortified building into a more comfortable manor house. In April of that year he wrote a letter to Major William Shairp of Houston which gives a small insight into the kind of person he was. A good-natured and affable man, he was no fool. Being a man of leisure, he had time to enjoy intrigue and gossip. He had written to Shairp warning him not to accept an offer which the Earl Marischal was planning to make him, giving him reasons why he should refuse it. What that offer was emerged more fully at a later date. He told Major Shairp not to breathe a word of what he had written to him until they met, asking him rather dramatically to lay his hand on his heart. The drama was heightened by his hinting that he had a 'mysterie' for him, but that he would 'forbeare to communicat it thus', because of lack of paper and time. His time had been restricted as he had sent the letter with Mr Robert Gordon who had been staying at Balquholly and who had left very early in the morning, the lady of the house 'not being out of her bed'.[19]

While George had been given Ardross, his brother, Joseph, had been given the lands of Fallside in the parish of Gordon in Berwickshire, shortly before their father's death. The lands had been acquired by Mr Roger Mowat from his good friend, James Mowat W.S. George's sisters had all married into good Lowland families. His Marjoribanks uncles and cousins all lived in and around Edinburgh. Life in Fife and Edinburgh and its surrounds must have seemed infinitely preferable to life on estates so far away in Aberdeenshire and Caithness. George seems to have been keen to divest himself of those estates and acquire a prestigious property close to Edinburgh. His plans to do so would have been hampered by the recession which prevailed during the Commonwealth. Once Charles II was restored, however, he was able to make a move. He was attracted by the estate of Inglishton in the parish of Kirkliston to the west of the burgh. In order to purchase it, he decided to rid himself of some of the lands he had inherited. During his lifetime his father had disponed a part of the Freswick lands to Magnus Mowat, grandson of James Mowat of Balquholly. At the beginning of 1660 George approached Magnus, offering to return the lands of Balquholly to him. George's factor in Caithness at that time was William

Sinclair of Rattar who was also Magnus's stepfather-in-law. George had recently redeemed Skriscarie and Sonsequouy, another part of the Freswick lands, from William Sinclair. The lands had previously belonged to the deceased Magnus Mowat of Balquholly's illegitimate son, Thomas, who had been forced to wadset them to William Sinclair.[20] George suggested to Magnus that the Balquholly estate should be split. Magnus would receive the lands of Balquholly in Aberdeenshire, while the Freswick lands in Caithness would be sold to William Sinclair. The money received for Freswick could then be used by Magnus in part payment for Balquholly. Shortly before this arrangement was mooted, however, Magnus had acquired the wadset of lands in Shetland belonging to Mr James Mowat of Ollaberry and perhaps should have hesitated before agreeing to George's terms.[21] He nevertheless agreed to the arrangement and on 11th July 1661 gave a bond to George Mowat for 21,000 merks (£14,000).[22] On the 11th July 1661 a Contract of Alienation was drawn up between them and, thereafter, the lands of Balquholly returned once more to the mainline family with the stipulation that if Magnus failed to honour their agreement, then the Balquholly estate would once again be owned by George.

Just over a year later the lands of Balmellie, which had caused so much conflict in the past, caused yet another problem. Magnus Mowat's great-uncle and namesake had pledged the lands to James Mowat of Ardo as security, after not repaying the loan of 5,000 merks which had been made to him in 1598. In 1603 James Mowat had obtained Letters of Inhibition against Magnus, having heard a rumour that he planned to dispose of Balmellie. The rumour had been well-founded, for Magnus had, in fact, subsequently sold the lands to John Urquhart tutor of Cromarty in 1612. In 1656, George Mowat had approached the Earl of Erroll, then owner of the teinds of Balquholly, with a view to purchasing them. Various 'meitings and co-mounings' had taken place and, in April and May of that year, a contract had been drawn up whereby the Earl agreed to grant George the right to the teinds. Unfortunately, the writer who drew up the document made use of an outdated charter of the Balquholly lands which included Balmellie. In 1662 the Earl of Erroll raised an action in the Court of Session against George Mowat and the new owner, Magnus Mowat, in an attempt to have the error rectified. Magnus argued that he had not inherited Balquholly, but had purchased the lands and that the contract had been part of the sale, but the Lords decerned that the contract should be produced and Balmellie deleted from it. (By 1680, the contract had still not been corrected.)[23]

George Mowat was able to purchase Inglishton a few months after he disposed of Balquholly and in 1662 sold his father's estate of Dumbreck to Walter Cochran elder, bailie of Aberdeen, and his wife.[24] At the beginning of 1665 he sold Ardross and Elie to James Muirhead, fiar of Broadhouse-holme.[25] During the previous year he had been made a baronet of Nova Scotia. It was a purchased honour, he having made a contribution to the settlement in Nova Scotia, a scheme initially projected by James VI. Thereafter he was known as Sir George Mowat of Inglishton. He did not enjoy his new title or estate for long. At the end of August 1666 he lay dying. He was then in his 40s and unprepared for death. Four days before he died he made a Translation of all his assets to his 'dearest wife'. Listed were several of the yet unredeemed bonds for large amounts which he had inherited from his father, as well as the bonds for all the money still owed to him by Magnus Mowat and William Sinclair of Rattar.[26] His testament, recorded the following July, reflects the suddenness of his death, the inventory not marrying up with the debts listed in the Translation to his wife.[27] It was fortunate for his widow that her brother was a lawyer and would be able to assist her in sorting out her husband's affairs. Their children were all under-age. In 1676 the eldest, Roger, went to Leyden to study. At the end of year he was no longer there, but staying in London, his presence in that city worrying his mother and his two uncles, Mr Archibald Hope and Sir John Harper of Cambusnethan, who were his tutors. An agreement was dispatched for him to sign, he having to promise not to alienate his lands or to contract any debts. He also had to concur that he

> being a young man subject to the frailtie of youth and understanding
> how easily may be deceived and circumvented be subtill and craftie
> persons who may intyse me to the dilapidence of my landis rentis goodis
> and estate . . . [should] use advyse and counsell of my best freinds . . . be
> whome I may be directed in my affairis.[28]

His 'best freinds' were, of course, his two uncles. Four years later he signed over all his movable heirships to Mr Archibald Hope.[29] He was dead by February 1683, when his brother, William, was served heir to him.[30] By 1704 their cousin, Captain William Mowat, who had succeeded to his father's lands of Fallside, had fallen heavily into debt to his uncle and aunt, Mr Daniel Robertson and Margaret Lyll, and had been forced to alienate Fallside to them.[31] In 1673, five years after his father had died, he had been taken to court by his cousin, Sir Roger Mowat of Inglishton, over a Bond for 1,000 merks which Sir Roger had acquired. It had originally been granted by his father, Joseph Mowat, to Mistress Grissel Toures of Innerleith in 1665, and his uncle, Sir George Mowat, had been his father's cautioner on that occasion. This document had found its way into the hands of Mr Robert Dicksone of Burnbrige, advocate, and had subsequently been purchased by Sir Roger Mowat. But he had been a minor at the time and its purchase and the action which followed had been the work of his uncles, Sir John Harper and Mr Archibald Hope.[32] Mr Archibald Hope appears to have been somewhat over-zealous in his capacity of guardian and it therefore comes as no surprise to find him later appearing as heritable proprietor of Inglishton. At the beginning of 1684 he disposed of it to Hugh Wallace, His Majesty's Cashkeeper. The sasines make no mention of the Mowats, despite the fact that Sir William Mowat of Inglishton was still very much alive and living in London then.[33] Interpreted differently, perhaps Mr Archibald Hope had been forced to take the helm. There are hints that his nephews were an irresponsible lot. They had certainly been cushioned by their grandfather's wealth. After the sale of Inglishton, all that was left was the baronetcy. In 1710 Sir William Mowat's only son, Winwood Mowat, was recorded as heir to his grand-uncle, Joseph Mowat of Fallside, as well as to his uncle, Captain William Mowat.[34] He did not register arms as the next baronet of Inglishton, however. It is ironic that all the lands which Mr Roger Mowat had acquired during his lifetime were sold and most of the wealth which he had generated was dissipated or found its way into other hands.

SOURCES

1. *RMS* iv, 1979
2. *Retours*, i, 241
3. *RMS* viii, 1246
4. RD1/522 f.258
5. CH2/1120/1
6. *The Book of the thanes of Cawdor* (SPC), 264
7. Seafield muniments (SRO) – GD248/401 – Information Robt Mollison anent his Claim on Balquholly
8. CS15/370 – Lord Bogie v Magnus Mowat
9. RD1/568 f.173
10. SC1/7/9 – 1 April 1651
11. *Ibid* – 30 July 1651
12. RD1/565 – 28 Jul 1652
13. RS2/2 f.158; RD1/565 – 16 July 1652; *RMS* x, 39
14. RD1/568 – 3 Aug 1652; RD1/609 – 2 Jan 1655

15. *Retours* xxi, 158
16. M Lynch – *Scotland, A New History*, 291
17. RD1/609 – 3 Jan 1655 (2 deeds)
18. RD3/29 f.131
19. Shairp of Houston muniments (SRO) – GD30/1711
20. RD4/16 f.505
21. SC1/7/24 – 23 Sept 1664; RD4/11 f.214
22. Seafield muniments (SRO) – GD248/218 – Inventar of papers produced by John Mowat, advocate
23. CS26/55 – 15 Dec 1677; CS26/58 – 1 Feb 1680
24. *RMS* xi, 155
25. CS22/33 – 26 July 1671
26. RD2/17 f.740
27. Edinburgh Commissary Testaments, CC8/8/73 – Testament of Sir George Mowat of Inglestoune – 26 July 1667
28. RD3/41 f.120
29. CS29; 4 Feb 1729 – Duff of Hatton v Creditors of Balquholly
30. *Retours*, xxxvii, 128
31. RD3/105 – 18 May 1705
32. RD3/18 f.170; CS22/42 – 30 July 1673
33. RS27/37 ffs.288, 290
34. RS3/99 f.207

CHAPTER SEVEN

The Rightful Heir

Magnus Mowat would have found it almost impossible to refuse Sir George Mowat of Inglishton's offer to return Balquholly to him. A descendant recorded that the long alienation of the lands had been extremely grievous to him.[1] Magnus had only been 14 when his father was killed at Alford, and from what he told the court in 1665, when Sir John Wemys of Bogie brought an action against him, he was very proud of the fact that his father had given his life for the King. He would have been brought up to be proud and conscious of the family's ancient roots and he must have been told stories about his forebears' exploits. Without a father or Mowat uncles, he must have felt very isolated at times. The only member of his father's family to have survived from the days when the family had been in possession of the estate was his aunt, Isobel. She too was an isolated figure. Three years after the lands had been apprised by Mr Roger Mowat, her father, James Mowat of Balquholly, had made provision of 2,000 merks for her in a bond in which he recorded that he had done so 'for fatherly love and affection and for her better provision and help to ane marriage quhen occasion sall offer'.[2] In the event, she did not marry. She would have been an unattractive prospect, merely having a bond for 2,000 merks to offer and one which was never likely to be honoured. She appears to have found a way to make ends meet by escorting Catholic children to the Jesuit colleges on the Continent and so led an itinerant existence, travelling to and from Scotland and France by way of London. In 1659 she employed James Mowat's associate in Paris, Francis Kinloch of Gilmerton, as her factor in an attempt to obtain the 2,000 merks promised to her in her father's bond. Both must have welcomed the return of the lands to her nephew, Magnus, in 1661. He was duly approached by Francis Kinloch who, according to Magnus, 'thundred me with bigg words and forced me to defend my self at law'. The outcome of an action brought by them in February 1663 was that the Lords decerned Magnus to make payment to his aunt.[3] Nothing was forthcoming and, while in London, Isobel Mowat assigned her father's bond to James Mowat in Paris. He agreed to maintain her for life, paying her £33/6/8d 'English money' at four terms of the year.[4] He explained to Magnus in a letter written at the end of 1667 that his actions had been 'to keep your a[u]nt off thir hands of thesse who intended no lesse than the ruin of your estate'. In his reply to James, written in January 1668, Magnus defensively wrote about the 'parlie' with his aunt, saying that 'she is a person with whom I have no credit to be hard, nather did my inclinations lead that way' and that he had often wished she would leave off her travels 'and com hence and live in hir fathers familie'. As heir to his grandfather, he was bound by the terms of the bond to pay his aunt, and when the bond was assigned to James Mowat in Paris, he was liable to pay James. On 29th February, James wrote to inform Magnus that his factor in Edinburgh, John Brown, had an account of all the money which had been disbursed to his aunt, suggesting that Magnus settle it. Magnus's answer was to object to doing business with John Brown for reasons known to various people he knew, but he did not elaborate.[5] He was obviously playing for time.

His mother's family would have contributed to his sense of isolation. Captain Alexander Copland was living at Aberchirder in the parish of Marnoch in Banffshire in 1640, his career as a mercenary having ended. Thereafter, he appears to have gone to live with his son, John, who had become the owner, through marriage to a widow, of the small lairdship of Haughs, to the east of Keith. In the nearby parish of Grange lived the family of Innes of Paithnick. The countryside thereabouts was, at that time, broken up into a number of small lairdships, a breeding ground for trouble. In 1646 John Copland was one of the accomplices of Walter Innes of Paithnick who attacked Alexander Gordon of Auchanachie who was walking in his own fields about a mile from his house. Their poor victim suffered in 'great dolour and pain' for five weeks before he died.[6] The incident had not been an isolated one, but was symptomatic of the insularity that existed in that area in those times. The Coplands would have been too caught up in their own affairs to show much interest in the young and impoverished Mowats.

Magnus's ownership of Balquholly only lasted for eight years. He was dead by the end of 1669. Before the Balquholly lands were returned to him, he would always have been conscious that his grandfather had named him as his heir. He was recorded in documents as 'Magnus Mowat of . . .' and as 'behavand as heir' to his grandfather, reflecting his uncertain status. His signature to several deeds and letters appears merely as 'Mowat', suggesting that he had also inherited more than a little of the Mowat pride. That pride would have been swelled when he had married into a notable Caithness family. Both his father–in–law and his father's cousin by marriage were sons of George Sinclair of Mey. His father's cousin, Christian Mowat, had married Sir John Sinclair of Geanies and Dunbeath, a wealthy merchant. Sir John had acted as guardian to the children of his brother, Alexander Sinclair of Latheron, after the latter's death in 1647. As he had no sons of his own, William Sinclair, his brother's eldest son, succeeded him. Sir John also appears to have shown an avuncular interest in the young Mowats. He had acquired Dunbeath c.1624 and had renewed the castle there, and Magnus and his brothers and sisters must have visited him and his wife while their father was still alive. After the loss of their father and grandfather, Mr Roger Mowat had disponed part of the Freswick lands to Magnus and thereafter he took the title 'of Freswick'.

On 22nd January 1651 the marriage contract between Magnus and Jean Sinclair, the young daughter of the deceased Alexander Sinclair of Latheron, was drawn up. They were to marry between that date and the following April. Sir John Sinclair of Dunbeath stood in for his deceased brother, agreeing to grant the young couple 5,000 merks out of the deceased Alexander Sinclair's readiest goods and gear at Whitsunday and Martinmas, to be paid a year and a day after the marriage.

Magnus for his part agreed, with the consent of Mr Roger Mowat, to infeft Jean Sinclair in the liferent of Tofts, Midtown of Freswick and the milne of Freswick and, in addition, the sequels of Auckingill and Stroupster.[7] Sir John Sinclair died in September 1651. A year had not passed since the marriage and, as a result, the tocher remained unpaid. At a much later date arguments arose as to whether Sir John Sinclair should have been responsible for paying it or whether it should have been paid by Jean Cunninghame, widow of Alexander Sinclair of Latheron, and her new husband, William Sinclair of Rattar, out of her deceased husband's estate. It was commented then that 'a persone of Dunbeithe's quality and estaite' could not have been suspected of circumvention. What was not recalled at that time was the fact that Sir John had died so soon after the marriage. The tocher appears never to have been paid.

Magnus led an impoverished existence in Caithness. Before his death, Sir John Sinclair of Dunbeath had drawn up a list of outstanding debts, among which were bonds amounting to 3,000 merks (£2,000) owed to him by Magnus's grandfather, James Mowat of Balquholly. He added to the entry – 'iff Mr Roger Mowat pay them not they ar disperatt'.[8] Magnus, as heir to his grandfather, would have been liable to repay the money. Sir John Sinclair's comment indicates that this would have been an impossibility. It was obvious that the Balquholly family had been propped up by Mr Roger Mowat for many years. In 1651, when his marriage contract was drawn up, Magnus, in addition to promising his wife the liferent of parts of the Freswick lands, also promised to grant any daughters of their marriage 2,000 merks each. To have made such promises indicates that he must have been relying on the future generosity of Mr Roger Mowat.

1661 marked a dramatic change in his life. In that year he was able to lend Mr James Mowat of Ollaberry £23,333/6/8d in return for the wadset of his lands of Ollaberry in Shetland. He was also able to grant a bond for 21,000 merks (£14,000) to Sir George Mowat of Inglishton, being part of his payment for the return of the Balquholly lands. With the acquisition of these properties came a rise in social standing. Through his marriage he found himself connected to several of the notable families in Caithness. His brother-in-law, for example, became the new laird of Dunbeath. Magnus may have become laird of Balquholly, but he and his family did not return there in 1661 nor did they remain in Caithness. They moved instead to Shetland to live on his recently acquired Ollaberry lands. There, they may initially have occupied the Mowat house at West Heogaland in North-maven, but they were soon settled on the island of Papa Stour, occupying and altering the old manor house called the Northhouse there. It was only in 1666 that he took his family back to Balquholly.

He did not remain there long, however, returning to Shetland the following year. It being the time of the Dutch War, he appears to have taken advantage of the degenerating situation, following the restoration of Charles II. Although he held no commission, he seized a Dutch ship and then had the temerity to institute an action against the governor of the fort at Bressay Sound who had commandeered the ship for the use of the garrison there.[9]

During all the time his family lived in Shetland and later at Balquholly, he had led an itinerant existence. In 1663, for instance, he had been on Lewis in January, in Shetland in March and in Edinburgh by September. While in Shetland and Edinburgh, he had borrowed money, but on Lewis he had stood as cautioner to a Kirkwall merchant. This involvement with a merchant partly explains his constant journeying. The Registers of Deeds from 1660 onwards contain a number of bonds and obligations involving merchants either made by Magnus or in which he is recorded as cautioner. His involvement, however, appears only to have been minor. Some of the money he borrowed was undoubtedly for his own use. Being involved in

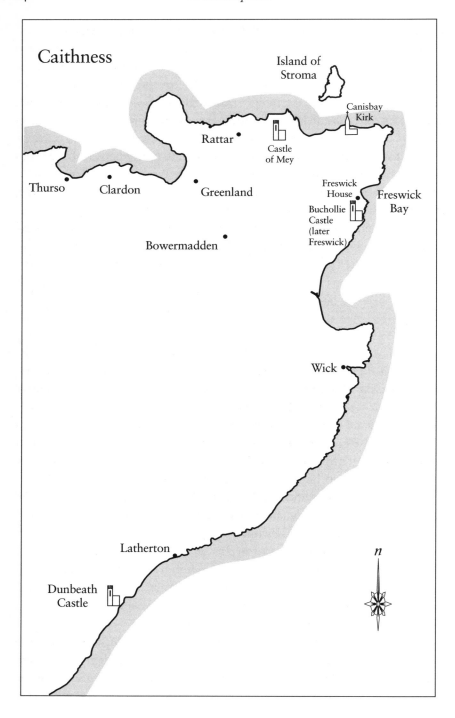

Caithness

Island of
Stroma

Canisbay
Kirk

Rattar •

Castle
of Mey

Thurso •   Clardon •   Greenland •

Freswick
House

Freswick
Bay

Buchollie
Castle
(later
Freswick)

Bowermadden •

Wick •

Latherton •

Dunbeath
Castle

n

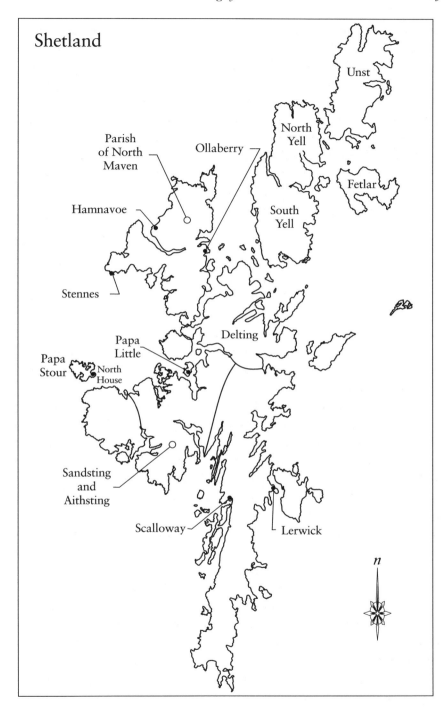

Shetland

Unst

North
Yell

Ollaberry

Parish
of North
Maven

Fetlar

Hamnavoe

South
Yell

Stennes

Delting

Papa
Little

Papa
Stour

North
House

Sandsting
and
Aithsting

Scalloway

Lerwick

n

the mercantile world carried with it an element of risk, and Magnus appears to have had no long-running partnership with any one merchant. He did, however, have close associations with two men who were merchants – Alexander Farquhar in Edinburgh and James Murray of Pennyland in Caithness. Alexander Farquhar was the son of James Farquhar, merchant and burgess of Aberdeen. Both he and Magnus stood cautioner for James Farquhar in 1662. Magnus also stood cautioner for Alexander Farquhar himself on several occasions. Had he survived, he would have found himself embroiled in the financial difficulties which beset Alexander Farquhar after his father's death. Two Caithness lairds, William Sinclair of Rattar and John Murray of Pennyland, had dealings with the Farquhars. John Murray of Pennyland had four sons, James Murray, the eldest, David Murray of Clardon, Francis Murray, a merchant in Thurso, and John Murray, a writer in Edinburgh. David Murray had married into Magnus's wife's family. He and his older brother, James Murray of Pennyland, were involved in trading with the islands of Orkney and Shetland, as well as with the Continent. Magnus joined forces with James Murray to purchase ships. They owned the *Swan* and a half share in the *Janet*, both skippered by Patrick Traill, an Orkney man.[10] Magnus also had a third share in the ship *The Young Tobias*. In 1668 he appointed Roger Mowat as his factor to pursue George, Earl of Linlithgow, in an action involving his part share in the ship.[11] Roger Mowat, the nephew whom Mr Roger Mowat had taken to Edinburgh, had become a writer there and was for two years Commissary Depute of Shetland. Magnus may have had some influence in his having been appointed, for James Murray of Pennyland and his brother, John Murray, writer in Edinburgh, were conjunct tacksmen of the Commissariot of Orkney and Shetland at that time.[12] Roger Mowat appears as witness to many of the bonds which Magnus granted and was employed by him to deal with his legal affairs. Roger Mowat, in turn, may have had some influence while deputy to William, Earl of Morton, in the appointments of Magnus as one of those to try witches in Shetland and of James Murray of Pennyland and George Mowat of Hamnavoe, Magnus's brother, as Commissioners of Excise and Justices of the Peace there in 1666.[13]

Another family in Caithness who had left Aberdeenshire were the Kennedies of Kermucks. They had been forced to flee north in 1652, following their quarrel with the Forbes of Waterton family. The dispute had begun over the cutting of a ditch, but had ended with the murder of Thomas Forbes of Waterton. They had settled on the island of Stroma, just off the north coast of Caithness. John Kennedy younger of Kermucks married Magnus's younger sister, Elizabeth. His sister, Elizabeth Kennedy, married George Forbes of Corse, an Aberdeenshire laird, and when Magnus and his family returned to live at Balquholly, their friendship grew. While staying at Corse castle, Magnus had made bonds of provision for his daughters which he had promised to make in his marriage contract, and he was there in March 1666 along with John Murray, writer in Edinburgh, and Jean Kennedy who was visiting her sister and her husband. On that occasion, Jean Kennedy, having decided to leave the island of Stroma and 'being perswadit of the fidelitie and cair that George Forbes of Cors will taik for me in my absence', had appointed him as her factor to obtain payment of the rents out of the two pennyland and three farthing land of Nethertown on the island which she had let to her brother, John, in 1662 and which he had never paid.[14] George Forbes extended this faithfulness and care towards his friend, Magnus Mowat, but later came to regret having done so.

Magnus had another sister who married into a very old Caithness family and two brothers. He appointed one of them, George, as his factor in Shetland to manage the Ollaberry estate.[15] George married Margaret Mowat, one of Mr James Mowat of Ollaberry's daughters, and Magnus attended their wedding in Shetland in November 1662.[16] He granted them the lands of Hamnavoe, Heogaland and Stennes, part of the Ollaberry lands in the parish of Northmaven.[17] He appears to have been very close to his younger brother, James, who married one of the daughters of Alexander Mowat in Redcloak. James had been a small boy when their father died and Magnus appears to have taken him under his wing. He was Magnus's companion on many occasions, making several trips up to Shetland with him, and was with him when he died in November 1669.[18] Magnus's death was sudden and unexpected and as a result his affairs were left in disarray.

As late as 1694 some of the debts he had left were still outstanding. In that year an account was drawn up listing the amounts still owed to the respective heirs of Sinclair of Rattar and Sir George Mowat of Inglishton. Magnus had granted four bonds to the latter between 1660 and 1663, part of which had been repaid, and William Sinclair of Rattar's family had ten unpaid bonds, dating from 1658 to 1665, in their possession. The debts, including interest which had accumulated since Magnus's death, by then amounted to £31,482/9/-.[19] These, however, had not been the only debts which had not been paid.

Magnus's fortune appeared to have turned full circle. The debts which he left far exceeded the amount he had lent to Mr James Mowat of Ollaberry in 1661. But had there really been such a change in his fortune? After his death, certain evidence emerged which threw a different light on some of the events during his life, especially with regard to his wadset of the Ollaberry lands in Shetland. In June 1677 Mr James Mowat of Ollaberry's daughters and their husbands sought to redeem their father's lands from Magnus's heir, William. The Heritable Disposition which had been drawn up between Magnus and Mr James Mowat in 1661 had stipulated that the Ollaberry lands were to be redeemed by James Mowat, second son (and heir) of Mr James Mowat, then living in Copenhagen. The debt was to be repaid 'haill togidder' and in one sum of gold. Magnus had to be given 60 days' warning personally in presence of a notary and, should he not appear to receive payment, then the money was to be left in the hands of the Dean of Guild of an unspecified place. Also left blank was the amount of interest which would have had to be paid at the time of redemption. James Mowat had died in Copenhagen before 1672. In that year his two sisters, Margaret and Barbara, were served heir to him. Then, in January 1677, the sisters had arranged for a Summons to be delivered to William Mowat, Magnus's heir who had come of age and was living in Aberdeen. Then, Letters of Supplement were read at the mercat cross in March, requiring him to go to Shetland to St Magnus kirk in Northmaven to receive repayment of the £23,333/6/8d in gold, plus the accumulated interest. On 3rd June the sisters and their respective husbands, George Cheyne of Esslemont and George Mowat of Hamnavoe, duly went to St Magnus kirk, carrying with them 'severall great bagis of money consisting of certan considerable sowmes'.[20] Also present were David Johnestoune, a somewhat elderly notary, and several witnesses. William Mowat did not appear and the following day George Cheyne and George Mowat consigned the 'considerable sowmes' into the safe-keeping of Gilbert Ollasone of Isleburgh, bailie of Northmaven, until such time as William Mowat appeared to claim the money. But what those 'great bagis' had contained was only 30 rix dollars worth less then £90.[21]

The Instrument of Consignation drawn up at St Magnus kirk on 3rd June at first presents a picture of the Shetland family wanting to do right by the Balquholly heir. They had apparently produced the money 'haill togidder' and in gold and had given him sufficient warning that they wished to redeem the lands. But the document had been drawn up at a remote venue by an elderly notary and certain suspect 'great bagis' of money had been produced. Moreover, the witnesses had all been men of little standing.

These anomalies throw an entirely different light on the whole event. They bring into question whether Mr James Mowat of Ollaberry had ever received £23,333/6/8d.

It seems remarkable that Magnus had been able to alter his impoverished state so rapidly that he was able to make such a large loan to Mr James Mowat and not long after that to contract to pay 21,000 merks to Sir George Mowat of Inglishton. What emerged much later was that there had, in fact, been little change in his fortune. By the 1660s Mr Roger Mowat's Apprising of the lands had, according to Magnus, 'outrun and long since expired' and his right to part of the Freswick lands been affirmed by Mr Roger Mowat's Disposition and Assignation to him. In April 1660, a month before Charles II was restored, he drew up a Minute of Contract with William Sinclair of Rattar whereby, with the consent of Sir George Mowat, he sold all the Freswick lands to him for 32,000 merks (£21,333/6/8d). William Sinclair agreed to use 2,000 merks of the money to repay a debt owed by Magnus to John Crawford, merchant. The remaining 30,000 merks (£20,000) was to go to Sir George Mowat to be used in part payment by Magnus for the Balquholly lands in Aberdeenshire. It was to be paid in instalments, the first, amounting to £10,000, to be paid the following Whitsunday. The first instalment was duly forthcoming from William Sinclair and was then paid by Magnus to Sir George. On 11th July 1661, when the Contract of Alienation was drawn up between Sir George and Magnus, it was recorded that, in addition to the 30,000 merks from the sale of Freswick, Magnus himself was to pay Sir George 21,000 merks. The previous day it had been arranged that William Sinclair was to pay an additional 9,000 merks (£6,000) to Sir George on Magnus's behalf, being the balance due on the Aberdeenshire lands.[22] The total amount due by Magnus, therefore, amounted to 30,000 merks: the same amount William Sinclair had agreed to pay for Freswick. Sir George, therefore, stood to gain 60,000 merks (£40,000) from the sale of both estates.

But had Magnus been engaged in some double-dealing? In April 1660 it had been arranged that he was to receive each of William Sinclair's instalments of the 30,000 merks and then pass the money on to Sir George. Did he then persuade Mr James Mowat to dispone the Ollaberry lands to him the following May, pretending that the money was his? Converted into pounds, 30,000 merks came close to £23,333/13/4d. However, two months later when the Contract of Alienation was signed, Mr James Mowat of Ollaberry had been present. It therefore seems unlikely that Mr James

Mowat would have been invited to witness the document and have agreed to do so, had Magnus pledged the 30,000 merks to him just a few months earlier.

Sir George Mowat had obviously intimated his intention to sell the lands long before July 1661. The plan to sell Freswick to William Sinclair in April 1660 had been his idea. The arrangement would have ensured that he would have received at least some payment for the sale of the lands. The passing of more than a year before the Contract of Alienation was signed does suggest a certain amount of hesitation on Sir George's part to finalise his plans. What probably contributed to his vacillation was the fact that William Sinclair of Rattar had had to wadset part of his new acquisition of Freswick to his father-in-law in order to find the money to pay the first instalment of the 30,000 merks.[23] It would also have caused Sir George some concern that Magnus might not have been able to pay his share for the Balquholly lands. What also may have worried him was that Magnus had already borrowed money from William Sinclair on several occasions and so there was always the prospect that William Sinclair might offer Magnus's bonds as part of his payment for Freswick. Magnus's acquisition of Ollaberry in May 1661, bringing in a yearly income, would certainly have provided Sir George with sufficient security to enable Magnus to pay him the 21,000 merks. So, had Mr James Mowat agreed to part with Ollaberry in order to help Magnus regain his family's lands and had Magnus even resorted to the old ruse of appealing to the 'weill and standing of the hous'?

Elizabeth Hope, wife of Sir George Mowat, was the granddaughter of Sir Thomas Hope of Craighall, the renowned Lord Advocate. During the 1630s Charles I had sought to recall all the church lands which his father, James VI, had given away during his reign. Sir Thomas Hope had suggested a way the landowners who had acquired those church lands could retain them, despite the Act of Revocation. They could wadset their lands to the King and in the contract could record that the King 'was indebted [to them] in great sums of money, whereas indeed he was never owing any'.[24] Had the Heritable Disposition drawn up between Magnus and Mr James Mowat taken this form? Had Magnus ever paid £23,333/6/8d to Mr James Mowat? Was the whole arrangement a fraud?

By 1661 Mr James Mowat of Ollaberry was getting on in years. He had been quite wild in his younger days. In the winter of 1638, he along with Ninian Nevin of Windhouse and his brothers had been involved in a skirmish with Mr Patrick Cheyne of Vaila, two of his brothers and several others at the castle yett at Scalloway. The Cheynes had come off worse and had brought an action against their aggressors three years later. At the end of 1641 the Nevins and Mr James Mowat waited in Edinburgh for ten weeks for the trial to begin, only to have it delayed because the Cheynes did not appear. They were then warded in the castle at Scalloway, but escaped. By June 1642 they were in lodgings in Edinburgh and the trial was set to resume, but once again an impediment occurred. This time, Mr James Mowat and Ninian Nevin were unable to appear,

> haifeing thair bodies and faices brunt with powder upon the saxt of Junii instant, quhairthrow they ar not of abilitie to cum out of thair ludgeingis for keiping of this court without haizert of thair lyves.

While they had been walking on the north side of the High Street, some gunpowder had exploded in one of the Luckenbooths. They had been thrown to the ground and had suffered burns. Their procurator, Mr Roger Mowat, delivered their excuse to the court. The trial finally got going in earnest in July, and on 5th August all three were found guilty. Mr James Mowat and the two Nevins were ordered to pay £1,000 to Mr Patrick Cheyne and his brother, Laurance Cheyne, in compensation for their each having lost fingers in the fracas. They also had to pay 300 merks (£200) to His Majesty's Treasurer for the crime of mutilation. The fines were paid shortly afterwards.[25] During their stay in the burgh, Mr James Mowat and his father had borrowed just over £3,000 from the Treasurer of the kirk rents and the Treasurer of the College of Edinburgh. The money had probably been intended to see them through their protracted stay and to pay the legal fees and fines. Almost ten years later, in August 1653, both men were put to the horn and an Inhibition was raised against them, as the money had still not been repaid.[26]

This debt appears to be the only large debt which Mr James Mowat had incurred, and so the payment of the £23,333/6/8d by Magnus in 1661 would have been more than enough for him and his wife to live on, and yet, in September 1662, he agreed to sell Magnus his liferent right to the Ollaberry lands which he had reserved in 1661. In exchange, Magnus granted him the use of Balquholly castle, the mains and its stock and the customs and services of the lands. The first arrangement drawn up between them allowed that should Mr James Mowat wish 'to returne to his countrey altogether', then Magnus would furnish him with part of the Ollaberry lands and 'such victual for maintenance of his house'. Margaret Sinclair appears to have been somewhat more perceptive than her husband, being 'not fullie satisfied' with the arrangement. To sweeten the pill, Magnus promised to pay her £1,000 on the death of her husband.[27] Both seem to have found living at Balquholly to their liking, and so another agreement was drawn up finalising the arrangement. Had Magnus pressurised the old man into drawing up a false wadset in 1661, and was his granting to him of the liferent of Balquholly a means of recompensing him or even of keeping him quiet? He certainly made sure that Mr James Mowat received the £1,000 payments promised in September 1662.

One further curious incident occurred five years after the wadset arrangement had been made. In July 1666, shortly before Mr James Mowat died, Magnus received a charter under the Great Seal of the lands of Ollaberry, following his apprisal of them.[28] However, Mr James Mowat had not borrowed the money pledging the lands as security. The arrangement had been in the form of a wadset and no term for repayment had been set. What had also been stipulated was that they were to be redeemed by Mr James Mowat's son after his death, so that technically Magnus had no right to apprise the lands. Mr James Mowat's approaching death must have caused him to act in this manner 'for his better security'.[29] Magnus had never been infeft in the Ollaberry lands and there was also reason to expect that Mr James Mowat's son might contest his claim to the property, for it emerged that Mr James Mowat had already disponed his lands to his son, prior to 1661, reserving his liferent of them.[30] The Heritable Bond of 1661, the work of John Murray (brother of James Murray of Pennyland), contained a clause listing an inordinate number of possible legal documents drawn up previously which were declared null and void. He and the servitors of each of the two men were the only people present. Had Magnus meant by his 'better security' that he was ensuring that once Mr James Mowat was dead and his son returned from Copenhagen he would be covered, should the son begin to ask some awkward questions?

In the autumn of 1669, Magnus and his brother, James, boarded a ship for Shetland. Some time after their arrival they sailed over to Norway. Magnus was never to return. He was murdered in November and his body buried there. He had lived for most of his life on credit, often delaying paying his debts. He had also been a man who could at times be somewhat economical with the truth. Both failings would have aroused a certain amount of animosity in many of those he had dealings with, so that he may have been the victim of a grudge. He could also have been the victim of a brawl.

SOURCES

1. Seafield muniments (SRO) – GD248/401.
2. RD1/528 f.314
3. Seafield muniments (SRO) – GD248/398/5
4. RD4/25 f.756
5. Seafield muniments (SRO) – GD248/398/6 – contains all the above correspondence
6. *TBFC* – May 13th 1935 – 'The Regality of Strathisla', 93; DI 30/4 f.131
7. SC14/50/3 f.136
8. Mey Papers (SRO) – GD96/683/1
9. Sir James Dalrymple of Stair – *Decisions of the Lords of Session*, 1683, pp.487–8
10. RD4/20 ffs.435, 469; RD2/37 f.468, SC10/4/8A
11. RD3/23 f.399
12. CS15/410 – Murray v Mowat
13. *RPC* ii, 136; 592 (third series)
14. SC14/50/2 f.370
15. Seafield muniments (SRO) – GD248/398/5
16. *Ibid.*
17. Bruce of Symbister muniments (Shetland Archives) – GD144/48/9
18. *Ibid* – GD144/187/16
19. Seafield muniments (SRO) – GD248/408/2
20. Bruce of Symbister muniments (Shetland Archives) – GD144/113/22
21. *Ibid* – GD144/114/6
22. RD4/162/1 – 2 June 1739 (error for 1738)
23. *Ibid*
24. T G Snoddy – *Sir John Scot of Scotstarvit, His Life and Times*, 122
25. J Irvine-Smith (ed.) – *Selected Justiciary Cases, 1624–1650* (Stair Society), ii, 464–484; a poor transcription of their Petition to the Council in RH1/2/838, (original in Shetland Archives)
26. DI 85/7 – 6 Aug 1653; RD1/576 – 1 Jan 1653
27. SC1/60/24 – 23 Sept 1664
28. *RMS* xi, 932
29. Seafield muniments (SRO) – GD248/402/2 – Memorandum of George Mowat of Hamnavoe
30. *Ibid.*

CHAPTER EIGHT

The Guardian

While Sir George Mowat of Inglishton may not have felt as strongly about his roots as his father had done, he still kept in touch with his northern relatives. Before his father's death, he accompanied him up north on several occasions. They were both in Aberdeen in May 1651, when they witnessed a bond for 1,000 merks being granted by John Mowat in Glithno to his son-in-law, Alexander Mowat in Redcloak.[1] Another witness on that occasion was Alexander's brother, Mr James Mowat, back in Scotland, taking a rest from accompanying his charges on their travels abroad. The previous October he had been at Balmuto in Fife, visiting his cousin, Margaret Mowat, and her husband, David Boswell.[2] In September 1652 he had been in Edinburgh but had thereafter gone to the Continent as governor and companion of Alexander Forbes, son of Alexander Forbes of Boyndlie. They were abroad for almost two years, during which time Mr James had great difficulty in obtaining money from the boy's father, and had finally decided to return with his charge, before the two years were up, fearing that Alexander Forbes was in danger of being 'corrupted'.[3] James was still unmarried in March 1656, when Sir George sold him his father's wadset of the lands of Logie.[4] Thereafter he designed himself 'of Logie' – a fitting title for a 'discreet gentilman'. By then he was in his mid-50s. It was probably during that earlier visit to Aberdeen that he renewed his acquaintance with his distant cousin, Margaret Mowat, one of the two surviving daughters of Thomas Mowat of Ardo. She was in her early 30s. Her younger sister, Elizabeth, had married William Douglas, master tailor in London, and it was probably during a visit to her newly married sister that Margaret's relationship with Mr James Mowat blossomed. He was certainly in London in 1659. They were duly married and settled in Aberdeen where their first child, John, was baptised in St Nicholas church on 8th November 1661. Margaret was expecting their second child when James died 'of the stone' on 5th March 1662.[5] The child Margaret was carrying was a girl and was baptised on 15th January 1663 and called Margaret. James was buried in Margaret's grandfather's tomb in St Nicholas church, and in July of that year she obtained permission to erect a stone to their respective memories. It was fairly elaborate and cost 103 merks.[6] The inscription to her husband read:

> Here awaits for a blessed Resurrection, Mr James Mowat of Logie,
> second Branch of the most ancient Family of Mowats, but second to few
> or none in Piety and all manner or kind of Virtue[7]

In his will James had appointed his brother, Alexander Mowat in Redcloak, as his executor and also as tutor and curator to his children. During his brother's absences abroad, Alexander had acted as his factor, collecting the rents from the Logie wadset. In 1661 he handed over £433/6/8d to James, being a year's rent from the property.[8] It had been relatively easy to oversee Logie. It was only two miles from Redcloak. Being an executor and guardian proved to be far more difficult, and Alexander appears to have felt uncomfortable in the role. He was a country dweller and not versed in the complicated procedures involved in winding up an estate. It was inconvenient for him to leave Redcloak for any length of time. He had married Sibilla, the only surviving daughter of John Mowat in Powbair. After her mother Isobel Hervy's death her father had moved to Glithno, part

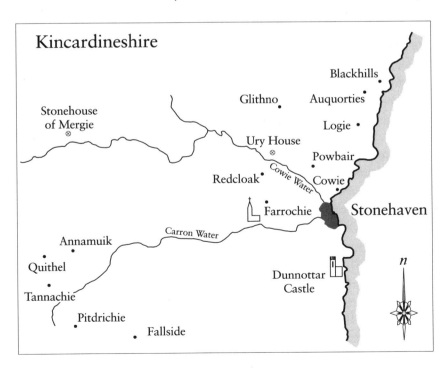

of the Earl Marischal's lands, where he had remarried. Glithno was a fairly substantial property to lease, the silver rent in 1650 being £100.[9] As a tenant of the Earl Marischal, John Mowat would have contributed to supplying the garrison at Dunnottar in the latter part of 1651. Thereafter, George Ogilvy of Barras held out against Cromwell's army until forced to surrender through lack of provisions in early 1652. That was the occasion when Christian Fletcher, wife of the minister of Kinneff, gained access to the castle under the pretext of visiting George Ogilvy's wife and smuggled out the Scottish regalia in some bundles of lint. John Mowat in Glithno died in 1655. The inscription on his tombstone records him as 'a godly and provident man'. When Sibilla had married Alexander Mowat in 1638, her father had given them his possession of the town and lands of Powbair, as well as 2,000 merks. At Aberdeen, in May 1651, he had added a bond for a further 1,000 merks and no doubt his thrift resulted in Sibilla inheriting even more. His 'godly' contribution took the form of 89 merks (£59/6/8d) mortified to the poor of the parish of Fetteresso.[10] Sibilla and Alexander invested some of the money in a wadset of the lands of Mergie in the neighbouring parish of Glenbervie in 1657, on which lands stood the house called the Stonehouse, still standing today. It was not a good investment. Not long after that the lands were sold by the owner, Sir William Douglas younger of Glenbervie, to Alexander Carnegie of Pittarrow who redeemed the lands prematurely from them for £3,000, thereby denying them a yearly income.[11]

In the August following his brother's death, Alexander went to Edinburgh to consult lawyers and to see his cousin, Sir George Mowat of Inglishton. His brother's estate had amounted to £21,604/4/-.[12] Part of it was tied up in unredeemed bonds, two of which had been granted by Sir George to Mr James for 2,000 merks and 1,000 merks in 1656 and 1657 respectively. Alexander possibly had not estimated how much ready money he would need for his sojourn in the burgh, as he had to borrow 50 merks (£33/6/8d) from Sir George, but, unlike his Balquholly cousins, he repaid it shortly afterwards.[13] Sir George was not so forthcoming with the 3,000 merks (£2,000) owed to Mr James's children, and in January 1664 Alexander took him to court, complaining that he had 'divers tymes requyred and desyred' payment of the amounts plus an annual interest of 240 merks (£160).[14] He was more successful in obtaining at least 100 merks (£66/13/4d) from Alexander Forbes of Boyndlie.[15]

Alexander spent much time and energy, thereafter, getting advice from lawyers. He was always careful to enclose their fee with his letters, usually a rix dollar. Although he could write, he could not be called an educated man. His spelling was eccentric even by seventeenth-century standards. Most of the time he employed William Auchinleck, a notary public, to write his letters for him. Alexander kept meticulous accounts of all his expenses and charged very little for his services. As executor, he was required to gather in all his brother's assets and then divide them three ways: two thirds would go to the children, John and Margaret, for their bairns' parts and a third to the widow, Margaret Mowat, for her terce. As the children were underage, they could only inherit the capital when they reached their respective majorities. Part of the money, however, could be used for their maintenance. Following his brother's death, it had been agreed between Alexander and his brother's widow that the children would each receive 100 merks (£66/13/4d) annually for their 'aliementing and entertaineing', and Alexander had duly paid her this amount until 1666 when he had stopped. In that year Margaret Mowat had remarried, to Mr Walter Copland in Ardneidly.

In October 1666, accompanied by his friend, Thomas Innes in Blackhills, Alexander journeyed to Aberdeen, ostensibly to make the annual payment to his charges, but before he went to Margaret Mowat's house he visited a notary where he had an instrument drawn up, requiring her to hand the children over to him 'to be keeped and educat be him as neirest of kin'. He felt that as he was their tutor, they should be living with him, as they had done just after his brother's death. (In a letter to a lawyer who sent him a 'soments' to go to Edinburgh at the beginning of 1668, he gave his reasons. He expressed resentment that he had 'now to mantene Mr Copland' and he also felt that the children could be 'cheper mantent' if they were living at Redcloak.) If Margaret refused to deliver them up, then he felt that he should no longer have to pay their maintenance. Margaret was furious at Alexander's request. She pointed out that their original agreement had stipulated that she would keep the children and receive an annual payment for their education. The children were still young and 'in a sicklie and tender condition', but even if they were strong and healthy, she would never agree to their going to Redcloak. 'It was ane remote mureland place wher ther is no convenience of breading or learneing', unlike Aberdeen where 'they have the convenience of education'. She also pointed out that since the annual payment for the children was 'so mean and inconsiderable', Alexander had 'no ground to quarrell the samen'. Perhaps he had 'some bad intention' towards them. After all he was their next of kin![16]

In 1666 Sir George Mowat of Inglishton had offered Alexander part of the bond which he had received from Magnus Mowat when he had returned Balquholly to the mainline family. Alexander obtained two bonds from Sir George, one of which was in the name of Margaret Mowat, posthumous daughter of his brother, James, and the other in name of his own three daughters, Margaret, Elizabeth and Marie.[17] Perhaps he had been foolish in agreeing to this arrangement, given the trouble he had encountered in not obtaining payment of the earlier bonds which had been granted to his brother, but his cousin moved in the best of circles and had a large estate just outside Edinburgh and he had obviously been flattered by the offer of part of the Balquholly deal. His brother's children had also inherited their father's wadset of Logie. Their mother as the widow was entitled to a third part of the liferent of the annual income. Alexander had initially made sure the children and their mother received that money, journeying to Aberdeen each year to receive their discharges. Since the original wadset had been made, the lands had been apprised by Mr James Beaton, M.D, who, in turn, had sold them to Andrew Arbuthnott of Fiddes. As a result, Andrew Arbuthnott wished to redeem them. This presented Alexander with a problem. If the wadset was redeemed, the annual income from his brother's estate would be reduced. In 1667 he journeyed to Aberdeen to consult 'men at law', hoping to find a way of delaying the redemption. The journey turned out to have been a wasted one, for in 1668 Margaret Mowat and her children were summoned to court as a result of several actions brought by Andrew Arbuthnott during that and the previous year and were forced to accept the 8,000 merks (£5,333/6/8d) redemption and give up the lands.[18]

To ensure that his nephew and niece continued to have a steady income, Alexander looked for another wadset in which to invest the money. In 1670, two months after Logie had been redeemed, he arranged with Sir David Carnegie of Pittarrow to become wadsetter of Mergie, the lands which he and his wife had possessed so briefly in 1657. He used the 8,000 merks which he had received on behalf of his charges from the redemption of Logie and added 1,000 merks of his own money, thereby becoming joint wadsetter with his nephew.[19] The lawyer who arranged the wadset was Robert Penman, writer in Edinburgh. He had made the arrangement at Pittarow's house in the burgh. It had been stipulated that Alexander was to keep the 'Stonehouse' in good repair. Obtaining an instrument of sasine had been delayed by Alexander's omission in sending his procuratory giving Penman permission to stand in for him. He had not forgotten the rix dollar, however.[20] In that year, Alexander held a meeting of the baron court at the Stonehouse. William Auchinleck acted as clerk and Thomas Innes in Blackhills as bailie. They appointed William Hunter as officer. Three years later they held another court at which the five tenants of Mergie appeared, summoned there on account of their tardiness in paying their rents.[21]

Sir George Mowat's untimely death, and the confused state of his affairs which ensued, further complicated Alexander's continuing struggle to administer his pupil's affairs. The question arose as to who was liable to pay the various bonds which had been granted by Sir George Mowat. Did Alexander pursue his heirs or Magnus Mowat of Balquholly? He was given conflicting advice by the lawyers, but in 1668 he was able to obtain £123/4/- for Margaret Mowat and £71/13/4d for his daughters from Magnus Mowat of Balquholly.[22] He had initially employed Mr Alexander Davidson, advocate in Aberdeen, but appears to have been fobbed off by him, although he did recommend a fellow advocate, Walter Reid, in his stead. In Edinburgh the obvious candidate had been his own brother, Roger Mowat, by then an established lawyer, but his brother had had other things on his mind and was often away from the burgh. Invariably Alexander's letters were answered by Robert Penman, informing him that his brother had not as yet returned and that nothing had been done about his 'persute'. The result was that the brothers fell out and Robert Penman took over. Remarking on the discord between them, Penman said he was 'reallie sorie for it'. What had fuelled the quarrel between the brothers had been an action by Alexander which Roger had deemed unwise. Harried by Margaret Mowat and learning of the unexpected death of Magnus Mowat of Balquholly in Norway in 1669, Alexander had decided to take matters into his own hands. He had obtained a decreet from the Sheriff Court in Aberdeen in 1670 and persuaded Mr Walter Copland, his sister-in-law's new husband, to make the journey to Balquholly to summon two of the tenants there, Alexander Ramsay and George Piery. In January, in the depths of winter, Walter Copland set off on horseback from Ardneidly just outside Keith. When he reached the Deveron, he had difficulty crossing, 'the water being great, hazardeing also my horse in causeing him swime not having convenience of any bot neir meit for the carying of horses'. On his arrival at Balquholly, he found the tenants hostile. In his letter to Alexander, written as soon as he returned to

Ardneidly, he reported that the tenants had complained that Alexander
had

> never came that lenth neither to craive them nor yit to asist them in the
> suffering Loss by the Laidy crying out befor all present (and ther wes no
> few present) that ye had dealt very unjustly and more that ye wes
> scaircely ane honest man in useing them so.

He had managed to persuade the two tenants who had been summoned to
meet him at Turriff the following day, where they had agreed to pay
Alexander the victual of crops 1669 and 1670, on condition that he 'wold
absolutly free them of the Laidy's trouble'. He had, however, noticed that
there appeared to be insufficient corn in their yards and that Alexander
would probably have 'to poynd the bestial'. He urged him to go to
Balquholly himself with his son-in-law, James Mowat, the deceased Laird
of Balquholly's brother, who would be sure to be more welcome than he
had been. It would be no use sending Thomas Innes in Blackhills in his stead.
He warned him that Magnus's widow, Jean Sinclair, had been very angry
and that the tenants 'favours the Laidy more then they doe you'. He
reported that she was planning to move into George Piery's house 'whether
it be right or no'.[23] She would have felt very vulnerable after her husband's
murder.

Thereafter, Alexander abandoned any further actions against the tenants
and instead turned his attention to the heirs of Sir George Mowat. He first
appealed to Sir Roger Mowat of Inglishton, but, having got nowhere, was
forced to institute an action against him in 1682. Sir Roger Mowat, or more
likely his uncle, Mr Archibald Hope, maintained that George Forbes of
Corse was liable. His connection will be revealed shortly.[24]

Because Mr James Mowat's children had been so young when he died,
Alexander had to spend over 20 years as their guardian. During all that time
he also had his farm to run and his own affairs to look after. For part of the
time he had been bailie of the baron court of Ury and so would have been
required to implement decisions of the court. He had also been an elder of
the kirk, and apart from attending the kirk on Sundays would also have had
to attend meetings of the Session. In 1670 he agreed to become factor to
James Auchinleck who was going to settle in Ireland.[25] In that capacity he
acted for James after his father's death when his mother wished to sell their
house in Cowie to the tutor of Leys.[26] Looking after James Auchinleck's
affairs was far easier than looking after those of his brother's family, however.

Alexander also lent out money. Elizabeth Douglas, wife of George Ogilvy of Barras who had held out against Cromwell at Dunnottar, for example, owed him £134/6/8d on her death in April 1657.[27]

Country life was hard. The farm of Redcloak, which was a mixed one, would have taken up a good deal of his time, although much of the labouring would have been done by servants. At the time of his death he employed five.[28] He was wealthy enough to own his own team of oxen for ploughing the land and he had several cows to supply the family with milk and butter. The surplus would be sold, thereby augmenting their income. If he wanted to journey to neighbouring farms or to Stonehaven, he had several horses to choose from. He had a sizeable herd of sheep which would graze on the common land. He grew oats, bear (barley) and a small quantity of rye. He would also have kept poultry to supply the family with eggs and enable him to pay his customs dues. His wife and daughters would have been employed in the running of the house, their spare time being taken up with spinning and knitting. Merchant goods and luxury items would have been ordered from Aberdeen and brought by local carriers.

In 1647 the Earl Marischal had purchased the barony of Ury. Redcloak was part of the barony, and in 1661 he attempted to evict Alexander and his family from the farm and the Waulkmill of Ury.[29] What had actually occasioned the Earl Marischal's action was that he owed money to Major William Shairp of Houston and had offered him Redcloak to offset the debt, once he had managed to evict the Mowats. Alexander argued that he was the tenant of Sir George Mowat of Inglishton, as heir to Mr Roger Mowat of Balquholly, and not of the Earl Marischal. His uncle, Mr Roger Mowat, had put the tenancy of the properties in his own name after his brother George's death in 1645.[30] Alexander also maintained that Redcloak had been tenanted by his family for over 80 years. The Earl Marischal retaliated by claiming that he possessed an Assignation and Renunciation of the properties by Sir George Mowat, but this had been a bluff for he had subsequently been unable to produce the documents to verify his claim. The court decided that Alexander had the right to continue in the tenancy. Before any action had taken place, wind of the Earl Marischal's plan had reached Sir George Mowat at Balquholly. In April 1659 Sir George had written to Major Shairp to inform him that he had heard that the Earl Marischal planned to 'pitch upon' him 'a rowme called Readcloak belonging to me by right', warning him not to accept the offer. Major Shairp had been pressurising the Earl Marischal to repay a debt to him. He needed the money urgently because he had used up his 'father's possessions with out his consent'. Sir George also impressed upon him that the 'small parcel' of Redcloak had been possessed by Mowats for 'above seven score years' (he probably meant seventy) and that the Earl Marischal 'hes no right in the Wald' to it.[31]

In 1668 Alexander and his wife lent 600 merks (£400) to Patrick Levingstone of Pitdrichie and his son, and in return were granted an annualrent out of the lands of Annamuick and Quithel in the parish of Glenbervie.[32] In that year he was summoned to Edinburgh to contest a case which had been brought against him by Margaret Mowat. To journey south, he told his lawyer, was

> ane thing imposebill to me to doe for senc I have your last [letter] my wyff and holl famellie hey bene bedfast and I never sane the kirk within senc as I hop the minester will attest.[33]

It is possible that Sibilla did not recover. She was certainly dead by the beginning of 1670.

Their eldest daughter, Margaret, appears not to have married. Their youngest daughter, Marie, married, fairly late in life, Andrew Moncur in Barnhill. Alexander granted them 2,000 merks (£1,333/6/8d) in tocher, but Marie appears to have died at the birth of her second child and Alexander, still owing 1,000 merks of the tocher, assigned it to his eldest grandchild, Robert Moncur, to inherit when he reached his majority.[34] In Marie Mowat's testament dative, it was recorded that she was still owed 1,632 merks (£1,088) by Magnus Mowat of Balquholly and his son which included 16 years' interest on the bond originally granted by Sir George Mowat in 1666.[35] Their middle daughter, Elizabeth, married James Mowat, Magnus Mowat of Balquholly's younger brother, and they settled at Redcloak. In February 1680 Alexander and his son-in-law were granted an annualrent of £64 out of the lands of Redcloak by Robert Keith of Redcloak, making their tenure even more secure.[36] Three years before that, Alexander had lost his good friend, Thomas Innes in Blackhills.[37] In 1681, in a letter to Dr James Leslie in Aberdeen, Alexander wrote:

> Sir, this fournicht bygon I have had extraorinerie aicken in my left leg and find that I may never goe nor lie upon the nicht nor sleep at all and especiallie upon the nicht I mey not keep my bead for extrordinerie pene.[38]

He struggled on for another four years, dying in the winter of 1685. His debts amounted to more than double his inventory. The inventory was estimated at £787, while he owed £1,822.[39]

But shortly before he died he had disposed of most of his assets. He had sold an Obligation to Andrew Strachan, sheriff clerk of Kincardineshire. It had been granted to him by the Earl Marischal in 1646 and had provided him with an annualrent out of the Earl's lands of Netherkirklands and two acres of Nether Toucks for over 40 years.[40] He had also granted bonds to his two surviving daughters, Margaret and Elizabeth, stipulating that Elizabeth's one was to go to her daughter, Christian, after her death. His son-in-law, James Mowat, did not survive him for long. Before he died he made over the annualrent of Redcloak to his wife and daughters, Christian and Jean. Elizabeth Mowat married again to Andrew Strachan, sheriff clerk, and moved to Netherkirklands. Thus came to an end the tenancy of Redcloak which had been in the Mowat family for almost a century. Andrew Strachan died in July 1697. Elizabeth Mowat soon followed him. In 1700 her daughters, Christian and Jean, sold their father and grandfather's annualrent of Redcloak to Margaret Ogilvy, the widow of Robert Keith of Redcloak.[41] There had been no one to carry on the farm. Christian married and moved to Aberdeen and Jean married a merchant in Stonehaven.[42] Their brother, James, left for America shortly afterwards where he established himself as a merchant in Maryland.[43]

SOURCES

1. SC5/1/3 − 18 June 1655.
2. RD1/573 − 24 Nov 1652
3. A Tayler − *The House of Forbes* (TSC), 356
4. RS7/6 − 3 May 1657
5. *SN&Q*, second series, vii, 52
6. Seafield muniments (SRO) − GD248/401
7. R Monteith − *An Theater of Mortality*, p. 92
8. Seafield muniments (SRO) − GD248/401
9. *Miscellany of the Third Spalding Club*, ii, 194
10. CH2/153/1 − November 1659
11. RD3/10 f.118; Fetteresso papers (SRO) − GD105/774
12. CS181 /3745 − Mowat v Mowat
13. CS150/111 − Mowat v Mowat
14. CS15/344 − Mowat v Mowat
15. Seafield muniments (SRO) − GD248/401
16. CS26/28 − 19 Feb 1668; CS15/401 − 8 Jan 1668
17. CS29; 26 July 1727 − Duff of Hatton v Mowats

18. CS15/408 – Andrew Arbuthnott v Mowat
19. RS8/7 f.159
20. CS150/111 – Mowat v Mowat
21. CS181/3824 – Mowat v Mowat
22. Seafield muniments (SRO) – GD248/217
23. CS150/111 – Mowat v Mowat
24. *Ibid.*
25. RD2/28 f.518
26. RD3/45 f.325
27. Brechin Commissary Testaments, CC3/3/6 – Testament of Elizabeth Douglas – 22 April 1657
28. St Andrews Commissary Testaments, CC20/4/15 – Testament of Alexander Mowat in Readcloak – 1 June 1686
29. CS15/305 – Earl Marischal v Mowat
30. Seafield muniments (SRO) – GD248/402
31. Shairp of Houston muniments (SRO) – GD30/1711
32. RS8/6 f.10
33. CS15/401 – Mowat v Mowat
34. SC5/58/1 – 29 July 1676; 22 Feb 1677
35. St Andrews Commissary Testaments, CC20/4/16 – Testament of Mary Mowat – 5 Nov 1695
36. Seafield muniments (SRO) – GD248/402
37. St Andrews Commissary Testaments, CC20/4/15 – Testament of Thomas Innes sometime in Blackhills – 23 Oct 1690
38. CS98/2132 – Mowat v Leslie
39. St Andrews Commissary Testaments, CC20/4/15 – Testament of Alexander Mowat in Readcloak – 1 June 1686
40. RD4/125 – 20 June 1719 – Contract of wadset, Earl Marischal to Andrew Strachan
41. SC5/58/7 – 20 Dec 1704
42. CS29; 23 Nov 1742 – Mary Keith v Christian Mowat
43. RS8/17 – 2 April 1702

CHAPTER NINE

Roger Mowat's Obsession

Mr Walter Copland was dead by May 1675. Although he was the tenant of a property just outside Keith, his wife, Margaret Mowat, owned a house in the Gallowgate in Aberdeen, and it was there that she continued to live after his death, being still alive in September 1695 when the poll tax was collected. Her daughter, Margaret, married Alexander Orem, a merchant and burgess of the burgh. Her son, John, when he grew up, had expressed the desire to train as an advocate. His uncle, Alexander, had arranged a consultation with an established advocate 'for going about it'. The cost of the exercise had been £4/6/–.[1] John had moved to Edinburgh to board with and be initially instructed by his other uncle, Roger Mowat, writer there, the expenses being met out of his father's estate.[2] Roger Mowat had been servitor to his uncle, Mr Roger Mowat, until the latter's death in 1653. Thereafter he appears to have been employed by Judge Broddie, being described as such when he was made a burgess of Edinburgh in 1659. In January of that year Roger had applied to become a notary public, painting a glowing picture of himself; as he said:

> for literature qualificatione and guid education he was become able and qualified to use and exercise the publict office of notarie to the people of the nation if he wer admited therto.[3]

On 1st May 1666 he was appointed Commissary Depute of Shetland for two years on the recommendation of Mr Nathaniel Fyfe, Commissary Principal of Orkney and Shetland, who had been assured of his 'qualification, sufficement and integrity'. Mr Nathaniel Fyfe had been concerned about the great distance between Orkney and Shetland and felt that there was the need for a deputy to serve Shetland itself.[4] Roger appears not to have remained in Shetland for the full term, being back in Edinburgh in August 1667 for his marriage at the age of 47 to Marie Logan, daughter of the deceased Mr Robert Logan of Mountlothian and Marion Logan. The marriage was to be the cause of his ruin.

Mr Robert Logan was the eldest son and heir of Robert Logan of Bonnyton.[5] In 1637 he married Marion Logan, daughter of the deceased

James Logan of Cowston.[6] James Logan was a member of a wealthy merchant family who owned lands in Newhaven and the mansion house of Sheriffbrae in the town of Leith.[7] The dowry given with Marion Logan amounted to 10,000 merks (£6,666/13/4d). On two separate occasions in December 1647 Mr Robert Logan lent George, Earl of Seaforth, just over £15,000 and in February of the following year, a further 3,300 merks (£2,200).[8] Some of the dowry money must have gone towards the loans. Thereafter, no sign of repayment was forthcoming from the Earl, and on 24th April 1650, at a Court of Apprising, Mr Robert Logan apprised the Earl's lands for the enormous sum of £59,405. The Seaforth lands covered a vast area and stretched from Kyle of Lochalsh northwards to Torridon, included such castles as Eilean Donan and Kishorn, lands in Ross and on the islands of Skye and Lewis – a mighty prize.[9] The Mackenzies, however, were not prepared to hand over any part of their lands or to repay any of the money, if they could avoid it. George, Earl of Seaforth, was in Holland when he died at Schiedam in 1651, having joined Charles II there.[10] By 1653 Mr Robert Logan too was dead, his son, Alexander Logan, his heir.[11] In March 1658 George Logan, merchant in Edinburgh and brother of Mr Robert Logan, apprised his brother's Apprising of the Seaforth lands for £18,750/15/6d, being granted a charter by Oliver Cromwell on 10th March of that year.[12] However, no mention of this was made when the marriage contract was drawn up in the Canongate on 6th August 1667 between Roger Mowat and Marie Logan. Marie's brother, Alexander, stood in for his deceased father, setting her dowry at 5,000 merks (£3,333/6/8d). The money was to come out of the bonds which the Earl of Seaforth had granted to their father and the subsequent Apprising. The arrangement was made with the consent of their mother, Marion Logan, who had the liferent. Alexander Logan then went abroad. Before he left, he made an arrangement which was to cause conflict amongst members of his family for the rest of their lives. As heir to his father, he was liable to pay his mother her terce. As his mother had the liferent of the Earl's bonds and the Apprising, it seems almost certain that her dowry money had been part of the loan her husband had made to the Earl. This meant that any income she was entitled to was tied up in those bonds. Her son, Alexander, was therefore her debtor. Alexander needed money to finance his plans to go abroad and in 1667 borrowed £3,000 from his brother-in-law, Roger Mowat, disponing to him and his wife all his money and property in liferent and to any son they might have in fee. Subsequent events indicated that by his actions, Alexander

Logan had indirectly granted the right to the Seaforth documents not only to his sister, Marie, but also to his other sister, Jean.[13]

Just two months after his marriage, Roger Mowat and his mother-in-law set out to journey north to see Kenneth, Earl of Seaforth, who was also Sheriff of Ross. They stayed at a tavern called Caddells, calling from there on the Earl and attempting to obtain some form of payment. Their lack of success resulted in Roger instituting an action against the Earl in the Court of Session in July 1669. Later that year he travelled north again, this time accompanied by his wife. He returned the following year and in January 1671 set out once again, once more accompanied by his mother-in-law. On that occasion they broke their journey at Brodie castle, where Marion Logan agreed to assign her marriage contract to Roger, on condition that her daughter, Jean, agreed with the arrangement. Whether Roger had used pressure or not, the acquisition of the marriage contract would have been a valuable asset to gain. It would have prevented his sister-in-law from making any claims on the Seaforth Apprising. When he and Marion Logan reached their ultimate destination, Roger had spent all the money he had taken with him and found himself in the embarrassing situation of having to borrow from the Earl's chamberlain. In 1672 they went north again. In 1673 his wife accompanied him instead of his mother-in-law, and this time

> he was detained 10 months under treisting and turned out in the mids of a great storme in Feb 1674 with his wyfe with out horse or money having got £60 from the Earl that January last.[14]

His mother-in-law had been more successful on one of their visits, having obtained 3,601 merks (£2,400/6/8d).[15]

It would appear that Roger had not only received his wife's dowry money in the form of a bond for which he could get no payment, but had also acquired a mother-in-law who did not know the meaning of thrift. She was a lady who, coming from a wealthy family, was used to having money, and when she needed she borrowed whether she could pay it back or not. She used to keep her papers 'in a bagg be itself upon the heid of . . . hir bed'. In it was a disposition of a third part of her tenement of land in the Canongate, dated 7th January 1658, made over to 'an blank persone'. This she used for 'disapoynteing riyval creditores'.[16] It was a successful ruse and she was able to borrow readily, even from her son-in-law. Many of the bonds she had granted later found their way into Roger's hands, he having rather foolishly purchased them from her creditors.

Jean Logan had not been at all happy about her mother's arrangement with Roger Mowat over the marriage contract. When they returned from up north to Edinburgh in 1671, she persuaded her mother to draw up a deed in her favour.[17] Thereafter relations between Jean and Roger and his wife became strained, borne out by a statement by the arbiters appointed to settle their quarrel that they wished to restore 'mutual love and duty between them'. When Marion Logan died, they squabbled over her effects. She had left all her movable goods and gear and household plenishings to Jean, together with a bequest of 5,000 merks. Roger Mowat accused Jean Logan of making use of her mother's 'blank' disposition, during her sister, Marie's, temporary absence from their mother's house.[18] Jean Logan questioned Roger's right to the tenement in the Canongate, accusing him of selling it to Hendrie Blyth or Agnes Hart. He avowed he had only heard about the disposal of the tenement while in 'the uther house' where he had happened on an action being heard involving the tenement.[19] Someone must have been guilty of removing the Disposition from the bag and filling in the blank space. The real cause of their quarrel was Alexander Logan's ambiguous arrangement over the Earl of Seaforth's bonds and the Apprising. They were the obvious source for the 5,000 merks left by Marion Logan to her younger daughter, Jean. Roger Mowat, himself, had a claim for the 5,000 merks promised in his marriage contract, and his brother-in-law had left him all his money and property in liferent. Moreover, Roger now had an heir, his young son, also Roger, who was due to inherit all in fee. As his son was yet a minor, Roger worked hard to ensure that he would receive what he was entitled to when he came of age. This meant attempting to exclude any claims his sister-in-law might have. But his son died long before he came of age, and in 1677 Roger obtained a charter of the Apprising in his own name and was duly infeft in the Seaforth lands.[20] He persuaded people that he now had the absolute right to them, and on the strength of this began to borrow money on account. He had already borrowed large sums prior to that, using the promise of the lands as security. Towards the end of 1677 he owed £8,031/19/-, his largest creditor being Patrick Taylfer, an Edinburgh merchant, to whom he owed £1,942.[21] He was, in effect, bankrupt. He was forced to hand over the Seaforth bonds and Apprising to Patrick Taylfer, although the arrangement specified that he was not to accept anything under £20,000 for the Apprising without Roger's consent. It was also agreed that Roger was to be given 200 merks (£133/6/8d) for his aliment over the next two years.[22] In 1681, Patrick Taylfer appointed Mr David Fearne, writer, to employ 'advocates, clerks, writers and others' to begin proceedings for the recovery of the money from the Earl of Seaforth.[23]

Meanwhile Jean Logan, now wife of Sir Ludovick Stewart of Minto, was still intent on proving that she had an absolute right to the bonds and Apprising. She even had Roger incarcerated in the Tolbooth in 1682, following his refusal to exhibit 'all and sundry gifts of escheat of George, Earl of Seaforth'.[24] She herself had been an inmate of the Tolbooth in 1673 for non-payment of £204 to William Nicol, vintner, and his wife.[25] The overcrowded and insanitary conditions in the Tolbooth would have been hard to bear. Roger was, by then, in his 60s. To effect his release, he was forced to draw up an Assignation to Jean Logan of the 5,000 merks left to her by her mother.

In 1684, no longer alimented by Patrick Taylfer, he approached Mr David Fearne for a loan 'in my urgent necessitie and for the expedeing of my lawfull affaires'. He was given £104.[26] He was still intent on prosecuting the Earl of Seaforth, despite all that had happened. In that same year he presented a Petition to the Lords complaining that he was 'being putt to many straits and difficulties in effundeing money for prosecuting the law against the said Earle'.[27] In November 1686 he was dead. Five months later Jean Logan, 'Lady Mintie', was dead. In 1687 Roger's widow, Marie Logan, petitioned the court. She said that her husband had spent 19 years pursuing the Earl of Seaforth

> but by reasone of the moyan which the said Earle used . . . could never get certification extracted nor get possession of any of the Earl's estate by reasone quhereof your petitioner and her said deceased husband wer depauperat and altogether befor his death rendered miserable having no other fortune nor estate for their subsistance but what soumes wer resting by the said Earl of Seaforth.

She had been left with two children 'destitute of bread' and had been unable to recover the papers belonging to her late husband which proved their right to the Apprising.[28] She died in June 1689. A few days before she died, she made a Disposition of all she possessed, including what was due from the Earl of Seaforth, to her only surviving daughter, Bethia.

When Bethia Mowat had been baptised in 1670, the witnesses to her baptism were Sir John Harper of Cambusnethan, Sir John Young of Lenie, Archibald Young, writer, and John Law, goldsmith. When her sister, Elizabeth, had been baptised in 1680, her baptism had been witnessed by Thomas and Alexander Dobson, saddlers, and John Dewar, wright. From

being a respected member of the legal fraternity in Edinburgh, Roger had
ended up becoming an outcast. The 5,000 merks promised in his marriage
contract in 1667, and the form in which it had been given, had resulted in
Roger's quest for obtaining payment from the Earl of Seaforth becoming an
obsession. He presents a somewhat ridiculous figure in his almost annual
journeys north to see the Earl, never realising that perhaps he was wasting his
time. He seems to have been unable to give up his quest. His legal practice
became neglected. No wonder his brother, Alexander Mowat in Redcloak,
found that he was of little help with regard to the settling of their other
brother, Mr James Mowat's, estate. When he did write to Edinburgh,
Robert Penman invariably wrote back that his brother was 'up north'; in
fact, during the period when Alexander most needed his help, he was
seldom in Edinburgh. A record of an action which Roger brought before
the Lords of Session at the beginning of winter 1670 illustrates his distracted
state. The action involved his debtors, John, Earl of Loudon, and Edward
Maxwell of Hills. The Earl of Loudon owed money to Roger's dead
brother, Mr James Mowat, for the three years he had been his governor on
the Continent, while Edward Maxwell of Hill's debt was owed to the
Logans. Neither could be called 'his' debtors. Small wonder the case did not
proceed.[29] Even Marie Logan appears to have inherited her husband's
obsession, remarking that they had no other fortune or estate for their
livelihood. She seems to have forgotten that her husband had been a lawyer
and notary public and, had he not been so distracted, could have earned a
living that way. After her death her daughter, Bethia, and her husband,
Alexander Campbell of Barvoline, sought legal advice about what they
could do to recover the money. They had come into possession of the bonds
and Apprising and were anxious to sell them. The obvious man to approach
was Bethia's cousin, Mr John Mowat, advocate. But John Mowat was also a
creditor of Bethia's deceased father and claimed that he too had a right to the
Apprising. In addition, he also owned a bond which Alexander Campbell
had granted to Robert Hamilton for 5,000 merks, and so was creditor of
Bethia's husband as well.[30] His comment on the Apprising was:

> I can have nothing for that Apprising, it is such a perplexed business: If I
> can when I dispose of it, I shall see to make something for you, if it
> should be but 500 merks.[31]

What had once been worth £59,405 had become virtually worthless, which
made a mockery of Roger Mowat's obsessive struggle. Mr John Mowat's

interest in trading bonds and apprisings was shortly to become part of events which would lead to the Mowat family losing their estate of Balquholly.

SOURCES
1. Seafield muniments (SRO) – GD248/401.
2. CS15/410 – Murray v Mowat
3. NP2/6 – 11 Jan 1659
4. Grant of Monymusk muniments (SRO) – GD345/714
5. *Ibid* – GD345/550
6. Trinity House of Leith muniments (SRO) – GD226/18/27; 82
7. Grant of Monymusk muniments (SRO) – GD345/550/13
8. *Ibid.*
9. *RMS* x, 646
10. Gordon Donaldson and Robert S Morpeth – *A Dictionary of Scottish History*, p.197
11. Grant of Monymusk Muniments (SRO) – GD345/550
12. *RMS* x, 646
13. CS229/M1/3 – Inventar of papers in actions of Reduction v Dame Jean Logan and her husband; CS226/5818 – Mowat v Stewart of Minto and his Lady
14. Grant of Monymusk muniments (SRO) – GD345/550
15. CS229/M1/3, no. 5
16. *Ibid* no.3
17. Grant of Monymusk muniments (SRO) – GD345/550
18. CS229/M1/3 no.3
19. CS226/5818 – James Mowat v Stewart of Minto and his Lady
20. CS233/L1/22 – Petition by Mary Logan; Grant of Monymusk muniments (SRO) – GD345/550
21. Grant of Monymusk muniments (SRO) – GD345/550
22. RD2/55 f.370
23. RD3/66 f.90
24. HH11/6 – 29 March 1682
25. HH11/5 – 8 July 1673
26. RD4/56 f.260
27. Grant of Monymusk papers (SRO) – GD345/550
28. CS233/L1/22
29. CS138/3529 – Roger Mowat v debtors
30. CS236/M1/8 – Petition for John Mowat
31. Grant of Monymusk muniments (SRO) – GD345/714

CHAPTER TEN

The Heir Apparent

When Magnus Mowat of Balquholly died in November 1669, his son and heir, William, was in France. Of all the lives of the Balquholly lairds, William's was the most tragic. His father appears to have been a capricious character, sending him to Paris to be under the care of James Mowat, 'being the best pledg[e]' that he could send to demonstrate that he intended honouring his grandfather's bond to his aunt, Isobel, and which she had assigned to James. In his letter to James Mowat, Magnus confessed that William was 'a litle younge yitt' and that he knew his wife

> will be dissatisfied with me but she being now at a distance, she shall not know till he be gone . . . On[e] thing I must desir you to doe for my exoneration at hir hands (becaus we ar severall judgements in religion and she may be aprehensive that hir sone may be broght [up] by hir principally) that ye would writ her a ligne giveing hir assurance that ye shall not divert him that way, if this is not done, she will put me to the charges of sending a person to attend him there.

William and a companion, John Farquhar, son of James Farquhar, merchant in Aberdeen, a boy 'bread a scholar', were put aboard a ship sailing from Leith to Rouen. An itemised account made of their expenses, from the time of their arrival until they left France at the end of August 1670, records that the very first items they bought were two swords, followed by a periwig and only after that a French/English grammar. Magnus had requested that they be sent to Saumur, having heard that it was the place 'fittest for thair breiding' and that they should want for nothing. He also asked James Mowat to send him two grey and two black hats and a periwig, 'of the best sort and fashione'. For someone who was having difficulty paying his own bills, this was a somewhat foolish request to make. When the bill for the boy's expenses was finally presented in September 1670, it came to £3,814/1/10d. It transpired that during his stay at Saumur, William had been ill for two months of a 'great sickness'. The bill for the doctor and apothecary on that occasion came to £300. Magnus's earlier letters to James begin with the flattering greeting, 'worthie and weilbeloved cousin', but one written in July 1668, several months after the boys had been in France, begins abruptly with 'cousin'. In it, Magnus expressed annoyance that the boys had been sent to Saumur when he had expressly wished them to remain in Paris. No doubt his wife had had plenty to say to Magnus when he had returned to Balquholly from Edinburgh and informed her that he had sent their son to France. He must have decided that it was best to tell her that their son was to remain in Paris under the watchful eye of James Mowat. His lie might have been believed had he not forgotten that he had requested James Mowat to write his wife a 'ligne'.[1]

At the beginning of 1670 William Mowat, still at Saumur and not yet 13, found himself the new laird of Balquholly. He left Paris in August, being given 60 livres by James Mowat for the journey to London. He was also to receive a further £20 sterling once there 'for the advancement of his voyage hommard', but did not return to Scotland immediately, remaining in London until April 1671. On his arrival in London, he ordered a new suit to be made for him by Mr Alexander Blair who also supplied him with stockings, hats, cravats, two pairs of shoes and a pair of galoshes. In November he took ill and required a visit from the apothecary and 'physick'. In March he ordered another new suit. It required six yards of 'drogat', and was to have a striped vest and breeches made of dyed cloth. For the making of it, Alexander Blair charged 14/-. The next month, he paid a visit to Hampton Court and on that occasion bought two bottles of wine. Ten days later, he was ill again while visiting William Douglas and Elizabeth Mowat. The illness lasted only four days, during which time the King's physician was summoned and charged 11/6d for his visit. William finally left London on 24th April 1671. The bill for his lodgings which included 'dyet, lodging, washing and other necessaries' came to £16/0/7d. He had been in London for 26 weeks and 5 days. He reached Edinburgh on 11th May and remained there for another month, finally arriving at Balquholly after a journey of six days, on 17th June, almost a year and a half after his father's death.[2] James Mowat in Paris and his associate, Alexander Blair in London, had paid for everything.

Before William had left France in August 1670, Balquholly castle had been invaded by George Forbes of Corse and his men. They had forced his deceased father's loyal servant, George Bruce, to surrender several coffers containing the Mowat family papers. Among them were bonds which George Forbes had either granted to Magnus or in which he had stood as cautioner for him. William Mowat, at a later stage, alleged that there were also some retired bonds among the papers which George Forbes had taken with a view to defrauding him. Despite this incursion, in 1673 George Forbes was able 'by his subtile insinuationes and pretences of friendschipe' to persuade William (by then studying at the university in Aberdeen) and his mother to pay him a visit at Corse castle. Once they were installed, he and his men, at dead of night, rode to Balquholly where they

> did most barbarously and inhumanely thrust the complainer's sisters and servants out off doores, scarcely allowing them any cloathes to cover their nakedness.

Thereafter, George Forbes and his men occupied the castle.[3] George Forbes was a desperate man. Before Magnus's death, he had 'ingadged for him in great soumes', standing as cautioner for him in several bonds which had remained unpaid.[4] There was a bond granted to Patrick and Malcolm Durward for £166/13/4d granted by Magnus at Stonehaven in 1669, one for 6037 merks and 10/- (£4,025/3/4d) made in a Bond of Corroboration to Elspet Mitchell, a bill of exchange for 11,000 merks (£7,333/6/8d) from James Mowat in Paris and another for the same amount in George Forbes's name granted to Patrick Andro of Cloakmilne which he had borrowed on behalf of Magnus as 'ane freind of the said Magnus Mowat alleinerly'.[5] Now that Magnus was dead and his heir still a minor, there was every likelihood that he would be pursued for those debts.

In 1681 he informed the Privy Council that he had been forced to sell his own lands of Corse to meet the payments. (He had, in fact, sold the largest part to his second cousin, Sir John Forbes of Craigievar, in 1670.) That he was short of money is borne out by a fair number of bonds which he had granted to his creditors being recorded at that time.[6] For his relief, he was granted a Gift of Recognition of the lands of Balquholly and a Back Bond by the Commissioner of the Exchequer in 1673, restricting the Gift to the amount he had had to lay out as cautioner.[7] His accounts presented in 1681 amounted to £20,879/5/5d.[8] Included were his legal expenses for getting the Gift and for stopping the appriseing of his own lands, bonds in which he had stood as cautioner to Magnus, as well as repairs and improvements he had made to Balquholly castle. His accounts also reveal the fact that he had alimented William Mowat and his servants with two horses from Whitsunday 1674 to 1675, which somewhat modifies William's accusation that George Forbes's friendship had been pretended. Between 1673 and April

1680, George Forbes peaceably occupied Balquholly, during which time he built a great barn, a kiln and kilnbarn and five byres on the estate. He also walled the barnyard of the mains, pointed and repaired the castle, victual house and doocot, slated the roofs and repaired and glazed the windows. William's father had led such a wandering and impecunious existence that it is likely he had not kept the buildings in good repair. In February 1680 Dame Elizabeth Hope, widow of Sir George Mowat of Inglishton, 'being assured of the abilitie and fidelitie' of William Mowat apparent of Balquholly, appointed him as her factor to uplift half the rents and duties from the tenants of Balquholly.[9] The Gift of the lands of Balquholly to George Forbes of Corse had also stipulated that the heirs of Sir George Mowat had an equal right to half the rents and duties of the lands, the debts owed to Sir George Mowat never having been paid in full.

It would have been too much to expect William Mowat to go to Balquholly in the humiliating role of factor, instead of as laird. By 1680 he was in his early 20s, no longer an ineffectual youth. In April he arrived at Balquholly and, gathering together a band of supporters, broke into the castle during George Forbes's absence. He had previously attempted to murder George Forbes as he lay in bed in William Meldrum's house in Turriff, according to George Forbes. Inside the castle they found George Forbes's son, William, whom they dragged out of bed, threatening him with swords and pistols, 'swearing they would ridle him if he did not quite the possession and goe out of the house'. They seized a chest containing Mowat and Forbes papers, and thereafter occupied the castle. William Mowat then turned his attention to the tenants. He drove 'thir haill horses and cattell violentlie into the close at Balquhollie and keiped them ther till they took tacks' from him and paid him their duties for the previous year.[10] George Forbes, in retaliation, travelled to Edinburgh to complain to the Privy Council, but while the hearing was in progress was persuaded by William Mowat

> to forbear farder insisting upon assurance that at his North-goeing he should be reponed to the possessione of his house, furnitur and papers and to the possessione of his lands as of befor.

George duly went north to take possession, but once there was refused entry. Not only had he not regained the lands, but he also stood to lose the crops he had planted in the fields on the mains. He returned to Edinburgh where he raised another action, but this time the witnesses who had been summoned did not appear. He suggested that although some may have been detained by the stormy weather, many, who were Balquholly tenants, would have been forcibly persuaded by William Mowat not to attend.[11] Thereafter, in April 1681, following a Decreet by the Sheriff of Aberdeen, the Sheriff's depute and his men went to Balquholly castle where they evicted William Mowat and repossessed bedding, clothing, spinning yarn, food, weapons and two young mares which George Forbes had brought from Corse castle. But the following month William returned with his accomplices. Once again, George Forbes was absent and his son in residence. This time they fired at his son and his servants, wounding several of them. They then garrisoned the castle, keeping 24 armed men in the garden.[12] In 1682 George Forbes once again regained possession and this time he installed John Erskine, brother of William Erskine of Pittodrie, and Alexander Forbes, burgess of Inverurie:

> be reasone of the necessar effars at Edinburgh and elsewhere [he] cannot reside within his owin propir dwelling in the mannor place of Balwhollie and considering that in the tyme of his absence the same has ben divers tymes invadit be William Mowat and . . . certaine his accomplices.[13]

John Erskine would have agreed readily to the arrangement, as he had lent William Mowat 1,800 merks (£1,200) in May 1680 while William was in possession of the lands and had not been repaid.[14] The situation was defused on 17th March 1683, when William Mowat drew up a Heritable Obligation in which he agreed to grant George Forbes an annualrent of £480 to be uplifted out of the lands of Meikle Colp, miln of Colp, Darra and Smiddyseat which would go towards the repayment of 12,000 merks (£8,000) owing to him. At the same time he recognised the Back Bond which had been granted to George Forbes by the Commissioners of the Exchequer on 15th April 1673.[15] In the following year William granted a Heritable Bond for an annualrent of £72 out of the lands of Lescraigie and Broadfoord to John Erskine.[16]

William Mowat's sisters who had been so unceremoniously ejected from the castle by George Forbes and his men in 1673 were Jean, Elizabeth and Helen. Their father, Magnus, had been staying with George Forbes at Corse in 1664 when he had executed bonds of provision for each of them to provide dowries for them or to give them an income when they were older.[17] They were in an even more precarious position than their brother, but nonetheless they managed to survive it all. Two did not marry. Helen, the youngest, married Robert Molysone, a merchant in Aberdeen.

After granting the Heritable Obligation to George Forbes, William once more installed himself at Balquholly. He began to lead the life of a country laird. He developed an interest in politics and channelled his energies into getting Sir Alexander Seton of Pitmedden chosen as Commissioner to Parliament. The successful Pitmedden, being very grateful to him, approached William Gordon of Pencaitland, Sheriff Clerk of Aberdeen, who was distantly related to William Mowat, enquiring of him whether there was some way he could repay William's efforts on his behalf. William Gordon informed him that although William Mowat represented

> ane ancient and honorable family yet his estate was incumbered and the greatest kyndness would be done to him wes to recommend him a suitable match that had a considerable tocher.

Pitmedden proposed his wife's cousin, niece of Mr William Lauder, his father-in-law, who was one of the Principal Clerks of Session. She could be expected to bring in a dowry of 20,000 merks (£13,333/6/8d). Moreover, if the marriage took place, he and Mr Lauder would be willing to advance William Mowat the money to clear his debts. The lady in question was Katherine Lauder, daughter of the deceased Robert Lauder, writer and town clerk depute of Dundee. The marriage took place in Edinburgh on 10th November 1685. 1,000 merks (£666/13/4d) were advanced by Mr Lauder for the 'profuse expense upon the marriadge'. The build-up was too good to be true. It, coupled with a splendid and elaborate wedding, is all William Mowat got. Soon after the marriage he discovered that the bonds and the disposition of a house in Dundee which made up the tocher had not been liferented in his favour. Instead they were liferented to his mother-in-law and were then to go to any children Katherine Lauder might bear. If there were no children, then they were to go to Mr William Lauder.[18] For William Mowat's part of the arrangement, he had been induced to agree to provide Katherine Lauder with 24 chalders of victual annually out of his lands as her marriage portion (the money value would have amounted to £1,600). Pitmedden and Mr Lauder withdrew their offer of advancing him money.[19] His plan to discharge his debts had come to nothing. Creditors began to hound him. He had lived on borrowed money ever since his first attempt to regain Balquholly in 1680. He had been forced to sign away a considerable part of the income from his estate. He was 'everyway disappointed'. His first child, a daughter, did not survive. The next, his only son, William, was baptised at Dundee on 8th January 1687. By then William had 'contracted a melancholly'. He died in November 1688, it being remarked that

> His death was certainly occasioned by the disapoyntment he mett with in that marriadge.[20]

He had made no effort to formalise the liferent arrangement for his wife. Katherine Lauder and her 10 month-old-son found themselves in an extremely vulnerable position. No one stepped into the breach. William's uncle, George Mowat of Hamnavoe, remained in Shetland. His other uncle, James Mowat in Redcloak, was dead by then. The enormity of her predicament did not become apparent to Katherine until her husband's creditors began to institute actions against her,

> I haveing [as she put it] contracted a great daill of debt for interteaning my selfe and sone since my husband's deceise and haveing my selfe and sone yett to meanteane and my proces to defend against my numerous and powerful enemies.

She singled out in particular 'those of the Colledge of Justice who are putt to no charges'.[21] Her remark contrasts sharply with the description of Sir Archibald Hope of Rankeillor, by then one of the Senators of the College of Justice, as a man who 'acquitted himself in every station of life with integrity and honour'.[22] She sought help from her uncle, Mr William Lauder, who, in turn, elicited help from Seton of Pitmedden. Perhaps their consciences were bothering them. In 1693 Robert Ross, Pitmedden's servitor, was appointed to act as her factor to contest actions which were brewing.[23] Meanwhile her infant son being a minor, the estate of Balquholly was in a state of ward. William Gordon of Pencaitland was granted the Gift of the Ward and Marriage. He, too, was in financial trouble and saw the Gift as a means of recovering the £3,298/1/10d owed to him out of the Balquholly estate.[24] He appointed John Gordon of Myrieton as factor to manage the property.[25] Katherine Lauder's uncle told her that William Gordon's action had been 'to apply it for securing of hir joyntur and ane aliment to hir sone'.[26] She, therefore, felt secure in this knowledge for several years. Nothing was forthcoming from William Gordon, however, and when she challenged him about his promise, he denied ever having made it. As a result, she said that she and her son had been reduced to 'extreem misery'. It transpired that the Gift had actually been taken in concert with Mr Alexander Leask of that Ilk, then minister of Turriff and also a distant relation to whom William Mowat had been in debt. William Gordon of Pencaitland had acted as the front man. He stated later that during the time he had had the Gift he had never received 'ane sixpence' for the whole enterprise. Mr Alexander Leask had attempted to recoup part of his loss shortly after William Mowat's death. He had gone to Balquholly where Katherine Lauder lay sick and removed 'a silver salver, caddell pott and eight spoons, ane silver tumbler and sex trincher salts'. Apart from the silver tumbler and two spoons which he had returned, as her 'third part', she was subsequently unable to recover the rest, the laird of Leask having 'sold his Estate and gone out of the Kingdome'.[27]

William Gordon had abandoned all interest in Balquholly by September 1695 when the poll tax began to be collected. The return for the parish of Turriff recorded, with regard to Balquholly, 'thar being no heritor nor factor within this parish'. In that year William Gordon was forced to sell his lands of Pencaitland to Hugh Dalrymple of North Berwick.[28] As a result, Robert Ross managed to secure 2,000 merks (£1,333/6/8d) for Katherine Lauder from him with a promise that the rest of the money owed to her in liferent would be paid.[29] She herself was living at Balquholly with her son and two servants, Patrick Watson and Janet Byth.[30] In that year the harvest failed, ushering in the great famine which was to last into the next century and to lead to a state of affairs in some parts of the country where 'Deaths and Burials were so many and so common, that the Living were wearied in the Burying of the Dead'.[31] By 1699 Katherine Lauder and her son had left Balquholly and moved to her native burgh of Dundee. In March 1705 she borrowed just over £150 Scots from Sir Alexander Seton of Pitmedden, her son witnessing the arrangement.[32] Young William Mowat did not live for much longer. He was dead before reaching his majority.

SOURCES
   1. Seafield muniments (SRO) – GD248/398/6.
   2. *Ibid*
   3. *RPC* vii, 49 (third series)
   4. Seafield muniments (SRO) – GD248/220
   5. Seafield muniments (SRO) – GD248/401
   6. SC1/60/25; 27; 28 – contain a number of bonds
   7. SC1/60/28 – 7 Oct 1685
   8. Seafield muniments (SRO) – GD248/401
   9. RD2/51 f.103
  10. Seafield muniments (SRO) – GD248/220
  11. *Ibid*.

12. *RPC* vii, 48 (third series); Seafield muniments (SRO) – GD248/225 -Inventory relative to Criminal Letters obtained by George Forbes against William Mowat
13. SC1/60/26 – 18 Feb 1682
14. RD3/60 f.34
15. SC1/60/28 – 24 Nov 1684
16. RD3/60 f.34
17. Seafield muniments (SRO) – GD248/408/2
18. CS181/3605 – Katherine Lauder v Mr John Mowat, advocate
19. Seafield muniments (SRO) – GD248/408/2
20. *Ibid.*
21. *Ibid.* – Answers for Commissary Elphinstone, Mr Robert Forbes and William Gordon of Pencaitland
22. G Brunton and D Haig – *Senators of the College of Justice,* 1532–1850, p. 444
23. RD2/78 f.1176
24. CS25; 17 Feb 1694 – William Gordon of Pencaitland v William Mowat of Balquhollie
25. RD2/78 f.1176
26. Seafield muniments (SRO) – GD248/402
27. CS181/3605 – Katherine Lauder v Mr John Mowat, advocate
28. RD3/108 f.264; RD2/79 f.766
29. RD3/84 f.264
30. *List of Pollable Persons within the Shire of Aberdeen,* ed. John Stuart, ii, 348
31. Gordon Donaldson – *Scottish Historical Documents,* p. 265
32. RD3/125 – 29 Dec 1710

CHAPTER ELEVEN

The Tenants of Balquholly

The famine years of the 1690s had a devastating effect upon the people. Some parishes lost a quarter or even a third of their populations. There was little in the way of relief. Everyone went hungry, whether they had money or not. Compared to England at that time, Scotland was a poor country and any event which upset the fine economic balance had a dramatic effect. The staple crop was oats and bear and when the harvest failed, the people went without food. The farm land was divided into the infield and outfield areas. These were not like the fields today but were divided into rigs, and on farms which had several tenants, one man's rigs would be interspersed amongst those of his neighbour. The infield lay nearest to the farm town and was not as large as the outfield. The crop grown on it was bear, a type of barley used to make ale. The infield was never left to lie fallow. Oats were grown on the outfield until the yield was extremely poor, and then it was allowed to lie fallow for a long period. John Allardyce, tenant in Lower Plaidy, a few miles north of Turriff, kept a diary in the eighteenth century and in 1771 wrote about the farming methods which had been used in his younger days and by generations before him:[1]

> When a piece of outfield ground had lain by six or seven years it was faughed and limed and then the unskilful farmer would take ten or perhaps fifteen crops off it after one very slim coat of lime, and then when it was reduced to ashes, he would let it out, as the term was, and then it produced a fine crop of red surak. It lay no doubt seven or ten years by and an acre would not have sustained an old ewe . . . The infield was little better used to advantage. It got indeed all the dung just as it fell from the cattle. A third part of the infields was always dunged and made bear, but it was never cleaned nor rested so that few had in good years three returns of bear and none except on some singular farms, exceeded four. A third or fourth of that, too, was black oats. The bear root crop, as it was called, was the only crop to be depended on and the second or aval crop, as they called it, was sometimes little more than two seeds.

Three returns meant that the farmer could never hope to increase his yield. As the old saying went, 'ane to graw, ane to gnaw and ane to pay the laird withaw'.

During the 1580s James Mowat, brother of the second laird of Balquholly, settled on the farm of Redcloak in Kincardineshire. At the beginning of 1612, when he died, he had 120 bolls of oats and 20 bolls of bear stored in his barn and barnyard. In 1622, when his widow, Agnes Auchinleck, died, she had 280 bolls of oats (infield and outfield) and 40 bolls of bear. Their son, George Mowat, continued to farm there. When he died in July 1645, he had 270 bolls of oats (infield and outfield) and 31 bolls of bear. Their grandson, Alexander Mowat, who took over after his uncle's death had, on his death in December 1685, 20 bolls of 'brokit' oats and 80 bolls without the fodder, making a total of 100 bolls and 18 bolls of bear with the fodder. Both Alexander and his grandfather died in the winter when the corn was stored in their barnyards and their inventories do not specify whether the oats they had stored had been grown in the outfield and so it is possible that the outfield was being allowed to lie fallow following the harvests of 1611 and 1684. But the weather had been more settled in the second half of the seventeenth century, and yet the yield at Redcloak had fallen. James Mowat in 1612 had had 16 bolls of meal stored in his girnels, while Alexander had only 10 bolls. A boll of infield oats had been worth £7 in 1622, and £4 by 1645. Outfield oats were valued at £6 in 1622 and 53/4d in 1645. Alexander Mowat's 'brokit' oats were valued at £3 the boll and a boll without the fodder 53/4d in 1685. As the prices were fixed each year, they would have varied in the intervening years, and it is possible that there were years in which Alexander Mowat got as good a price as his grandmother had done in 1622, but as the yield had fallen, he would never have had as good an income as his grandmother and uncle had had. James Mowat's 'utencils and domicils' had been valued at £66/8/4d, his wife's inventory of the 'plenishings' of the house of Redcloak had been valued at £266/3/4d, while Alexander Mowat's 'utencils and domicils' were worth £60. Again, it would appear that Alexander's standard of living had fallen compared with that of his grandparents.

All four had sufficient oxen to pull the old heavy ox-plough. Tenants usually had to pool their oxen when it was time to plough the lands.

James Mowat in 1612 had:

16 drawing oxen valued at £13/6/4d each.

3 horses and mares valued at £11 each.

6 cows, some in milk and some farrow, valued at £10 each.

6 two or three year old heifers and steers valued at £6 each

120 young and old sheep valued at 40/- each

Agnes Auchinleck in 1622 had:

22 drawing oxen valued at £16/3/4d each.

9 cows and their calves valued at £16 each.

7 young beasts valued at £8 each.

4 horses and 2 mares valued at £33/6/8d each.

60 ewes valued at 43/4d each.

60 hogs (young sheep) valued at 40/- each.

40 wedders valued at £3 each.

George Mowat in 1645 had:

13 drawing oxen valued at £16/3/4d each.

10 cows and their calves valued at £16 each.

6 yeld nolt (barren cattle) valued at £6 each.

6 horses and mares valued at £35/16/8d each.

22 wedders valued at £3 each.

36 hogs valued at 40/- each.

62 ewes valued at 53/- each.

Alexander Mowat in 1685 had:

21 oxen and cows valued at £10 each.

2 stirks valued at £4 each.

3 horses and 1 mare valued at £10 each.

2 staigs and a mare foal valued at £18 each.

75 head of sheep valued at 33/4d each.[2]

They would all have kept poultry to pay their customs dues, their original tack specifying 18 capons and 18 poultry. Their corn would have had to be ground at the mill they were thirled to and they would have had to pay multures and sequels to the miller and his servants. In addition to the poultry, they would have to pay £20 silver rent at Whitsunday and Martinmas, 4 bolls of bear, 4 wedders, and 3 bolls of horse corn out of their annual income. They were also required to labour on the Mains of Ury and supply a good horse and equipage when required.[3] There were also servants' wages to be met. Alexander Mowat owed his servants, Robert Edward £20, John Craig £12, Elspet Williamson and Isobel Foderingham £6 each and Agnes Hill who had worked at harvest time £5/6/8d. A hundred years before, William, Earl Marischal, had paid £20 to his chamberlains and to the important servants in his household. A tenant farmer in 1592 had owed each of his servants £4 on his death.[4] Servants' wages had obviously risen during the seventeenth century.

The rents in money and kind were delivered to the landowner and the surplus grain and stock would then be sold by his factor or chamberlain. The money received together with the silver rent became the landowner's annual income. Without this income and tenants who generated it, the landowner would have had no means of support. The Mowats of Balquholly may have entertained romantic notions about their family's long history and been proud of the Norman blood in their veins, but in reality none of this would have mattered if they had not had tenants on their lands of Balquholly and Freswick (until it was sold) who paid their annual rents and dues to them. It was the tenants who enabled them to live the way they did, to wadset their lands and to borrow money. The factors who collected the rents and set tacks made sure that the money came in. Magnus Mowat who died in Shetland in 1669 had appointed a particularly conscientious man, George Bruce, the previous June who kept affairs in order immediately after his death.[5] He had been left in charge of the writs coffer when Magnus had made his last journey to Shetland and which George Forbes of Corse had purloined before William Mowat had returned from France.

The lands of Balquholly which were rented out were:

Forelands – Mains of Balquholly (only in the second half of the seventeenth century), Broadfoord, Darra, Boggieshalloch, Over and Nether Smiddyseat, Meikle Colp, Quarrelhill, Ardin, Mill and Mill ploughgate of Colp.

Backlands – Lendrum, Nether Brownhill, Rushhead, Ewebrae, Jackston, Backmilne (of Balquholly), Broadgreens and Lescraigie.[6]

There were mills on some of the lands, such as at Colp, which were leased out separately. Tenancies were held by one or two people who in turn sub-let to their own tenants, so that each possession would have a fair number of people on it. In September 1695, when the poll tax was collected, for example, the tenant of Darra was Walter Catto, but there were 11 people living there (not including children under 16 living *in familia* and those on the poor roll who were exempt from the tax). George Mowat and William McKie had the joint-tenancy of Mill of Colp where 29 people were living. The Mains was leased to Harry Gordon of Avochie whose sub-tenant was John Black, and 24 people, mainly servants and cottars, lived there.[7]

Over a hundred years before, in 1576, Patrick Mowat of Balquholly, the second laird, had brought an action against his tenants:

Robert Cassy and Thomas Cassy in Rushhead
Alexander Hat in Ewebrae
Robert Anderson and Elizabeth Barclay in Jackston
Donald Piry in Lendrum
Andrew Jerat in Woodend
Adame Duncan in Middlethird of the mill and mill lands of Colp

His intention had been to have them legally warned to remove from their possessions.[8] However, in 1584 Donald Piry or Pierie was still on the lands of Lendrum, indicating that he had either paid his arrears, following Patrick's action, or that the action had been ineffectual. In that year Patrick Mowat had brought a further action against five of his tenants: John Gray, Donald Pierie (again), John Murray, John Cassy and David Anderson. (His bailie at that time had been Mr Andrew Mowat who had acted as reader at Turriff kirk for a while.) John Gray had been able to produce a 'set and assedation' which had been granted to him by Patrick Mowat, thereby proving that he had a right to remain as tenant of Brownhill until the following Whitsunday. The others appear to have had no leases and were there by the tolerance of their master. They were therefore in the precarious position of having to remove whenever Patrick required them to. That is what he had been attempting to do at that time. He also appears to have been planning to raise the rents. John Gray was allowed to remain at Brownhill 'for payment of the auld duty', but he may not have been able to pay the new rent and as a result would have been forced to quit his possession.[9] Brief glimpses of tenants and indwellers in Balquholly during the first half of the seventeenth century occur in the records. It is interesting to follow those in Brownhill. In 1601 a Magnus Mowat, was in Brownhill.[10] In 1603 Walter Mowat, servitor to Magnus Mowat had had his 'plenishings' stolen from his steading there by Magnus's brother, James Mowat, and William Smith in Newburnhill. In 1612 William Smith and his son, Andrew, were granted the wadset of the property by Magnus.[11] He may very well have been William Smith in Newburnhill, having been successful in causing Walter Mowat to leave his steading. In 1650 an Alexander Mowat and his eldest son, John Mowat, were in Brownhill.[12] By 1673 there were three tenants on the property.

After George Forbes of Corse had forcibly occupied Balquholly, he had held a meeting of the baron court. In the late sixteenth century Patrick Mowat of Balquholly had resigned his lands into the King's hands so that a united barony could be made out of the separate baronies of Balquholly and Freswick. Minutes of the earlier meetings of the court have not survived, but on 9th October 1673 the court met to establish under what conditions each tenant held his possession. Birlaymen (to act as a jury) were appointed on that occasion, they being William Mackie in Darra, John French in Lendrum, John Androw at the Mill of Jackston and George Wood in Broadfoord. John Androw had the lease of the land and miln of Colp which he had possessed since 1668 and was able to produce discharges of his rent which had been granted by George Bruce, Magnus Mowat's trusted servant, apart from one dated October 1669 which had been granted by George Simpson of Idoch who had replaced George Bruce. Jackston was let to two men, George Wobster and James Hatt. James Pierie was in Broadgreens, having entered at Whitsunday 1669. Alexander Panton's lease of Lescraigie had begun at Whitsunday 1667, Andrew Greive had the lease of a ploughgate of Nether Brownhill which had begun in 1663, and George Milne and William Reid had entered their respective half 'pleughs' in 1669. At a meeting of the court on 10th January 1674, John Androw at the Backmill of Balquholly had complained against the suckeners of his mill, they not having contributed towards its repair.[13]

By the time the 1696 poll tax returns were made, the lands could be divided into three sections:

1. Those that were not burdened with wadsets were: Mains of Balquholly, Broadfoord, Darra, Boggieshalloch, Over and Nether Smiddyseats, Meikle Colp, Quarrelhill, Ardin, mill and mill croft of Colp, Mill ploughgate of Colp.
2. Those that were wadset to Mr Adam Hay, minister of Montquhitter, were: Lescraigie, Broadgreens, Backmill of Balquholly, Jackston, Nether Brownhill, Ewebrae and Rushhead.
3. The remaining lands of Little Colp, Woodend, Lendrum, Over Brownhill and Keithin were wadset to others.[14]

The lands which were not burdened were let as follows:

MAINS OF BALQUHOLLY to Harry Gordon of Avochie whose sub-tenant was John Black – John Black paid 20 bolls of ferme meal, 4 bolls of wheatmeal, 4 bolls of bear and 50 merks.

DARRA to Walter Catto – paid 5 bolls of meal, £20/6/8d, 2 wedders, 2 lambs, 1 dozen hens and 1 dozen capons.

MILL OF COLP to George Mowat and William Mackie/McKie. George Mowat paid 2 bolls of ferme meal, 4 bolls of ferme bear, 20 merks, a milne swine, 1 dozen hens and 1 dozen capons. William Mackie paid 20 bolls of ferme meal, 4 bolls of bear, a wedder, a lamb in wool, 1 dozen hens and 1 dozen capons.

MEIKLE COLP to Peter (or Patrick) Pierie – paid 40 bolls of ferme meal, 6 bolls of bear, a wedder, a lamb in wool, 2 dozen capons, 2 dozen hens, a stone of butter, 50 merks for cess and other public burdens.

ARDIN to Isobel Massie – paid 14 bolls of ferme meal, 25 merks, a wedder, a lamb, 1 dozen capons and 1 dozen hens.

BOGGIESHALLOCH to George Pierie – paid 10 bolls of ferme meal, 25 merks, a wedder, a lamb, 1 dozen capons and 1 dozen hens.

BROADFOORD to William Barclay – paid 40 merks, 10 merks maill and duty for the pasturage of the Mains, 1 boll multure meal, a stone of brew tallow and 1 dozen chickens.

QUARRELHILL to Alexander Scot (erroneously rendered Granrvhill by the transcribers of the 1696 poll) – no details recorded in 1694.[15]

In 1697 John Thomson of Haremoss and William Mackie at the mill of Colp drew up a rental of the three sections of the lands – those that were unburdened, those which were possessed by Mr Adam Hay, and those which were wadset to various others.[16] At that time, bear wheatmeal and ferme meal fetched 100 merks per chalder; wedders and lambs 3 merks; mill swine 10 merks; capons £3 a dozen; hens 30/- a dozen; a stone of butter and tallow £4. Some of the tenants of the wadset lands had to render leets of peats and each leet was calculated at £6.

The annual rents for each section amounted to:

The unburdened section £1,358/13/4d
Mr Adam Hay's section. £532/10/–
Other wadsets £494/3/4d
The total rent being £2,385/6/8d

By 1698 John Black was still tenant of half of the Mains of Balquholly, but the other half had been taken over by William Shand. James Cantly's wife rented the yard at the Mains. Over and Nether Smiddyseat had been let to George Burnett and Andrew Esslemont. (In 1695, it appears to have lain empty.) Magnus Mitchell was at Little Colp, the wadset of which appears to have been redeemed by then. The rest of the lands were tenanted by the same people.[17] The famine was beginning to have an effect, however. By the end of 1698, for example, both William Shand and John Black were unable to pay their year's maill and duty and were forced to grant obligations to Mr John Mowat.[18] It was recorded that there was a 'sterilitie and scarcity of tennants att that tyme'.

In 1705, a rental was drawn up recording when the tenants had received their tacks from Mr John Mowat of Balquholly, advocate:

The Mains was tenanted by Alexander Gordon of Auchreddie who had been appointed factor in that year.

BROADFOORD – Alexander Wallace – entered Whitsunday 1704.

DARRA, including Whitehillock – Walter Catto – had a 5-year tack from Whitsunday 1705.

BOGGIESHALLOCH – William Gordon and John Fordyce – had a 5-year tack from 1703.

OVER AND NETHER SMIDDYSEAT – George Burnet – no details given.

MEIKLE COLP – Patrick Pierie – tack to end Whitsunday next.

QUARRELHILL – John Greive – 'hes no standing tack'.

ARDIN – Isobel Massie – 'this year is a violent possessor being warned legally to remove'.

MILL OF COLP AND MILL CROFT – John Thomson – 5-year tack from 1703.

MILL CROFT – not tenanted, but used partly by Walter Catto and John Greive, the garden and glen there having been set to James Chevis, gardener for 5 years from 1705.

LESCRAIGIE to Alexander Panton – 5-year tack from 1705.

BROADGREENS – waste – untenanted.

EWEBRAE – Alexander Prott and John Mair – 5-year tack, 1705 being their 2nd year.

BACKMILL AND MILL CROFT – William Mitchell – his tack had expired.

JACKSTON – Alexander Mitchell – had 3-year tack from Whitsunday 1705.

NETHER BROWNHILL – 2 pleughs – 1 occupied by James Mitchell who had no standing tack; other set to Thomas Milne and John Gerrard for 3 years from Whitsunday 1704.

NETHER BROWNHILL CROFT, known as Smith's croft – John Horn, smith – no tack.

RUSHHEAD – waste.

LENDRUM – Isobel Muir and William Hepburn – set for 5 years from Whitsunday 1705 – but not including Heatherybanks.

HEATHERYBANKS – George Allan and James Gabriel – 7-year tack from Whitsunday 1705.

MOSS OF LENDRUM – Robert Beattie had the liberty to cut peats for 'serving himself att Balwollie for the space of fyve years' – he had to pay one and a half bolls meal yearly.[19]

In 1725 Katherine Lauder instituted an action of maills and duties and of removing against the last laird of Balquholly, his mother and her second husband and the tenants of Balquholly. Those tenants were:[20]

MAINS OF BALQUHOLLY – Andrew Morison, Bessie Chalmers, Jean Hepburn, William Wilson, James Gray and James Halket.

MEIKLE COLP – William Morison.

OVER SMIDDYSEAT – Alexander Morison and William Wilson.

NETHER SMIDDYSEAT – William Barclay and William Woodman.

JACKSTON – Alexander Milne.

BACKMILL OF BALQUHOLLY – Arthur Dingwall.

DARRA AND BOGGIESHALLOCH – Patrick Ramsay.

LESCRAIGIE – Alexander Grieve.

MILL OF COLP – William Hepburn.

MILNLPLOUGH OF COLP – John Grieve.

LITTLE COLP – Alexander Panton.

ARDIN – William Panton.

There had been many changes of tenants over the 20 years. Many had moved away from Balquholly, perhaps to avoid actions for arrears which were pending. One former tenant who had occupied part of Miln of Colp during the famine years was courageous enough to contest such an action. He was George Mowat who had left Balquholly at the turn of the century with his wife, Isobell Greig, and their son, John, and moved north to the lands of Craigfintray.[21] Most tenants, however, would have been unable to do what he did.

Throughout the seventeenth century the tenants had seen many changes and had had much to bear. Those who had rented lands during the lifetime of Magnus Mowat of Balquholly who died in 1634 had had to endure raids by the Gordons of Gight and much confusion as Magnus wadset and redeemed parts of his lands so frequently. On his deathbed, however, he had discharged them all of their debts to him, with the exception of John Scot.[22] Then in the 1640s they had suffered losses when the castle had been garrisoned. After the second Magnus Mowat's death in November 1669, they had paid their rent to the factors until William Mowat's return, but then in 1674 had found that George Forbes of Corse and Dame Elizabeth Hope, widow of Sir George Mowat of Inglishton, were both entitled to a half-share of the rents and duties of the lands. At times they were possibly coerced into paying more than they should have. In September 1695 there was no factor or heritor in the parish and the country was about to suffer years of famine. In July that year food had been plentiful and Parliament had even passed an act encouraging the export of food, allowing it to go duty-free. In August the crops were stricken by an easterly fog, and the resulting harvest produced little and poor grain. In the following years the seasons, whether summer or winter, were cold and barren. A boll of meal in 1696 cost £24 and bear, wheat and rye £14. (A boll of oats had been worth £3 in 1685.) There were years when the rents were not collected. There were other years when the tenants found themselves being taken to court for arrears. Factors changed frequently. After the death of the depressed William Mowat, there were at least six 'owners', as well as two widows claiming their liferent out of the lands. No wonder parts of the lands lay untenanted for years. 'The haill lardschipe and leving of Bolquhollie' was finally 'in gret danger'.

SOURCES

1. *TBFC* – 4 March 1930 – 'A Northern Diary', p. 34.
2. Testament of James Mowat in Redcloak – CC20/4/5; Inventories of Agnes Auchinleck and George Mowat in Redcloak – RH15/37/95; Testament of Alexander Mowat in Redcloak – CC20/4/15
3. RD1/343 f.21
4. Gordon Donaldson – *Scottish Historical Documents*, p. 163
5. SC2/59/3, no.1044 – Factory
6. Seafield muniments (SRO) – GD248/218
7. *List of Pollable Persons within the Shire of Aberdeen*, ii, 348
8. SC1/2/2 – 26 June 1576
9. SC1/2/4 – 23 June 1584
10. Mey papers (SRO) – GD96/305
11. Seafield muniments (SRO) – GD248/217
12. SC1/60/14 – 29 Jan 1652
13. Seafield muniments (SRO) – GD248/402
14. *Ibid*
15. Seafield muniments (SRO) – GD248/216; *List of Pollable People within the Shire of Aberdeen*, ii, 348
16. Seafield muniments (SRO) – GD248/402
17. Seafield muniments (SRO) – GD248/216
18. SC1/61/49 – 6 Dec 1698 – Obligation William Shand of Woodend to Mr John Mowat, advocate; 6 Dec 1698 – Obligation John Black to Mr John Mowat, advocate
19. Seafield muniments (SRO) – GD248/216
20. CS29; 13 July 1725 – Lauder v tenants
21. CS29; 21 June 1705 – Mowats v Mowat
22. Mey papers (SRO) – GD96/683/1

CHAPTER TWELVE

The Creditors

George Mowat of Hamnavoe, in Shetland, was next in line to the deceased youth, William Mowat. In 1661 his brother, Magnus Mowat of Balquholly, had become the wadsetter of the Shetland lands of Mr James Mowat of Ollaberry. By doing so, Magnus had gained the income from the Ollaberry estate which consisted of lands in the parishes of Northmaven, Delting and Sandsting, the islands of Papa Stour and Papa Little and parcels of lands on Yell, Fetlar and Unst.[1] In the following year he had appointed his brother, George, as his factor, and in that same year George had married Margaret Mowat, daughter of Mr James Mowat of Ollaberry.[2] The marriage more than likely took place in St Magnus kirk, burial place of Mr Gilbert Mowat of Garth, Margaret's grandfather. After their marriage, Magnus had given them the 36-merk lands of Hamnavoe, part of the Northmaven lands. Thereafter George had taken the title 'of Hamnavoe'. Until recently the ruins of an old haa house could still be seen there which may have been built by George.[3] In 1666 he had been appointed one of the Commissioners of Excise and a Justice of the Peace for Shetland, many of the Justices of the Peace by then having become 'aged and infirm'.[4]

After Magnus and his family had returned to live permanently at Balquholly, he frequently returned to Shetland. As a result of his sudden death in November 1669, many of the bonds he had granted to Shetlanders had not been paid. After his death his brother, George, set about repaying them. In December 1669 he purchased an Obligation which Magnus had granted to Gilbert Murray of Laxe for 100 rix dollars, and the following year a Bond which had been granted to Thomas Leslie of Burwick for £294, one for £500 originally granted to Gilbert Nevin of Scousburgh, a Bond for £3,247/5/4d which had been granted to Robert Hunter, chamberlain of Shetland, and one to David Murray of Clardon for 200 merks (£133/6/8d). In addition, he possessed a Bond for 3,000 merks (£2,000) which had been granted by Magnus to Mr James Mowat of Ollaberry and two discharges of bills which he had paid on Magnus's behalf to Colonel William Sinclair, governor of the garrison of Shetland, and James Brown, carpenter who had done some work for his brother.[5] There were also unredeemed bonds which Magnus had granted to various people in Edinburgh: one for £1,309 to William Carmichael, merchant and burgess, one for 400 merks (£266/13/4d) to Adam Christie, writer, one for £124 to George Gibson, son to Sir John Gibson of Pentland, and one for 250 merks (£166/13/4d) to David Bruce, indweller in Leith, which had been assigned to him by John Bruce, merchant in Edinburgh. George also acquired these bonds. In addition, he and his wife were still owed 3,000 merks (£2,000) which Magnus had promised them on the occasion of their marriage in 1662, and George had further acquired a bond for £216/16/8d which Magnus had owed to John Cunninghame, tailor in Edinburgh.[6] Altogether, they added up to a considerable sum. After following the usual legal procedures of obtaining Letters of Horning, Inhibition and Charge to Enter Heir addressed to his nephew, William Mowat of Balquholly, George Mowat had obtained a Decreet of Apprising for £11,872/12/4d on 11th June 1674 and thereby claimed ownership of part of the Shetland lands.[7] Given that his brother's heir, William Mowat, was very young and appears to have had no one to act for him, this action was somewhat underhanded.

George Mowat was not the only one who was interested in the Shetland lands. When his brother, Magnus, had received the lands of Balquholly from Sir George Mowat of Inglishton in 1661, part of the arrangement had been that Freswick was to be sold to William Sinclair of Rattar. It emerged, later, that Magnus had borrowed considerable sums of money from Sinclair of Rattar, before and after Freswick had been sold to him. After William Sinclair's death, his widow Jean Cunninghame, Lady Rattar, in need of money, obtained a Decreet of Apprising in January 1672 against Magnus's son and heir, William Mowat, for £12,753/10/-. The court ordained that she was to receive payment out of the maills and duties of the Shetland lands, consisting of rent in money and in kind – butter, oil, and grassing, fish and rent of fishing booths, as well as the parsonage teinds, amounting to 2,000 merks annually.[8] In that same year George Mowat of Hamnavoe, who had been somewhat slower off the mark, obtained Letters of Inhibition against his nephew, but it was only in June 1674 that he was able to obtain his Decreet of Apprising. He had done so in his role of creditor to his brother.[9]

So by the middle of 1674 there were two creditors who had major claims on the Ollaberry estate. George Mowat, however, had another role. Not only was he his brother's creditor, but he was also owner of half of the lands through his wife, the other half being owned by his sister-in-law and her husband, George Cheyne of Esslemont. In 1672 Margaret and Barbara Mowat had been served heir to their brother who had died in Copenhagen. In this capacity they had summoned William Mowat of Balquholly to St Magnus kirk in Northmaven in 1677 to receive repayment of the £23,333/6/8d which his father had apparently loaned to their father. His failure to appear had resulted in the two sisters and their husbands becoming firmly entrenched on the Shetland lands.

As a result, when two years later, in January 1679, Jean Cunninghame brought an action for non-payment of 11,000 merks (£7,333/6/8d) due to her out of the maills and duties of Ollaberry for five years, it was raised not against William Mowat of Balquholly, but against George Mowat of Hamnavoe and George Cheyne of Esslemont and his son.[10] Later in the year she made her son, James Sinclair of Freswick, her assignee who, in December, obtained a Decreet of Adjudication against them, it having been recorded during the hearing that George Mowat was by then 'reall and natural' possessor of the lands.[11] In 1684 George Mowat drew up a Memorandum preparatory to his attempting to have James Sinclair's Decreet suspended. He did so in his role as husband of Margaret Sinclair, his role as creditor of his brother having by then fallen into abeyance. He claimed that the Decreet should be suspended because Mr James Mowat of Ollaberry's disposition of the lands to his son, James Mowat in Copenhagen, prior to wadsetting them to Magnus Mowat, had not been 'clogged' with the burden of the debts. William Mowat of Balquholly, still trying to retrieve his father's money, had joined forces with James Sinclair of Freswick, claiming that the burden of the debts had been included in the arrangement.[12] William Mowat's unexpected death and the turmoil which followed, coupled with James Sinclair's death in France, suspended further action. James Sinclair's heir, his brother, David Sinclair, decided very wisely to dispose of his mother's Apprising. George Mowat of Hamnavoe and George Cheyne of Esslemont, unopposed, continued to occupy the Ollaberry lands.

Two other people had lesser claims on the Shetland lands. One was Patrick Con in Paris who had purchased the bond which James Mowat of Balquholly had granted to his daughter, Isobel, in 1637 and which she had then sold to James Mowat, merchant in Paris. In December 1674 Patrick Con obtained a Decreet of Apprising of the Ollaberry lands to the value of the bond together with the accumulated interest.[13] The other claimant was Mr Alexander Dunbar, sometime minister of Inveraven and, by 1672, minister of Delting to whom Magnus had granted a back bond in July

1668 for £1,688/1/4d, at the same time promising to pursue the parishioners of Inveraven for 520 merks (£346/13/4d), the amount owed by them to Mr Dunbar for his stipend for the year 1668.[14]

So the property due to be inherited by the youth, William Mowat, had he come of age, would have consisted only of the lands of Balquholly in Aberdeenshire. Freswick had long ago become the property of the Sinclairs, and the Shetland lands by then had been claimed by his great-uncle and aunt, George Mowat of Hamnavoe and Margaret Mowat and her sister, Barbara Mowat and husband, George Cheyne of Esslemont. Any claims which creditors of the Mowats had could only be made upon the Aberdeenshire estate.

When his grand-nephew died, George Mowat, his heir, was an elderly man and reluctant to leave Shetland. It is doubtful whether he appreciated or was much interested in the complex state of the Balquholly estate. There were, however, many people who were very interested in the foundering estate. There were those whose interest was touched with anxiety – the creditors, large and small, who faced the possibility of losing their money. There were also those whose interest was enhanced by the prospect of making money. They were the lawyers who were involved in the speculative business of buying and selling bonds. If sufficient burdens on an estate could be purchased, then the estate could be theirs. Acquiring a heavily burdened estate, while a gamble, promised the possibility of even greater returns. In 1667 the valued rent of Balquholly had been £1,147/15/8d, and that was without Lendrum, Brownhill, Colp and Keithin.[15] In 1673 the money rent had amounted to £2,358/16/4d.[16] In modern terms, the Balquholly estate could be likened to a company in financial difficulties and about to be the subject of a takeover bid, those wishing to acquire the company attempting to purchase a majority of the shares. The valuable assets of such a company are those which are fixed – the property and plant. Balquholly's fixed assets were the lands and the castle. Potential income could be generated by the tenants. The shareholders were the creditors. In a modern takeover bid the most valuable shares to acquire are those owned by large shareholders. In the case of Balquholly, those creditors who had major claims were, in effect, the substantial shareholders.

Who were these major creditors? To ascertain who they were, it is necessary to go back to 1661 when Sir George Mowat of Inglishton returned the Balquholly lands to the main line. The 21,000 merks which Magnus Mowat had agreed to pay had only been partially repaid. £4,000 was still outstanding. The 9,000 merks which William Sinclair had agreed to pay directly to Sir George Mowat had never been paid during Sir George's lifetime. His widow, Dame Elizabeth Hope, had at first attempted to obtain the money from William Sinclair of Rattar's heir, John Sinclair, and had then instituted an action against James Sinclair of Freswick, eldest son of his second marriage. Thereafter, just over half the amount was repaid.[17] On the death of Sir George, the bonds which had been granted by Magnus passed to his widow, Dame Elizabeth Hope. In March 1678 she transferred them to her brother, Sir Archibald Hope of Rankeillor.[18] When her son, Sir Roger Mowat of Inglishton, came of age, he signed over all the movable heirships to his uncle, his action being ratified by his brother, Sir William Mowat of Inglishton, who succeeded him. Their younger brother and sister also made their uncle their cessioner and assignee.[19] Sir Archibald Hope was, therefore, one of the major creditors.

Part of the bond which Sir George Mowat had received from Magnus Mowat in 1661 had been transferred to Alexander Mowat in Redcloak, in the form of two bonds, together worth £4,000. One had been in the name of Margaret Mowat, daughter of the deceased Mr James Mowat of Logie and the other in the names of Alexander Mowat's three daughters. In 1685 Alexander had assigned the latter bond to his only surviving daughter, Elizabeth, in liferent and to her daughter, Christian, in fee.[20] They also had an interest in the estate.

Then there was Magnus's friend, George Forbes of Corse whose finances had been so sorely stretched by their friendship. He had a Back Bond which he had obtained from the Commissioner of the Exchequer, as well as the Heritable Obligation which William Mowat of Balquholly had granted him. Both of these were substantial assets to have.

Stretching even further back to Magnus's grandfather, James Mowat of Balquholly, there was the bond which he had granted to his daughter, Isobel, which she had sold to James Mowat in Paris, and by so doing had obtained a steady income for herself. In March 1663 James Mowat had sold the bond to Patrick Con, but he had made a claim on the Ollaberry lands. However, James Mowat in Paris, himself, had a claim for all the money he had laid out for William Mowat's aliment while he was at Saumur and for his subsequent stay in London and journey back to Edinburgh. He was also, no doubt, still owed for the four hats and the periwig.

After William Mowat had regained Balquholly from George Forbes of Corse, he had been short of money and had wadset the lands of Lendrum in

1683 to Mr Alexander Leask, minister of Turriff, who in the following year had sold the wadset to Mr Adam Hay, minister of Montquhitter. Three years later, Mr Adam Hay had also acquired the wadset of Lescraigie.[21] He was yet another creditor.

Others included people such as William Gordon of Pencaitland who had had the Gift of the Ward in October 1688. There were some whose claims extended as far back as 1620. Jean Ross, daughter of George Ross, merchant in Aberdeen, and granddaughter of John Ross, Treasurer of the burgh, had a claim through a wadset granted by Magnus Mowat at that time to John Wallace elder, in Turriff of the lands of Little Colp.[22] There were many other smaller creditors, among whom were some of the tenants. Those who should not be forgotten were the members of the immediate family. Her son may have died, but Katherine Lauder was still alive and still unprovided for. There were her sisters-in-law who had never received the money promised in the bonds of provision their father had executed at Corse. One of them, Helen Mowat, wife of Robert Molysone, had sold hers to Christian Mowat, daughter of James and Elizabeth Mowat in Redcloak, in 1692, but Christian had assigned it back to her in 1699.[23]

Interest by the lawyers in the bankrupt estate began even before the death of the melancholy William Mowat of Balquholly. In August 1687 Alexander Deuchar, an Edinburgh lawyer, purchased the Heritable Obligation which William had granted to George Forbes of Corse and the Back Bond granted to him by the Commissioners of the Exchequer in 1673. William's death in November of the following year required Alexander Deuchar to follow certain procedures before he could make further moves. He had to obtain Letters of General Charge for William's son to enter as his heir within a year and a day. These he obtained in 1689. The infant, William, could not have been expected to decide whether to enter as heir or renounce the succession, and so there was no obstacle to Alexander obtaining Letters of Special Charge in 1690.[24] In 1694 Alexander Strachan of Auchmull was empowered to draw up a 'Reasonable Compecture of what may be paid to the Creditors', and the list placed Alexander Deuchar as the man who would be due to receive the largest payment.[25] Finally, on 17th December, Alexander Deuchar obtained a Decreet of Adjudication (a replacement for Apprising). To consolidate his holding, in July 1697, he purchased the Bond of Alienation of 1661, and other bonds granted by Magnus Mowat to Sir George Mowat, Sir George Mowat's Assignation to his wife and her Translation and Assignation to her brother, Sir Archibald Hope of Ran-

keillor. He now had a marketable package. In August 1697 he sold all he had
acquired to Mr John Mowat, advocate. The following January, Sir Alexander Seton of Pitmedden, his Lady, and Katherine Lauder presented a
Petition questioning Alexander Deuchar's right to sell the Heritable Bond
which had belonged to George Forbes of Corse. It was arranged for the
matter to be discussed at Alexander Deuchar's house in the Lawnmarket.
Alexander Deuchar's defence, on that occasion, was that the arrangement
had not been formalised.[26] It was, however, shortly afterwards.

The entry for John Mowat in the Scottish Record Society's *Faculty of
Advocates* lists him as 'of Mergie'. He had become joint wadsetter of the lands
of Mergie with his uncle, Alexander, in 1670, the arrangement being
reaffirmed after he came of age in 1684.[27] In that same year he and his
uncle had sold their wadset to Patrick Irving of Bealtie, arranging for him to
hold the new wadset from them as well as from Sir David Carnegie of
Pittarrow, superior of the lands.[28] John Mowat's link with Mergie was
therefore somewhat tenuous and he did not use the title for long. His links
with his family in the North-East continued after he had moved to
Edinburgh. In October 1685, when he went abroad on business, he
appointed his brother-in-law, Alexander Orem, merchant in Aberdeen,
to see to his affairs during his absence.[29] It is more than likely that he met his
wife through his sister and her husband. She was Helen Mitchell, a native of
Aberdeen, daughter of a former Provost, and they were married in 1689.
They set up house in the Canongate in Edinburgh in premises which they
rented from Thomas Cleghorn, goldsmith.[30] Three of the children born to
them survived.

Before John Mowat had purchased the package of documents from
Alexander Deuchar, he had already become part-owner of the Decreet of
Apprising of the Ollaberry lands which had been obtained by Jean Cunning-
hame, widow of Sinclair of Rattar, in 1672 and which had subsequently
become the property of her second son, David Sinclair of Freswick. He and
Mr William Lauder had paid 9,000 merks (£6,000) for it.[31] As George
Mowat of Hamnavoe and his brother-in-law had been successful in holding
onto the Shetland lands, this acquisition had not been of any particular value.
But their error of judgement was of little consequence, after John Mowat
acquired the package of documents from Alexander Deuchar. He added to
them in February and March 1698 by purchasing Mr Adam Hay's wadsets of
Lendrum and Lescraigie at a 'verie great loss' to Mr Hay.[32] Mr Hay had
previously joined with other creditors under the direction of Mr William

Mitchell, minister in the Canongate, in an attempt to bring an action in the courts.[33] He had obviously decided that it was better to sell out even if it meant at a loss. By 1700 John Mowat was calling himself 'of Loscraigie' and then, having gained the majority of the preferential rights, changed his title soon after to that 'of Balquholly'. Several people when referring to him at that time prefixed this with 'pretended'. Among the documents he acquired was the, by then, very old bond for 5,000 merks which had been granted to his maternal great-grandfather, James Mowat of Ardo, by Magnus Mowat of Balquholly in 1598.

Outwardly, it appeared that Mr John Mowat was attempting to emulate his great-uncle, Mr Roger Mowat, whose philanthropic action had rescued the estate almost 60 years before, and that once more a member of a cadet branch was coming to the aid of the main line. In reality, he had no such reason. His acquisition had been purely speculative and he had every intention of selling the estate. Perhaps he had periods of conflicting emotions which made him delay temporarily. He may have been swayed by the thought of the 'weill and standing of the hous'. That he was vacillating is suggested by his appointment of Nathaniel Gordon of Noth as his factor, whom he replaced with Alexander Gordon younger of Auchreddie in 1705.[34] He also employed a painter, glazier and mason to repair the castle or manor house, as it was called by then.[35]

In 1707 his aunt, Elizabeth Mowat, who had outlived two husbands, died. He was served heir to her in 1708. In that year Lendrum and Lescraigie became the property of Sir Samuel Forbes of Foveran.[36] In 1697 Sir Samuel Forbes had stood as surety for John Mowat when he had borrowed 15,000 merks (£10,000) from Mr James Elphinstone of Logie, one of the Commissaries of Edinburgh. In 1705 he had been forced to grant Sir Samuel Forbes an Obligation of Relief, not having been able to repay the money at the agreed term.[37] Sir Samuel Forbes had then had him incarcerated in the Edinburgh tolbooth, agreeing in May 1708 to his release, despite the fact that he had still not received any payment.[38] The outcome was that John Mowat was forced to grant him Lendrum and Lescraigie and to hand over various documents, including Sir George Mowat's Contract of Alienation, to Mr James Elphinstone. A year later, while on a visit to Aberdeen, he took ill and died. He had made a will, naming his wife and brother-in-law as executors. His children were still young and he requested that they be well educated and brought up 'in the fear of the Lord'.[39]

Had he lived he would certainly have had to sell Balquholly. His widow confirmed this when she submitted an account of all the money which had been expended on acquiring and maintaining the estate. It amounted to £22,952/13/8d.[40] She stated that her husband owed debts on the estate far in excess of its value.[41] According to the terms of her marriage contract, made on 28th September 1689, her husband had bound himself for his part to provide 6,000 merks and to add a further 4,000 merks, making a total of 10,000 merks (£6,666/13/4d) to be invested in 'well-holden land'. Whoever survived would have the liferent of the money, and thereafter it would go to their children.[42] Their son, James, who called himself 'of Balquholly' briefly, perhaps to avoid the repercussions of his father's unexpected death, had left the country by the end of 1715. Helen Mitchell and her two daughters were left to face the ensuing confusion. Her husband's servitor, John Hay, stated in a Petition to the Lords in December 1709 that he was unable to hand over his master's papers, because 'no person can nor will medle with his writs', and that, moreover, several of his papers were in the hands of Sir James Elphinstone and the laird of Foveran.[43] (John Mowat had emphasised in his will that he did not want Samuel Forbes of Foveran to meddle in his affairs after his death.) Helen Mitchell was no match for all the other contenders. She could not even write. Balquholly had certainly not been 'well-holden' land.

Margaret Mowat, John Mowat's sister, also found herself in difficulties following the death of her husband, Alexander Orem, in March 1712. Under the terms of her marriage contract, she was to receive the liferent of 8,000 merks (£5,333/6/8d). She was unlikely to receive anything, however, as her husband had died in debt. His assets were the stock in his shop and debts which were owed to him. Among those debts was one for £549 which his sister-in-law, Helen Mitchell, had borrowed from him. It was never likely to be honoured. His merchant stock consisted of a cask of starch valued at £16; a barrel of indigo at £70; half a cask of vinegar at £13; a small barrel of Dutch doits; 16 matts (of undressed flax?); and a barrel of merchandise which John Pratt shipmaster had brought from Holland the previous month valued at just over 333 guilders. He also had '£400 value in John Anderson's ship from Bostoun'. He owed money to nine creditors, mostly fellow merchants, who were not long in taking his widow to court.[44] Margaret Mowat soon found herself in the same predicament that her sister-in-law, the 'pretended' Lady Balquholly, was in.

SOURCES
1. RD4/11 f.214.
2. F Grant – *Zetland Family Histories*, p. 196
3. Inhabited until 1934; only the north gable is now standing (photograph by Tammy Thomson of Braehoulland)
4. *RPC* ii, 375 (third series)
5. Seafield muniments (SRO) – GD248/398/5
6. CS15/472 – 10 Feb 1672; CS26/40 – 10 Jan 1672
7. Seafield Muniments (SRO) – GD248/398/5
8. CS21 – 6 Dec 1679 – Sinclair v Mowat and others
9. Seafield muniments (SRO) – GD248/398/5
10. CS18/75 – 9 Jan 1679 – Cunninghame v Mowat and Cheyne
11. CS18/78 – 6 Dec 1679; CS21 – 6 Dec 1679 – Sinclair v Mowat
12. Seafield muniments (SRO) – GD248/398/5
13. Seafield muniments (SRO) – GD248/408/2
14. CS26/40 – 21 Feb 1672
15. A. and H. Tayler – *The Valuation of the County of Aberdeen for the year 1667* (TSC), p. 28
16. Seafield muniments (SRO) – GD248/402 – Information Robt Mollison anent his Claim on Balquholly
17. *Ibid*; CS22/61 – 15 Jan 1677; CS22/65 – 7 Feb 1678
18. RD2/54 f.529
19. RD3/63 f.393; RD3/74 ffs.18; 24
20. Seafield muniments (SRO) – GD248/402
21. *Ibid.*
22. CS29; 7 Jan 1704 – Ross v Mowat
23. Seafield muniments (SRO) – GD248/402; SC5/62/1 – 9 Dec 1699
24. Seafield muniments (SRO) – GD248/218
25. *Ibid.*
26. *Ibid.*
27. RD4/53 f.703
28. SC5/58/1; RS8/12 – 16 July 1684
29. Seafield muniments (SRO) – GD248/401
30. CS271/16494 – 13 April 1710
31. RD2/78 – 24 Aug 1694
32. Seafield muniments (SRO) – GD248/408
33. Seafield muniments (SRO) – GD248/220
34. CS149/159 – 14 Feb 1711
35. CS238/M2/81 – John Ritchie Reid v Mowats
36. Seafield muniments (SRO) – GD248/402
37. RD3/105 f.148
38. RD4/103 – 15 Sept 1708
39. Edinburgh Commissary Testaments, CC8/8/24 – Testament of Mr John Mowat of Ballquholly – 12th October 1709
40. CS226/6269 – Mowat v Mitchell
41. CS236/M1/20 – Petition George Mowat of Balquholly
42. CS29; Box 450 – 16 Feb 1716 – Mitchell v Mowat
43. Seafield muniments (SRO) – GD248/218
44. CS229/F1/22 – Forbes of Puttachie and others v Margaret Mowat

CHAPTER THIRTEEN

The Last Mowats of Balquholly

The state of Balquholly's affairs left George Mowat of Hamnavoe with no choice. He was still the heir. In a Memorandum dated 9th June 1710, it was recorded that on 22nd May 1710 he had been served heir *cum beneficio*, the deceased William Mowat never having been infeft in the Balquholly lands. Living in Shetland, 'at a great distance and being ane aged man', he was unable to travel to the mainland to take actual possession of the lands and thereby be infeft. He requested that he be allowed to take his oath in Shetland upon the Inventory of the lands instead, but this request was initially refused by the Sheriff of Aberdeen, it being unprecedented. An Act had been passed in 1695 requiring an heir to make up an Inventory of the lands and estate within a year and a day of his predecessor's death and then to depone within the shire in which those lands lay. A Petition to the Lords, however, resulted in a commission being addressed to the Stewart-depute of Shetland (bypassing the sheriff in Aberdeen), allowing George Mowat to take his oath in Shetland. It being a time of war when very few ships were sailing to the islands, the Lords' decision had been hasty, in order that the commission could be sent with the fleet which was lying at Leith, ready to sail for Orkney.[1] When his oath was taken at his house on Papa Stour on 5th August that year, George Mowat was unable to write, 'being so weik and tender of bodie'.[2] He was obviously dying.

He was succeeded by his son, Patrick, to whom he had already disponed his right to the Balquholly lands in April 1710.[3] Robert Molysone, husband of Helen Mowat, recorded of Patrick, her cousin, that he

> sold Balquhollie's Lands in Zetland which he and his father had possessed for 42 years without compting for the same, came over to Balquholly and charged the Creditors thereof to produce their Rights and possessd the said Lands till his Death[4]

It was not quite as simple as that. In a Memorial for Arthur Nicolson of Lochend written in 1802, Patrick Mowat was described as 'an extravagant man', so much so that he had 'before he succeeded to Balquholly sold and disponed away much of his lands in Zetland and also contracted considerable debts'.[5]

By 1677, when William Mowat of Balquholly had failed to appear at St Magnus kirk to receive repayment of his father's money, Patrick's mother and his aunt had divided the Ollaberry lands between them. His parents' share included the islands of Papa Stour and Papa Little and they appear to have made the former their permanent home. The old manor house called the Northhouse stood on the island, close to the eastern shore at Housa Voe. Its shell had been used for a new house, erected by George's brother, Magnus.[6] In 1818 the gateway to the house was still standing, decorated with the family's armorial bearings and their Norman name of Monte Alto.[7] When the poll tax was collected in 1696, George Mowat was recorded as living at Papa Stour and owing £12. He claimed that 'he was never refractorie and consignit his poll judiciall, at least made offer thairof'.[8] He remained there, till his death, turning the house into a fortress, erecting 'mounted guns on his gate' in readiness for deforcing any court messengers attempting to serve him with summonses.[9] He was succeeded by his eldest son, Patrick, who inherited Papa Stour.[10] His other sons, James and Hector, received Stennes and Hurdaback respectively. In 1690 Patrick had wadset part of his family's land in Aithsting to Thomas Gifford of Busta, but had certainly not sold all his lands before he left for the mainland as reported by Robert Molysone.[11]

It is more than likely that Patrick's financial troubles spurred him on to leave the island and head for Balquholly. He must have been unaware of the fact that far greater burdens faced him there. In October 1710 he and his second wife and six-year-old child sailed for the Scottish mainland. On the 13th of that month at Lerwick, shortly before they sailed, Patrick made a Disposition of the island of Papa Stour and its manor place to that child, his second son, John Mowat.[12] The 'dangerousness of the passage' proved just that, for they were shipwrecked en route and it was only the following May when they finally reached Balquholly. They found the castle in a state of decay, a tenant occupying the lower floor. Patrick and his wife and son moved into the upper floor. He felt it was necessary for them to stay there to prevent the house becoming completely ruinous. Almost immediately he was presented with petitions from the tenants. He then began legal action in the Court of Session. His estimate of the burdens on the estate was £43,777/8/6d and he was anxious to have the estate sequestrated.[13] In December 1712 he agreed to pay Helen Mitchell a yearly sum of £200, following a Decreet of Removing which she had obtained from the Court of Session against him.[14] By 1715 he was in great need of money and was forced to wadset the whole island of Papa Stour to Arthur Nicolson of Bullister for £13,000, returning to Shetland to sign the necessary documents.[15] It emerged that his parents had gifted only two-thirds of the island to him, the remaining third, consisting of the 72-merk lands, having been granted to his two brothers, James and Hector. On the death of Hector, he and James had disputed who should inherit Hector's share. James had been successful and was served heir to Hector in July 1711. Patrick appears to have resented the outcome, for his subsequent wadset of Papa Stour to Arthur Nicolson in 1715 makes no mention of the fact that he was owner of only two-thirds of the island. That had not been the first time the island had been alienated. His parents had granted a heritable bond for £786/11/- to Thomas Cushney, late Dean of Guild in Aberdeen, as far back as 1683.[16] In June 1715 Patrick's daughter, Katherine, was born, her baptism being witnessed by Mr Roderick Cheine,'chaplane at Balquhollie'. Patrick had obviously made some changes at the ruinous castle.

In October 1715, in support of the Old Pretender, he sent a dark bay horse 'with sadle pistols and furnitor to be made use of in the Kings service' to the Marquis of Huntly.[17] In the following year he was dead. In May 1716, two months before he died, he drew up two deeds in his wife's favour, a new marriage contract and a Gift of Tutory to her, as his heir, John, was still a minor. In the latter he stated categorically that he wished to debar 'all brothyrs german, brothyrs in law, cusin germans and all othyr freinds and relations' of him or his wife 'from medling with or negotiating any of his [son's] affairs' other than as tutors and curators during his minority. It had been necessary for him to draw up a new marriage contract, as his wife had renounced their original one. There is no doubt that her husband's financial difficulties had occasioned her renunciation. In the new contract she was given the liferent of the mains of Balquholly and the castle and the multures and sequels of Darra, Boggie-shalloch, Over and Under Smiddyseat, Meikle Colp, Ardin, Quarrelhill and Broadfoord.[18] Patrick did not forget Ursula, his only surviving daughter of his first marriage. In June he made provision for her, leaving her 1,000 merks (£666/13/4d) out of the Balquholly lands of Broadfoord and Whitehillock.[19] (His other daughter, Margaret, and her husband, John Scott, had been lost at sea on a voyage from Shetland to Leith just after they had been married.) Robert Molysone gave Patrick credit for having managed to clear some of the creditors during his lifetime. Had he lived longer, it is doubtful whether he would have been able to achieve much more, given the enormous debts which had accumulated and the complex problems which had arisen as a result.

His heir, John Mowat, was still a young boy. His widow, Barbara Cheyne, remarried to James Erskine in Dorlaithers, brother of John Erskine whom

George Forbes of Corse had employed to guard Balquholly castle in 1682. James Erskine became the owner of the Heritable Bond which William Mowat of Balquholly had granted to his brother and he also acquired the Bond of Provision which Patrick Mowat had granted to his daughter, Ursula.[20] Ursula remained at Balquholly for a while, but by 1723 had moved back to Shetland. Her stepmother sent her her love in a letter which she wrote to James Mowat of Stennes in November of that year.[21] The letter had concerned the tithes of Papa Stour to which Barbara Cheyne and her son were entitled and which James Mowat of Stennes, as their factor, collected for them.[22] Patrick Mowat's other son, Robert, died in Edinburgh in March 1722. He had been ill since the previous November and had been attended by George Cheine, 'chirugeon' in Leith, who appears to have prescribed large quantities of 'chirie, clairet and whit wine' for the ailing youth.[23] He and his elder brother, John, had been sent to Edinburgh to be educated, where they had boarded with Grizell Scott, the widow of a goldsmith. By April 1726 John Mowat had reached his majority and was charged to enter as heir to his father but, in July, was freed by the Lords from doing so, on condition that he paid Katherine Lauder her liferent of the lands from the time of her husband's death in 1688 until 1725, amounting to the enormous sum of 64,800 merks (£43,200).[24] He married Agnes Keith, heiress of James Keith younger of Keithfield (formerly Tilligonie). The marriage contract caused much debate among the lawyers with regard to the conditions it should contain. It was finally drawn up in December 1727. What had concerned them was

> Balqholy being burthened with his own debts and 14,000 merks of Keithfeilds if Keithfeild should die quhereby Balqholy succeds to the half of the Ladys joynture it's observed that Balqholys creditors could afect this joynture and reduce the Lady Keithfeild to a small subsistance and incapacitate her to opose the creditors of Balqholy or relieve her grandchildren.

Her father had not been helping matters. He had been busy 'squandering his means and estate'.[25] In the event, what had concerned the lawyers never happened, for John Mowat had, by then, formally resigned the Balquholly estate to Katherine Lauder.[26] Katherine Lauder had tried repeatedly after her husband's death to obtain payment of her liferent out of the lands. She had obtained a charter under the Great Seal on 28th July 1690 and had been infeft on 17th October that year.[27] She had then raised two actions in the Court of Session against the tenants of Balquholly. In 1704 she had even recorded the marriage contract which her husband had been remiss or reluctant to record. Finally, on 26th March 1726, she sold her liferent right to George Dempster, merchant in Dundee. On 17th February 1727 George Dempster, with the consent of Katherine Lauder, sold that liferent right to Alexander Duff of Hatton.[28] The following July, John Mowat of Balquholly resigned the lands to Katherine Lauder, a mere formality. By then Alexander Duff of Hatton had become the owner of the estate and had begun the process of establishing 'in himself all Competent Rights and Titles'. On 1st November a Deed of Consent and Ratification was drawn up between him and the Balquholly heir. John Mowat recorded therein that the lands of Balquholly had

> for many years yea for severall ages past been incumbered and burdened att the instance of many just and lawfull Creditors and whose Rights and dilligence still affect the same even to a greater extent than the worth and value of the Subject itself and in such Circumstances it being very unsafe amid me the appearand heir and Representative of the family of Ballquholly to Inmix or Concern myself personally But being heartily willing that the Estate and Subject should be brought to the best account for the benefit of these having Intrest therin and Alexr Duff of Hatton being Resolved out of goodwill to the memory of my predecessors and in Justice to their lawful Creditors to Establish a Sufficient absolute heritable and irredeemable Right therto in his own person and that in the way of a legall sale before the Lords of Council and Session or in some othyr manner competent in Law and to Transact and Clear the Just and lawfull debts affecting the samen in such a way as the Creditors and he will agree and in Consequence of this Resolution he having already paid and Transacted very Considerable debts affecting the said Estate and is about to do the like to the othyr Creditors having Intrest therin.

He therefore ratified all actions which had been taken by Alexander Duff and approved all those which he intended taking.[29] Even in defeat, he appears to have been unable to admit that, to a large extent, the estate had become so heavily encumbered with debts through his forebears' mismanagement. His statement that Alexander Duff's actions had been out of goodwill towards the memory of his predecessors demonstrates that he too had inherited his family's obsession with who they were. In November 1729 an application for a Judicial Sale before the Lords of Council and Session was heard, instituted by Alexander Duff.[30] It heralded the end. The ancient house of Balquholly had finally fallen.

One of the witnesses to the Deed of Consent and Ratification was Alexander Garioch of Mergie, a lawyer in Edinburgh, who had dealt with some of John Mowat's earlier affairs. Several of his accounts have survived addressed to 'Mr John Montealto'. He appears to have addressed them in that manner to humour the last young laird who, after becoming heir, in youthful intoxication insisted on signing himself 'John Montealto of that Ilk'. In September 1723 he wrote to his uncle, James Mowat in Stennes, informing him that 'I have gott my Coat of arms from Edinburgh which pleases me verry weel'.[31] At least the Mowat pride had not been dampened. He did not live long, dying in 1736, leaving a young family. His widow found herself in the same position as so many of the earlier Mowat wives – being left with very little and having to face creditors. In January 1737 she applied to the Commissary Clerk of Aberdeen for an executor to be appointed to draw up an Inventory of her husband's estate, but by February was having to petition for all 'outsight and insight plenishings and other effects' to be rouped or disposed of to pay off debts. In October 1738 she once again petitioned the Commissary Clerk. On that occasion she requested the seals of the cabinet of the deceased George Keith, advocate in Aberdeen, to be broken in order to ascertain whether there was a receipt or obligation amongst his papers for 7,000 merks (£4,666/13/4d) which she maintained she and her husband had deposited with him 'to extinguish their debts'.[32] (John Mowat had, in fact, deposited 6,200 merks with George Keith, but that money had been destined to pay off his father-in-law's debts.)[33]

John Mowat's heir, his son, John, changed his surname to Mowat-Keith, further emphasising the end, although in the 1760s he 'was incited to make some enquiry about the estates which belonged to his ancestors'. The man who was responsible for inciting him to do so was his brother-in-law, William Chalmers, collector of customs at Lerwick, who according to Arthur Nicolson of Lochend 'was a man very much disposed to fish in muddy waters'.[34] He had discovered the Heritable Bond which Mr James Mowat of Ollaberry had granted to Magnus Mowat in 1661. In 1762 he lent his brother-in-law £2,000 Sterling and two years later, still unpaid, charged him to enter as heir to the Shetland lands.[35] Whether the incitement had resulted in the loan or whether the loan had led to the incitement, John Mowat-Keith found himself in a difficult situation and in November 1767 renounced his heirship to his father. What may have spurred him on to do so was a pending action by Arthur Nicolson of Lochend. William Chalmers had obviously been unaware that much had happened with regard to the Ollaberry lands since 1661. Arthur

Nicolson, heir to his uncle Arthur Nicolson of Bullister (later of Lochend), had fallen heir to several bonds which had been granted by Patrick Mowat of Balquholly. It appears that in 1710, when Patrick Mowat had left Shetland for Balquholly, he had borrowed £692/4/- from Mr John Otto Bossawe, merchant in Heldwick and later in Hamburg. This loan had been followed by another in 1711 for £400. The bonds which had been drawn up had then been acquired by Arthur Nicolson of Bullister, together with a Bill for £144 which had been drawn and receipted by Patrick Mowat on Alexander Brock, tailor and burgess in the Canongate, Edinburgh in 1714.[36] Arthur Nicolson's acquisition of these documents had obviously led to Patrick Mowat's subsequent wadsetting of the whole island of Papa Stour to him in 1715. At that time he was already owner of a wadset of 4 lasts of land on the island, having lent 6,000 merks (£4,000) to Patrick in 1711. In 1716, he also aquired a Heritable Bond for £2,064/7/4d upon the whole island which Patrick had granted to John Scot of Scotshall.[37] It would have been wiser for John Mowat-Keith not to listen to his brother-in-law. As late as 1811 his son, George Mowat-Keith, was having to face litigation by Arthur Nicolson of Bullister's great-grand nephew.

Two years before he died, John Mowat-Keith was living 'in the Town of Peterhead in a mean condition without business'.[38] In 1803 his widow, Margaret Mowat-Keith, wrote to Thomas Bolt in Lerwick, tutor to Arthur Nicolson, grandson of the Arthur Nicolson of Lochend who had brought the action in the 1760s, recalling that many years before, when they had been living at Faichfield near Peterhead, she and her husband had been visited by Mr Gifford of Busta who had tried to buy the redemption of the Shetland lands from them. He had become the owner of the third part of Papa Stour which had belonged to Patrick Mowat's two brothers and had been keen to consolidate his holding. She also pointed out to him that the Mowats were and had been

> a much injured family who for many centries past have been strugling with a sinking fortune, a family who have had the highest offices in the Kingdom with honour to themselves and benefit to their country.[39]

More than a century before, Patrick Mowat of Balquholly's fear of litigation and concern about the loss of the lands had been 'in caice the saidis soumes be not payit at the termes to cum appointit for payment'. Their inability to honour their debts at the agreed times had been the Mowats' biggest problem. It was the cause of their 'sinking fortune' and had ultimately led to the loss of their lands.

But the actual losers were all those people from whom the Mowats had borrowed money, including those who had disposed of their documents to the lawyers. Some, like Elspet Mitchell, lost all their money. In the 1620s James Mowat of Smiddyseat and his son, Patrick (grandfather and father of Magnus Mowat of Balquholly), had borrowed 1,450 merks (£966/13/4d) on two occasions from Elspet's parents, Thomas Mitchell, merchant in Turriff, and his wife, Elspet Mowat. On 15th July 1651 Thomas Mitchell had assigned the bonds to Elspet Mitchell, his only daughter. She, like Isobel Mowat, was a maiden lady and in need of an income to support herself. By 1651 the original amount, augmented by interest, would have amounted to a tidy sum. In January 1658 she obtained a Decreet from the Commissioner for the Administration of Justice against Magnus Mowat, as heir to his grandfather, but not yet owner of Balquholly, ordering him to make payment to her.[40] Following litigation in the courts in January 1668, during which Magnus had asserted that he and Isobel Mitchell and her cousin, Thomas Mitchell, bailie in Aberdeen, had 'entered in freindlie trysting anent the said soumes', Isobel was finally able to obtain a Bond of Corroboration from Magnus in July 1669. There he reiterated the original arrangement which had been made between his grandfather and father and Isobel Mitchell's father and agreed to pay her 6037 merks and 10 shillings (£4,025/3/4d) by Candlemas 1670.[41] His cautioner on that occasion had been his friend, George Forbes of Corse, who became liable for the debt after Magnus's death in November 1669. George Forbes estimated in 1681 that he would have had to pay £5,846/18/10d to Elspet Mitchell.[42] In the event, she appears to have died before the final stage was reached, never having received any form of payment. Both she and George Forbes and all the other creditors would have benefited from the advice given by Polonius to his son, Laertes:

Neither a borrower, nor a lender be;
For loan oft loses both itself and friend:
And borrowing dulls the edge of husbandry.

SOURCES

1. Press cutting – Irvine of Midbrake collection (Shetland Archives) – 392/71/3.
2. Seafield muniments (SRO) – GD248/401
3. SIG/113/42; RS3/100 f.2
4. Seafield muniments (SRO) – GD248/401 – Information Robt Mollison anent his Claim on Balquholly

5. Nicolson papers (Shetland Archives) – Memorial for Arthur Nicolson of Lochend, October 1802
6. Bruce of Symbister muniments (Shetland Archives) – Papa Stour writs
7. Samuel Hibbert – *Description of the Shetland Islands*, p. 287
8. SC12/6/1696/2
9. CS236/M1/28 – John and James Mitchell v James Mowat
10. E S Tait Collection (Shetland Archives) – D6/131/6/8
11. RS3/97 f.210
12. RD4/192/2 – 29 Oct 1762
13. CS226/6269 – Petition by Patrick Mowat of Balquholly
14. Seafield muniments (SRO) – GD248/401
15. RD4/192/2 – 29 Oct 1762
16. RS3/59 f.13
17. Gordon Papers (SRO) – GD44/51/500/11/16
18. RD3/151 – 18 June 1717; RD4/136/part 2 – 14 Nov 1724
19. Seafield muniments (SRO) – GD248/408/1; RS3/29 f.595
20. RS3/122 f.27; RS8/20 f.595
21. Nicolson papers (Shetland Archives) – Letter from Ursula Mowat to Arthur Nicolson dated 16 April 1720
22. Bruce of Symbister papers (Shetland Archives) – GD144/137/7 – Letter Barbara Cheyne to the Laird of Stennes; RD4/141 – 9 Jan 1727 – Factory by John Mowat of Balquholly to his uncle
23. Seafield muniments (SRO) – GD248/408/1
24. CS29; 4 Feb 1729 – Duff of Hatton v Creditors of Balquholly
25. Haddo muniments (SRO) – GD33/29/3
26. CS29; 20 July 1727 – Lauder v Mowat
27. RS3/61 f.331
28. RD4/141 f.2
29. RD4/147 – 12 Jan 1730
30. CS29; 11 Nov 1729 – Decreet of sale of lands of Balquholly in favour of Alexander Duff of Hatton
31. E. S. Reid Tait collection (Shetland Archives) – D6/131/6/7
32. CC1/7/1 – 13 Jan 1737; 17 Feb 1737; 13 Oct 1738 (Petitions)
33. SC1/61/76 – Jan 1742
34. Nicolson papers (Shetland Archives)
35. CS29; 27 June 1764 – Chalmers v Mowat-Keith
36. CS29; 29 June 1768 Nicolson v Mowat-Keith
37. Nicolson papers (Shetland Archives) – Memorial for Arthur Nicolson of Lochend, October 1802
38. Gardie House Papers – Extract from a letter from Mr Murdoch Mackenzie dated 14 June 1786
39. Nicolson Papers (Shetland Archives) – Letter from Margaret Mowat-Keith to Thomas Bolt of Lerwick, tutor to Arthur Nicolson of Lochend, 23 May 1803
40. RD4/27 f.754
41. CS22/23 – 9 Jan 1668
42. Seafield muniments (SRO) – GD248/401

Postscript

Among the Balquholly papers which Mr John Mowat, advocate, had acquired at the end of the seventeenth century had been the Assignation by Alexander Mowat in Redcloak to his daughter, Elizabeth, of the bond which had been granted to him by Sir George Mowat of Inglishton. Elizabeth Mowat's elder daughter, Christian, married William Mowat, a merchant in Aberdeen. Their youngest son, William, was born in 1712 and followed his father into the mercantile trade. He acquired the property of Colpnay and was Provost of the burgh from 1754 to 1755.[1] He was the founder of a company known as William Mowat and Co. and was engaged in various other ventures, such as the Whale Fishing Company of Aberdeen.[2] His mercantile interests also included the importing of tobacco from America,[3] and he was a partner in the Aberdeen Banking Company.[4] One of its customers was the kirk session of Fetteresso, native parish of many of the Mowats. They had invested £105 of the kirk's money in the bank. The minutes of the session record their growing concern as rumours reached them that 'the credit of Provost Mowat and Co had fallen under great suspiscion'.[5] The Sheriff Court Deeds for the period take on a familiar pattern. They contain records of many bonds having been granted by William Mowat. That the company was in trouble is reflected in the number of times he and his fellow merchants were put to the horn shortly before it foundered. The outcome was that the company was declared bankrupt in the 1760s, the repercussions of which were felt for many years afterwards.

In the year in which William Mowat of Colpnay was born, the Apprising of the Earl of Seaforth's lands which had so obsessed Roger Mowat and his wife and which had passed to their daughter, Bethia, finally passed out of Mowat hands. It became the property of William Martine of Harwood, he having apprised it from Bethia and her husband. He had obviously not been aware of the trouble it had caused nor that it was no longer of any value.[6]

A later inscription on the Ardo tomb in St Nicholas kirk recorded that Margaret Mowat and her husband, John Stewart of Inchbreck, Professor of Greek at Marischal College, were buried there in the 1820s. Margaret

Mowat was described as the 'last' of the family of Mowats of Ardo and Logie. She was the daughter of George Mowat younger, merchant in Aberdeen, and Marjory Burnett. Her grandfather, George Mowat elder, had been born in the 1670s.[7] Ardo had been disposed of long before then.

Another Mowat descendant registered arms in March 1811, as heir male and representative of the ancient family of Mowat of Balquholly. He was George Mowat, Captain in the Royal Navy, eldest grandson of James Mowat of Stennes.[8] He, poor man, had been insane for many years and under the care of Joseph Proud, an apothecary in Bilston.[9] He named as his heir his brother, James Mowat of the Bengal Engineers. No one has claimed arms since that date.

The lands may have fallen into other hands and the family's struggle ended, but pride, in the name of Mowat, even if at times misguided, lingered on.

Finally, on a plan of the lands in the vicinity of Balquholly castle drawn up in 1769, there is a field just behind the castle called 'Make Him Rich Infield'. Unfortunately for the Mowats, this never happened.

SOURCES

1. A. M. Munro – *Memorials of the aldermen, provosts and lord provosts of Aberdeen, 1272–1895* – entry for William Mowat of Colpnay, Provost 1754–5
2. SC1/61/89 – 27 Dec 1756 – contract of copartnery – partners: William Mowat, James Dun, Alexander Osborn, George Alexander, Alexander and Peter Reid
3. E 371/54 – 15 April 1757 – William Mowat, George Alexander, James Abernethy and John Elphinstone
4. CC1/16/3 – Partners: William Mowat, William Brebner, James Ligertwood, Alexander Osborn, John Dingwall, John Elphinstone, and John Duncan – all merchants and bailies of Aberdeen; RS64/8 – 7 May 1752 – Partners – Mr Alexander Livingstone, William Mowat, William Brebner, James Ligertwood, Alexander Osborn, John Dingwall, John Elphinstone and John Duncan
5. CH2/153/3 – November 1758
6. RS3/114 f.408
7. A. M. Munro – *Memorials of the aldermen, provosts and lord provosts of Aberdeen* – entry for William Mowat of Colpnay, Provost 1754–5
8. *Register of Arms*, vol ii, 66 (Lyon Office)
9. Gardie House papers – evidence of Murdoch McKenzie

Mowat Lands

Balquholly

'Maines of Bolquhollie toure and fortalice of the samyn, The Landis of Colp, mylne of Colp, mylnelandis and multures of the samyn, The Landis of Mekle Colp, Lytill Colp, Smiddiesait, Landis of Jackistoun mylne, mylnelandis and multures thairof, Landis [of] Yowbraye, Lytill Brounhill, Mekle Brounhill, Lyndrum, Wodend, Keithin, Ruschheid'(RD1/75 f.456 – 4 Nov 1600)

[Not included were the lands granted to Magnus Mowat and his wife in 1596. The charter to Mr Roger Mowat, advocate, dated 17th March 1635, includes: 'Loscragie, Darauche, Boggieshallauch, Bomalie and Ardine'(*RMS* ix,295)]

Freswick

'All and haill the Landis of Freschwick toure and fortalice of the samyn, the maynis of Burnesyde mylne mylnelandis and multures of the samyn, The Landis of Harley, Middiltoun of Freschwick, Skriscarie, Sonsequouy, Toftis, Maynes of Toftis, Landis (of) Overlie, Astriwall, Blayberriesquoyis, Landis of Harvisdaill, Okkingill, milntown of Okkingill, Landis of Strowbister'(RD1/75 f.456 – 4 Nov 1600)

Mowats of Balquholly (alias Loscraigie)
Mowats of Loscraigie

1309 PATRICK DE MONTE ALTO received charter of lands of Loscraigie (*RMS*, App 2,36)

1410 WILLIAM DE MONTE ALTO, Lord of Loscraigie. John de Monte Alto, his son, granted charter of confirmation of Freswick lands (*RMS* i,929). Murdered in the chapel of St Duthac at Tain.

1433 ALEXANDER MOWAT OF LOSCRAIGIE on retour of James, Lord Abernethy (Alexander Fraser, Lord Saltoun – *The Frasers of Philorth*,ii,305)

1457 JOHN MOWAT OF LOSCRAIGIE involved in unlawful retour of late, Robert, Lord Erskine (RH6/348)

1495 ALEXANDER MOWAT OF LOSCRAIGIE (*ADC*,487), heir to his cousin, William of Clyne, in lands in Ross (GD96/8)

1500/1 JOHN MOWAT OF LOSCRAIGIE, son and heir to above (*ibid*), also heir to uncle, William Mowat, canon of Aberdeen (NSC – *Sh Crt Recs*,i,34). Had younger brother, Alexander Mowat, m. Isabella Leslie (GD305/1/19/1–3), they had no issue, their grand-nephew, Patrick Mowat, heir in 1543 (GD305/1/19/8). John Mowat possibly killed at battle of Flodden in 1513.

1516 MAGNUS MOWAT, son of deceased John Mowat of Loscraigie, given gift of relief and non-entries of the lands (*RSS* i,2781). Reputed to have married a daughter of Forbes of Pitsligo (*John O'Groat's Journal*, 28 May 1948). He d. 1526 (*RSS* i.2781). His heir, Patrick Mowat, a minor.

Mowats of Balquholly

1. Patrick Mowat of Balquholly, b.c.1511 – d. 1564 (*RMS* iv,1379), in 1532 had sasine of Freswick and Harpsdale, in 1545 confirmed in lands of Balquholly, m. Margaret Cheyne, dau of Patrick Cheyne of Esslemont and Isobel Bad (*RMS* iii,3072; NRAS – 0925, no.273). Margaret Cheyne m.(ii) James Dempster of Auchterless, c.1566/7 (CS7/39 f.41).

They had:

(i)   Patrick Mowat, heir

(ii)   James Mowat (see Mowats in Redcloak)

(iii)   Magnus Mowat (see Mowats in Cowie and of Ardo)

(iv)   Beatrix Mowat m. (i) Alexander Mortimer of Auchinbady, m.con 1565 (RD1/8 f.365), she relict by Sept 1577, m. (ii) Patrick Dalgarno (CS7/85 f.365)

(v)   Margaret Mowat m. John Craig of Craigfintray, divorced him 18 Nov 1562, because of his impotency, ran off with his uncle, Mr John Craig, parson of Kincardine in Speyside in Dec 1562 (R Pitcairn – *Criminal Trials*, vol i, part ii ★459)

Relationship not able to be determined, may have been a sons and daughter of Patrick Mowat of Balquholly:

(vi)   George Mowat in Loscraigie, d. by March 1608 (DI 21/14 f.96) – had (a) Walter Mowat whose future spouse in 1608 was Eister Cuming, dau of the deceased William Cuming of Inverallochy and Isobel Grant (RD1/157 f.40), possibly the Walter Mowat buried St Nicholas, Aberdeen, 21 Oct 1606 'being hurt be Mr Pa. Cheyne' (St Nich OPR), (b) Elspet Mowat ?, m. Thomas Mitchell, merchant in Turriff (DI 21/14 f.96), they had only dau, Elspet Mitchell (RD4/27 f.754)

(vii)   Thomas Mowat in Balquholly had (a) Thomas Mowat, merchant in Turriff; (b) Elspet Mowat m. Robert Melvill, son of the deceased Mr Thomas Melvill, sometime in Kildrummy in Mar (RD1/204 f.210)

(viii) Janet Mowat, m.(i) Thomas Copland, portioner of Idoch, second wife?, he d. by 1574 (NSC – *Sh Crt Recs*.i,220). She m.(ii) John Roy Grant of Carron (RD1/20 f.351)

[Thomas Copland had by first wife ?: (i) Patrick Copland of Idoch, m. Elizabeth Auchinleck (*RMS* vii,205). Their son, Alexander Copland, captain in Poland; (ii) Alexander Copland, a freebooter (RS4/3 f.447); (iii) William Copland in Laverockhills (ibid)]

[Patrick Mowat (1) had a sister, Margaret Mowat, who had two illegitimate sons, Patrick and John, by William Sinclair of Mey, legitimised in 1607 (*The Scots Peerage*,ii,342; *Caithness MIs, parish of Canisbay*,15)]

2. Patrick Mowat of Balquholly, son of Patrick Mowat above, d. by June 1603, m. Christine Ogilvy, dau of Walter Ogilvy of Boyne c.1559 (*RMS* iv,1379)

[Walter Ogilvy, 3rd of Boyne (c.1504 -c.1561), m. in 1525, Christian Keith. They had:(i) Alexander Ogilvy, 4th of Boyne, m. (i) Mary Beaton, one of Mary Queen of Scots' ladies and m. (ii) Lady Jane Gordon, dau of George, 4th Earl of Huntly, m.con 10 Dec 1599, (he, her 3rd husband). He d. c.1601; (ii) Walter Ogilvy of Baldavie; (iii) Margaret Ogilvy m. Master of Buchan (killed at Pinkie); (iv) Marjorie Ogilvy m. James Dunbar of Tarbat; (v) Barbara m. Alexander Ogilvy of Cardell whose son, Walter, became 1st Lord Deskford (*TBFC* – 15 March 1933 – 'The Ogilvies of Boyne')]

They had:

(i)   Magnus Mowat, heir

(ii)   James Mowat of Smiddyseat, heir to brother, Magnus (i) above

(iii) Christian Mowat, eldest dau, m. James Gardin, son of Alexander Gardin of Blackford, m.con 13 Mar 1591 (CS7/409 – 28 Mar 1628)

(iv)   Isobel Mowat, d. 19 May 1601 (*Caithness MIs, parish of Canisbay*,15), m. William Bruce of Stanstill, [he m.(ii) Jonet Murray (GD96/367)]

(v)   Elizabeth Mowat (RD1/91 f.71) m. George Crawford of Annochie (NSC – *Sh Crt Recs*.ii,98)

(vi)   Jean Mowat m. Alexander Calder of Asloun (*ibid*, 99, 245)

3. Magnus Mowat of Balquholly, d. March 1634 (GD96/683/1), m. Elizabeth (Isobel) Cheyne, dau of William Cheyne of Arnage and Margaret Irvine, sister of Alexander Irvine of Drum (*RMS* iii,1233), m.con 3 Nov 1592 (GD96/240). [Isobel Cheyne was the widow of John Kennedy of Kermucks, buried in St Nicholas churchyard 6 Nov 1591 (St Nich OPR). They had: (i) James Kennedy of Kermucks (d. 1608), m. Elspet Forbes, dau of William Forbes of Monymusk, [she m.(ii) Alexander Annand of Auchterellon (A and H Tayler – *The House of Forbes*,301)]; (ii) John Kennedy (RS6/2); (iii) Hugh Kennedy m. Susan Hay

(GD96/451); (iv) Margaret Kennedy (CS7/226 – 19 Feb 1607), she m.(i) Alexander Con in Woodend, son of Patrick Con of Auchry (Dl 21/14 – 20 June 1608), and m.(ii) Robert Merser, minister of Ellon (*Fasti.*vi,190); (v) William Kennedy in Borrowley – had dau Elspet (SC1/7/8 – 15 July 1642)]. Elizabeth (Isobel) Cheyne d. post July 1642 (*ibid*).
They had:

(i) Elizabeth (Elspet) Mowat (GD96/449), d. by 1634, m. (John ?) Forbes of Asloun (GD248/401)

(ii) Christian Mowat, m. Sir John Sinclair of Geanies and Dunbeath by 1627 (GD248/401; GD96/683/1), he second son of George Sinclair of Mey. She d. 'prematurely in the bloom of life', buried at Latheron (J Henderson – *Caithness Family Histories*,83); tomb built by John Dirom, master mason post 26 Sept 1642 (GD96/573). [Sir John Sinclair of Dunbeath m.(ii) Katherine, dau of Hugh, Lord Lovat, m.con 2 June 1643 (GD96/575). He d. Sept 1651 (GD96/683/1). He had a natural dau, Barbara Sinclair who m. William Bruce of Stanstill, m.con 29 May 1640 (RH9/7/15)]
They had:

(a) Margaret Sinclair, only dau m. Hugh Rose of Kilravock, m.con 12 Feb 1640 (SPC – Rev H Rose – *A Genealogical Deduction of the family of Rose of Kilravock*,329). In Sept 1651, she was described as heavily diseased (GD96/683/1) and d. Nov 1654. Hugh Rose d. May 1649 aged 29
They had:
(1) Hugh Rose
(2) John Rose
(3) Magdalen Rose m. Mr William Robertson of Insches. She d. 12 Mar 1669, leaving an only dau who d. as a child (*A Genealogical Deduction of the family of Rose of Kilravock*,340)

[Magnus Mowat (3) had an illegitimate son, Thomas Mowat (RS37/1 f.272), m. Marjorie Gardin, dau of James Gardin of Blackford and Christian Mowat – (see 2 (iii) above) (CS7/409 – 22 Dec 1627). They had: (a) Elspet Mowat, m. Alexander Coghill in Bowermadden (GD96/667); (b) . . . Mowat, m. Findlay Groat of Skirscary (RD4/16 f.505) – she may have been (a) and he, her second husband]

4. James Mowat of Smiddyseat, brother of Magnus above, of Ardin in 1611 (GD96/365), of Balquholly (post-1634) (*RMS* viii,295), d. between Aug 1642 and Mar 1643 (RD1/536 – 8 Jan 1644; CH2/1120/1 – 9 Mar 1643), m. Lucy Gordon, one of seven daus of William Gordon of Gight and Isobel Ouchterlony (J Malcolm Bulloch – *House of Gordon*, ii,16;67)

[William Gordon, 5th laird of Gight (d.1604), had sons – (i) George Gordon; (ii) John Gordon of Ardlogie; (iii) William Gordon; (iv) Patrick Gordon; (v) Adam Gordon; (vi) Alexander Gordon; (vii) Robert Gordon, and daus – (i) Christian Gordon m. Sir Adam Gordon of Park and Glenbucket; (ii) Lucy Gordon above; (iii) Marjorie Gordon m. Alexander Innes of Cults; (iv) Elspet Gordon m. James Cheyne of Pennan; (v) Janet Gordon m. the goodman of Harthill Leith; (vi) Anna Gordon m.(i) Alexander Gordon of Tulloch and (ii) Thomas Gordon of Pittendreich, brother of the laird of Cluny; (vii) Jean Gordon m. George Gordon of Cushney (*ibid* – his source the Balbithan MS)] They had:

(i)   Patrick Mowat, only son (SC1/7/13 – 14 July 1661)

(ii)   Isobel Mowat (RD1/528 f.314), d. unmarried, possibly abroad (*The Blairs Papers*, App 111, 245)

(iii)   Christian Mowat m. William Lindsay, brother-in-law of Mr Alexander Lindsay, servitor to Patrick Lindsay, Archbishop of Glasgow (RD1/504 – 26 Dec 1636)

5. Patrick Mowat, son of James Mowat of Smiddyseat above, designed himself 'apparent of Balquholly' (RD1/553 – 8 Jan 1644), killed at battle of Alford, July 1645 (GD248/401), m. Helen Copland, dau of Captain Alexander Copland of Idoch, mercenary in Poland (SRS – *Lyon Office Genealogies*) [Captain Alexander Copland in Aberchirder in 1640, in Haughs in 1649 (CC16/19/1 – 4 July 1649). He had John Copland of Haughs (CC16/9/1 – 9 Oct 1648; 10 June 1651), m. Isobel Gordon, relict of Leonard Leslie of Haughs (RS16/7 ffs.13,44). Their possible sons – William Copland m. Annas Innes (RD4/27 f.101) and Mr Walter Copland m. Margaret Mowat (see Mowats in Cowie and of Ardo)] They had:

(i)   Magnus Mowat, heir to grandfather, James Mowat above

(ii)   George Mowat of Hamnavoe (see 9 below)

(iii)   James Mowat (see Mowats in Redcloak)

(iv)   Barbara Mowat, m. Malcolm Groat, portioner of Duncansby (Caithness sasine index)

(v)   Elizabeth Mowat, m. John Kennedy younger of Kermucks (also younger of Stroma), m.con 18 Aug 1663 (GD144/187/16). She in parish of Thurso, 29 Nov 1663, (SRS – *Parish Registers of Canisbay*). She d. by 1678 (*SNQ*, 3rd series,109)

        They had:

        (a) George Kennedy, bap 14 Feb 1664 (*ibid*)

        [John Kennedy was son of John Kennedy elder of Stroma, and Janet Forbes, dau of William Forbes of Craigievar. Elizabeth Mowat was

his second wife. His first wife was Margaret Burnett by whom he had
Thomas and John Kennedy (SC14/50/2 f.199). His third wife was
Jean Mackenzie, eldest daughter of Bishop Mackenzie of Orkney, m.
15 May 1678 (*SNQ*, 3rd series,v109). John Kennedy elder of
Kermucks and Stroma also had three daughters, (i) Elizabeth m.
George Forbes of Corse, [they had (a) William Forbes d. young; (b)
Elizabeth Forbes; (c) Mary Forbes; (d) Henrietta Forbes (A and H
Tayler – *The House of Forbes*,317)]; (ii) Jean Kennedy, second dau; (iii)
Margaret Kennedy, youngest dau (SC14/50/2 f.199)]

6. Magnus Mowat of Freswick, of Balquholly (post-July 1661), heir to James
   Mowat of Balquholly (GD96/600), born c. 1631 (GD248/401), in Shetland
   1669 (*RPC* vii,49 (3rd series)), murdered Nov, buried in Norway (SRS – *Lyon
   Office Genealogies*), m. 1651, m.con 22 Jan 1651 (SC14/50/3 f.136) Jean Sinclair,
   dau of deceased Alexander Sinclair of Latheron (d.1647) and Jean Cunninghame, dau of John Cunninghame of Broomhill and Geise, Admiral Depute and
   Sheriff of Caithness and his second wife, Elizabeth Sinclair, dau of Sir John
   Sinclair of Greenland and Rattar (J Henderson – *Caithness Family Histories*,201)
   [Jean Cunninghame m. (ii) her cousin, William Sinclair of Rattar, as his second
   wife (J Henderson – *Caithness Family Histories*,47). He d. by Jan 1677 (CS22/61
   – 15 Jan 1677). By his first wife, Elizabeth, dau of John Sinclair of Ulbster, he
   had: (i) John Sinclair of Rattar, his heir (CS22/65 – 7 Feb 1678). By Jean
   Cunninghame, he had: (ii) James Sinclair of Freswick, said to have d. in France,
   having been taken prisoner, while on his way to Edinburgh to be married (*Scots
   Peerage*,ii,353); (iii) Robert Sinclair (RD4/162/1 – 3 June 1738); (iv) David
   Sinclair of Freswick, heir to (ii) (RD2/78 – 24 Aug 1694) and (iii) in 1696, m. (i)
   Barbara, dau of Sir William Sinclair of Mey and (ii) Sophia, dau of William
   Stewart of Burray; (v) Janet Sinclair m. John Sinclair of Ulbster; (vi) Anne
   Sinclair, m. (i) Robert Sinclair of Durran and (ii) John Campbell of Castlehill (J.
   Henderson – *Caithness Family Histories*,44].

   [Alexander Sinclair of Latheron's brothers were: William Sinclair of Mey and
   Sir John Sinclair of Geanies and Dunbeath, all sons of George Sinclair of Mey (J
   Henderson – *Caithness Family Histories*,83). Alexander Sinclair of Latheron and
   Jean Cunninghame had sons:(i) William (heir to Sir John Sinclair of Dunbeath)
   m. Elizabeth Sinclair, dau of deceased William Sinclair of Canisbay and Dame
   Elizabeth Leslie, m.con 25 and 28 July 1656 (RD2/109 – 16 Dec 1718); (ii)
   John; (iii) Alexander;(iv) George, and daus (v) Jean (see above) and (vi)
   Elizabeth m. Walter Bruce of Ham, m.con 1 May 1657 (RH9/7/491); (vii)
   Helen; (viii) Margaret (SRS – *Lyon Office Genealogies*)]
   They had:

(i) Patrick Mowat bap 30 Nov 1654 (SRS – *Parish Registers of Canisbay*) – died

(ii) William Mowat bap 18 Oct 1656 – heir (*ibid*)

(iii) Jean Mowat bap 10 Jan 1658 (*ibid*)

(iv) Elizabeth Mowat (GD248/398/5)

(v) Helen Mowat, m. 6 Jan 1691 Robert Molysone, merchant in Aberdeen (St Nich OPR)

They had:

    (a) Robert Molysone, merchant in Aberdeen (CS29;26 Nov 1739)

    (b) Jean Molysone, m. George Ramsay, excise officer, Lochaber, son of Hugh Ramsay in Crieff (GD248/398)

    (c) James Molysone bap 21 Nov 1708 (St Nich OPR)

7. William Mowat of Balquholly bap 18 Oct 1656 – d. Nov 1688 (CC1/6/9), m. 10 Nov 1685 (Edin OPR) Katherine Lauder, dau of Robert Lauder, town clerk depute of Dundee (d. by Jan 1676 (CS18/65 – 25 Jan 1676)) and Euphan Bathgate (RS35/5 f.334). [Robert Lauder's brother was William Lauder, writer in Edinburgh and Clerk of Session. (His only daughter, Margaret, m. Sir Alexander Seton of Pitmedden, 11 March 1669 (Margaret D Young (ed.) – *Parliaments of Scotland*,ii,628)). Euphan Bathgate liferentrix of Dudhope (CS181/3605 – Katherine Lauder v Mr John Mowat, advocate). She m.(ii) John Benjamin Jorrens, captain in Lord Lindsays's regiment at Dundee, 30 May 1694. (He a bigamist, m. first wife, Mary Dudyon 10 Sept 1684 at The Hague). Their marriage dissolved 1 June 1705 (CC8/5/1 f.639)]. Katherine Lauder heir to her mother – 23 June 1718 (*Services of Heirs*)

They had:

(i) a dau who died as an infant (GD248/408/2)

(ii) William Mowat bap 8 Jan 1687 (Dundee OPR),

8. William Mowat, son of above, bap 8 Jan 1687 – alive in September 1695 (*List of Pollable Persons* ii,348), d. post-March 1705 (RD3/125 – 29 Dec 1710)

9. George Mowat of Hamnavoe, brother of Magnus Mowat of Balquholly (6), served heir and retoured 1710 to grand-nephew, William Mowat (7 above) (SIG 1/113/42), m. Margaret Mowat dau of Mr James Mowat of Ollaberry by his first wife, Margaret Sinclair, m.con 10 Nov 1662 (GD248/398) George Mowat d. in Shetland by Oct 1710 (GD248/408). Margaret Mowat d. 1713 (D6/131/6/8).

They had:

(i) Patrick Mowat, heir

(ii) James Mowat of Stennes and of Hugoland (GD144/48/10), served heir

to brother, Hector, 2 July 1711, m. Elizabeth Mackenzie (*SN&Q*, first series,xii,94; GD144/135/7), dau of Commissary Mackenzie [he second son of Bishop Mackenzie of Orkney (Gardie House papers – Letter to Mr Murdoch Mackenzie, 1786), his sister, Jean McKenzie m. John Kennedy younger of Kermucks, 15 May 1678 (*SN&Q*, 3rd series, v 109)]
They had:

(a) George Mowat of Stennes, commander of a merchant ship, d. c.1774. Living in England in 1786 (Gardie House papers – Letter to Mr Murdoch Mackenzie, 1786)

Left two sons:

  (1) George Mowat, Lieut, later Captain RN (CS25;21 June 1788, no.2; *Register of Arms*, ii,187)

  (2) James Mowat, Bengal Engineers (*Register of Arms*, ii,187)

(b) William Mowat, commander of a ship *Charming Jane of London*, trading with America and the West Indies, m. Agnes Spense, daughter of deceased Thomas Spense of Dalvennan, writer in Edinburgh and Margaret Roehead [their m. con 3 Oct 1707; their other children: Sophia Spence m. John Marshall, tanner in London and Jean Spence (RD4/179/1 – 21 Mar 1753)], 19 Dec 1742 (SRS – *Edin Marr*, RD4/171/2 – 19 June 1745), m. con 23 Dec 1742 (RD4/179/1 – 24 Mar 1753). William Mowat in South Carolina in 1752 (RD3/212 f.473)

They had:

  (1) James Mowat, went to live with grandmother in Scotland after mother's death (*ibid*)

  (2) Alexander Mowat (*ibid*)

(c) Patrick Mowat commanded the *Dolphin*, one of the ships that went round the world along with Commodore Byron. Left 5 sons; eldest and third sons in Navy, second son a clerk in public offices, fourth son a Lieut in the Marines and youngest son a Lieut in the Corps of Engineers, HEIC, Bengal establishment (Gardie House Papers – Letter to Mr Murdoch McKenzie)

(iii) George Mowat, alive in 1696 (RS45/5 f.126), d. young

(iv) Hector Mowat of Hurdaback, Ollagairth and Averagairth (GD144/78/1), d. by 1711 (GD144/78/2) – no issue

(iv) Margaret Mowat d. by July 1705, seised in lands of Papa Little, sister Helen, her heir (Nicolson papers)

(v) Helen Mowat m. Mr James Dunbar of Weatherstay, seised in lands in parishes of Northmaven and Delting (Nicolson papers; GD144/48/10)

10. Patrick Mowat of Hamnavoe and of Balquholly, served heir to father, George Mowat of Hamnavoe in Balquholly lands in 1710 (SIG 1/113/42), d. July 1716 (GD248/401), m.(i) Marjorie Bruce, dau of Andrew Bruce of Muness (F Grant – *Zetland Family Histories*,190)

They had:

   (i)   Margaret m. c.1711, in Shetland, John Scott, merchant in Dundee. They both lost at sea on a passage to Leith. She seised in Papa Little 12 June 1711 (Nicolson papers – Letter – Margaret Mowat-Keith to Thomas Bolt,1803; Extract copy memorial Mr William Chalmers to Mr Walter Scott, W.S, Nov 1767)

   (ii)   Ursula Mowat (GD248/408), at Balquholly April 1720 (Nicolson papers – Letter by her to Arthur Nicolson, 16 April 1720), in Shetland by 1723

He m.(ii) his cousin, Barbara Cheyne, dau of George Cheyne of Esslemont and Barbara Mowat (Gardie House papers – Letter to Mr Murdoch McKenzie). Her brother, John Cheyne (GD144/135/17). [She m.(ii) James Erskine in Dorlaithers (CS29; 13 July 1725), brother of William Erskine of Pittodrie and John Erskine to whom William was served heir (RS3/122 f.27)]

They had:

   (iii)   Patrick Mowat (RS45/7 f.274), d. young

   (iv)   James Mowat, eldest son ? (RD4/131 – 10 Jan 1722),d. between Nov 1709 and Oct 1710

   (v)   John Mowat, second son and heir, born 1704 (CS226/6269)

   (vi)   Robert Mowat (RD4/131 – 10 Jan 1722), d. Edinburgh Mar 1722 (GD248/408)

   (vii)   Elizabeth bap 19 Mar 1714 (Turriff OPR) – died?

   (viii)   Katherine bap 11 June 1715 (*ibid*) – died ?

11. John Mowat of Balquholly, son of above, d. 1736 (CC1/6/8; CC1/6/1A (Testament); Nicolson papers – Letter – Margaret Mowat-Keith to Thomas Bolt,1803), resigned lands of Balquholly in 1727 (GD248/401), m. c.1723 Agnes Keith, heiress of James Keith younger of Keithfield and Agnes Gordon, dau of Gordon of Craig, m.con 23 and 27 Dec 1727 (DI 22/7 – 2 April 1747) [She m.(ii) James Glass in Keithfield (SC1/11/1 – Feb 1750)]. Keithfield sold to the Earl of Aberdeen who, in 1765, granted her an annuity of 700 merks (SC1/61/104 – 20 June 1770). She d. 11th July 1783 (F Grant – *Zetland Family Histories*,190)

They had:

   (i)   James Mowat (CC1/6/1A), b. 1727 – d. 1744 (Nicolson papers – Answers to Memorial,1803)

   (ii)   John Mowat (CC1/6/1A), b. 1729, heir to father, following brother James's death (Nicolson papers – Answers to memorial,1803)

(iii)   Barbara Mowat, (CC1/6/1A; GD33/29/3), d. by 1765, m. William
        Anderson, land surveyor to the Duke of Gordon. They had a son,
        Alexander (SC1/61/104 – 20 June 1770)

(iv)   Agnes or Anna Mowat, youngest dau, m. John Wilson, hecklemaker in
        Aberdeen, m.con 1762 (SC1/61/104 – 20 June 1770), living in Montrose
        in 1765 (SC1/61/104 – 20 June 1770)

(v)   William Mowat (CC1/6/1A)

(vi)   Alexander Mowat d. in Jamaica in 1762 (CC8/8/121/1 – 8th Feb 1768)

(vii)   Mary Mowat (CC1/6/1A), died.

(viii) Francis Mowat, b.c.1734/5 (*ibid*), apprenticed to James Chalmers,
        printer in Aberdeen – 14 June 1751 for 5 years (SC1/61/104 – 20 June
        1770)

Mowat-Keith

John Mowat, son and heir of John Mowat of Balquholly, changed his surname to
Mowat-Keith. He m. Margaret Chalmers, dau of William Chalmers, merchant and
provost of Aberdeen, 7 Sept 1761 (St Nich OPR). He d. 1788 (*SN&Q*, first
series.,xii,94).

They had:

(i)   John Mowat-Keith bap 18 Aug 1762 (St Nich OPR)

(ii)   George Mowat-Keith bap 29 Feb 1764 (*ibid*). Heir to brother, John
        Mowat-Keith above (CS238/N/2/23)

(iii)   Helen Mowat-Keith bap 11 July 1765 (St Nich OPR)

(iv)   Agnes Mowat-Keith bap 5 April 1767 (*ibid*)

(v)   Margaret Mowat-Keith bap 6 July 1768 (*ibid*)

(vi)   Veramina Mowat-Keith bap 22 Dec 1769 (CH2/699/11)

(vii)   Isabella Mowat-Keith bap 20 Sept 1771 (*ibid*)

(viii) Cecilia Mowat-Keith bap 1 July 1774 (*ibid*)

(ix)   Katherine Mowat-Keith bap 27 July 1777 (*ibid*)

[(vi) to (ix) born at Faichfield, near Peterhead]

Mowats in Cowie and of Ardo

Magnus Mowat in Cowie, in Glithno c.1559 ? (NSC – *Sh Crt Recs* i.188), d. c.1596/
7 (CC8/8/31), m. Isobel Hay (*RMS* iv,2191). She buried 2 Sept 1615 in Aberdeen
(St Nich OPR)

They had:

1. James Mowat of Ardo, d. 1636 (Tombstone in St Nicholas church), writer in
    Edinburgh, then advocate in Aberdeen (NSP – *Advoc of Abn*), burgess of

Aberdeen, 3 Sept 1596 (*Misc NSC*,i), chaplain of the chapel of Holyrood (GD1/12/35), solicitor for the ministers of the kirk (PS1/60 f.84), m.(i) Isobel Strang (RS25/2 f.120; CS7/123 – 16 June 1590), dau of Andrew Strang (tutor of Balcasky ?) (d. March 1567 (CC8/8/2)) and ? (the widow of Martin Balfour, burgess of Pittenweem). [Andrew Strang had (i) Alexander Strang of Pittenweem; (ii) Janet Strang m. Mr John Kene, WS (GD1/12/35). His brother was Mr Richard Strang, advocate, burgess of Edinburgh m. Janet Balfour (SRS – *Fac Advoc; Edin Burg Roll*)]. Isobel Strang d. by 1593. James Mowat m.(ii) by April 1594 (RD1/50 – 28 July 1595) Jonet Hay, m.con 1596 (GD225/35), dau of Mr George Hay, minister of Eddleston and then Rathven and Marion Henrysoune (RD1/97 f.201; RD1/63 – 14 Mar 1597). [Mr George Hay and Marion Henrysoune had: (i) Mr George Hay d. by 1586; (ii) Mr James Hay of Rannes m. Katherine Dunbar, dau of Dunbar of Grange and Katherine Reid (*TBFC* – 7 Feb 1889); (iii) William Hay (RD1/63 – 14 Mar 1597). Marion Henrysoune d. Oct 1577 (CC8/8/31)]. Jonet Hay d. 21 Aug 1599 (CC8/8/29) They had:

(i)   Bethia Mowat (RD1/97 f.201) m. 25 Oct 1614 (as his second wife) Mr David Wedderburn, master of the Grammar School in Aberdeen, author of Latin Grammar chosen as universal text book, son of William Wedderburn and Marjorie Annand bap 2 June 1580. [His first wife was Janet Johnston, m. April 1611, she buried 23 Oct 1613. They had a son bap 25 Mar 1612 (St Nich OPR)]. David Wedderburn d. 13 Feb 1646 (ibid) They had:

    (a) Bethia Wedderburn bap 31 Jan 1616 – buried 6 June 1616

    (b) William Wedderburn bap 25 Jan 1617

    (c) David Wedderburn bap 8 Dec 1618

    (d) Margaret Wedderburn bap 20 Dec 1619

    (e) Jean Wedderburn bap 16 Feb 1629

    (f) Bethia Wedderburn bap 12 June 1630

    (g) 'new born bairn' buried 7 Jan 1632 (all St Nich OPR)

    (ii) Jonet Mowat (RD1/97 f.201)

James Mowat of Ardo, m.(iii) Katherine Forbes, dau of James Forbes of Bridge (NSC – *Advoc of Abn*). She still alive 1639 (*RMS* ix,1799) They had:

(iii) Thomas Mowat bap 17 Oct 1602 (St Nich OPR) – (see 'A' below)

(iv) Alexander and Agnes Mowat (twins) bap 21 April 1605 (*ibid*). Agnes buried 16 April 1606 (*ibid*), Alexander, infant burgess of Aberdeen (*Misc NSC* i), d. by 1635 (*RSS/9* f.450)

(v)   Robert Mowat bap 24 Mar 1607, infant burgess of Aberdeen (*Misc NSC* i), d. by 1640 (*RSS/11* f.458)

(vi)   child unnamed bap 25 April 1609 – buried 7 Nov 1610 (St Nich OPR)

(vii)   Isobel Mowat bap 10 Jan 1614 (*ibid*)

(viii) Margaret Mowat bap 19 Jan 1614 (*ibid*), m.(i) 8 Oct 1632 Mr Andrew Strachan, Doctor of Divinity (*ibid*)

They had:

(a) Jonet Strachan bap 29 May 1635 – buried 17 Dec 1635 (*ibid*)

Margaret Mowat m.(ii) 19 Feb 1637 (St Nich OPR) Alexander Hay of Bilbo, second son of John Hay of Crimonmogate (RS5/10 – 27 May 1637)

(ix)   James Mowat bap 9 Feb 1616 (St Nich OPR), infant burgess of Aberdeen, 6 Oct 1620 (*Misc NSC*,i), mentioned in a bond in 1637 (*NSC – Sh Crt Recs*, ii, 445), (possibly learned tailoring from Alexander Blair, tailor in Aberdeen), merchant, tailor and banker in Paris, burgess of Aberdeen, 5 Aug 1652 (*Misc NSC*,ii), m. French wife who predeceased him. He d. post 1680.

They had:

(a) John Francis Mowat, only son, ran away from Douai in 1659 (M. V. Hay – *Blairs Papers*, p.244), burgess of Aberdeen 23 July 1667 (*Misc NSC*,ii)

(b) Gawdon (Gordon?) Mowat, a dau (GD345/505), married (CS181 Misc 10/3)

(c) Susane Mowat, youngest dau (*ibid*)

2. William Mowat, tacksman of half the Kirklands of Fetteresso (*RPC* v, 630), in Logie in 1602 (RD1/91 f.74), in Crackenhill (RD1/235 – 20 June 1617), buried 28 Oct 1633 in Aberdeen (St Nich OPR)

He had:

(i)   John Mowat in Powbair, then in Glithno, chamberlain to Francis, Earl of Erroll?, burgess of Aberdeen, 24 Aug 1630 (*Misc NSC*,i), m.(i) Isobel (Elspet) Hervy (RD1/278 – 9 Sept 1618), she dau of Mr James Hervy of Blanok and Elspet Stewart. [They also had James, William and Jean Hervy. Elspet Stewart m.(ii) Robert Burnett in Mongatehead (*ibid*)] Isobel Hervy d. 1 June 1650 (*Kincardineshire MIs*) He m.(ii) Elspet Burnett, relict of Andrew Strachan in Yetsyde (SC5/1/1). John Mowat d. 6 July 1655 (*Kincardineshire MIs*)

By his first wife, Isobel Hervy, he had:

(a) Bethia (Bessa) Mowat (RD1/592 – 22 Nov 1652), m. Leonard Leslie 'a good man and merchant in Aberdeen' [Probably son of Gilbert Leslie and Marjorie Merser (m. 22 Dec 1604), he bap 14 Nov 1607 (St Nich OPR), d. Aug 1647 (R Montreith – *Ane Theater of Mortality*,95)]

They had:

(1) Gilbert Leslie bap 5 May 1634

(2) Isobel Leslie bap 15 May 1636

(3) Marjorie Leslie bap 27 Feb 1639

(4) John Leslie bap 16 April 1640 – buried 16 Oct 1641

(5) John Leslie bap 17 July 1642 – buried 19 Sept 1642

(6) Bethia Leslie bap 26 Nov 1643 – buried 4 Oct 1645

(7) Elspet and Bethia Leslie bap 13 July 1645 (St Nich OPR)

(b) Sibilla Mowat, m. 1638 Alexander Mowat in Redcloak (see Mowats in Redcloak)

3. John Mowat in Powbair, student of grammar in 1583 (CS7/96 -11 June 1583, had gifts of chaplainries of Moray and Navity (PS 58/84 – 2 Nov 1587), d. by Sept 1621 (SRS – *Edin App*)

He had:

(i) John Mowat apprenticed to Alexander Hangitsyde, skinner in Edinburgh, 21 Sept 1621 (*ibid*)

(ii) Jonet Mowat, m.(i) . . . Mowat (d. by Jan 1624), son of John Mowat in Powbair (see Appendix 3) m.(ii) John Rait, merchant and burgess of Aberdeen 18 Jan 1624 (Fetteresso OPR), m.con 13 Jan 1624 (RD3/374 f.460), he d. 7 May 1647

They had:

(a) William Raitt b.1628

(b) John Rait b.1630

(c) Elspet Rait b.1632

(d) Margaret Rait b.1635 (St Nich OPR)

4. Isobel Mowat, d. 23 Aug 1597 (CC8/8/21), m.(i) Bartill Winton at Fetteresso, 20 Dec 1575 (St Nich OPR)

They had:

(i) Thomas Winton (CC8/8/21), burgess of Aberdeen (RD3/374 f.460), m. Katherine Alexander, dau of George Alexander and Katherine Stewart (she m.(ii) David Bryson, mason (RD1/231 – 13 Dec 1614))

(ii) Margaret Winton (*ibid*)

Isobel Mowat m.(ii) John Foullarton in Cowie, sheriff clerk of Kincardineshire.

They had:

(iii) Richard Foullarton (*ibid*)

(iv) John Foullarton (*ibid*)

A. Thomas Mowat of Ardo (son of James Mowat of Ardo above) bap 17 oct 1602 – d. 27 Dec 1648 (St Nich OPR, burials), heir to brother Alexander (RS5/9 f.450) and brother Robert (RS5/11 f.458) m.(i) Janet Ogilvy, dau of Thomas Ogilvy, citiner of Brechin, shortly after 11 Sept 1626 (RS1/20 f.55), m.con 17 and 23 Aug 1626 (RD1/438 – 27 Jan 1631) [Thomas Ogilvy had another dau, Katherine Ogilvy m. Thomas Hunter of Reswallie, son of Thomas Hunter of Reswallie, m.con 28 Aug 1624 (*ibid*)]. She d. between 1642 and 1646 (RS5/11 f.458; RS5/13 f.228).

m.(ii) Margaret Forbes, eldest dau of John Forbes of Craigton, future spouse 18 Nov 1646 (RS5/13 f.228). She d. 11 Sept 1662, buried at Turriff (A Jervise – *Epitaphs and Inscriptions*, 223 – although he erroneously describes her as first wife)

By Janet Ogilvy he had:

(a)   child – still-born, buried 23 July 1627 (St Nich OPR)

(b)   Margaret Mowat bap 20 Jan 1629 (*ibid*) – d. 7 Mar 1700 (Ardo Tomb, St Nich). She m.(i) Mr James Mowat of Logie (see Mowats in Redcloak) m.(ii) Mr Walter Copland in Ardneidly, 5 Oct 1666 (St Nich OPR), he of Maislie in 1668 (RD2/50 f.136), graduate of King's College 1662, possibly student of Divinity (CS26/41 -17 July 1672) grandson of Captain Alexander Copland and son of John Copland of Haughs ? He d. by May 1675 (RD3/50 f.136). She heir-portioner to her father, Thomas Mowat.

(c)   a child buried 17 July 1632 (St Nich OPR)

(d)   Thomas Mowat bap 24 Dec 1632 – d. June 1633 (*ibid*)

(e)   Isobel Mowat bap 11 Mar 1634 (St Nich OPR) – died

(f)   Janet Mowat bap 31 Mar 1635 (*ibid*) – died

(g)   Elizabeth (Elspet) Mowat, possibly b. at Auquorties – d. 19 April 1707 aged 70 (SRS – *Greyfriars Interments*), m.(i) William Douglas tailor, St Martins, London, m.(ii) John Maxwell, tailor in Edinburgh, 22 July 1680 (Edin OPR), m.con 16 July 1680 (RD2/54 f.385). He d. 1703 (RD3/112 f.338). She liferentrix of Chanrahill (CS26/53 – April 1679) and heir portioner to her father, Thomas Mowat with sister Margaret above.

(h)   Andrew Mowat bap 7 Aug 1642 – died, probably child buried 15 Nov 1643 (St Nich OPR)

Mowats in Redcloak

James Mowat in Redcloak, b. c.1532 – d. 3 Feb 1612 (CC20/4/5; *Kincardineshire MIs*), m. Agnes Auchinleck, sister of George Auchinleck of Balmanno. [George Auchinleck m.(i) Elizabeth Auchinleck, dau of William Auchinleck of Gallowhill, (he d. 7 Nov 1579 (CC8/8/9)) and m.(ii) Jean Erskine, dau of laird of Gogar (CC8/

8/29). He d. 1595 (*Ibid*). Other brothers: (ii) Archibald Auchinleck m. Jean Sleich (of Cumledge) (*RMS* iv, 2445, CC8/8/26); (iii) Adam Auchinleck (*RMS* iv, 2288); (iv) James Auchinleck (*ibid*); (v) John Auchinleck (*ibid*); and a sister, (vi) Elizabeth Auchinleck m. John Orchardtoune in Annamuick, he d. April 1590 (CC8/8/26). Their cousin, William Auchinleck of Shethin, m. Elizabeth Cheyne. George Auchinleck of Balmanno, his heir in 1574 (*RMS* iv, 2288). William Auchinleck's natural son, Robert, legitimised, 21 Sept 1574 (*RSS* vi)]. Agnes Auchinleck d. 1622 (RH15/37/95).

They had: (all sons named in RD1/217 f.432)

1. John Mowat, d. 1633 (C22/13 – 22 Nov 1633), servitor to George Auchinleck of Balmanno (RD1/52 f.101), in Tannachie (RD1/130 – 18 Mar 1607), in Pitrichie (CC3/3/4), finally in Auquorties (C22/13 – 22 Nov 1633), m. 1596, Agnes Gardyne, dau of Thomas Gardyne, minister of Tarves by his first wife, Isobel Chalmers, m.con 9 July 1596 (CS7/349 – 20 Jan 1621). [Thomas Gardyne was son of Robert Gardyne of Ballimore, (legitimised 19 Nov 1622). He m.(i) Isobel Chalmers. They also had Elizabeth Gardyne, m. George Merser in Old Aberdeen (CS7/468 – 6 Feb 1635). Thomas Gardyne m.(ii) Violet Layng, (dau of John Layng, burgess of Aberdeen and Elspet Thornetoune), m. 18 April 1620 (St Nich OPR), m.con 13 Mar 1620 (RD1/488 – 20 July 1635). He d. by 1633]. Agnes Gardyne d. Sept 1622 (CC3/3/4). They had:

   (i)   Mr James Mowat of Logie (See 'A' below)
   (ii)   George Mowat – Captain (RS7/6 – 26 Mar 1656)
   (iii)   Alexander Mowat in Redcloak (See 'B' below)
   (iv)   William Mowat (CC3/3/4)
   (v)   Roger Mowat, writer in Edinburgh, b. c.1620 (NP2/6) (See 'C' below)
   (vi)   Elspet Mowat (CC3/3/4)
   (vii)   Isobel Mowat (*ibid*)
   (viii) Agnes Mowat (*ibid*)

2. Alexander Mowat, writer in Edinburgh, ('Saunders' Mowat), servitor to George Auchinleck of Balmanno (RD1/29 -25 May 1594), servitor to Mr John Hay in 1595 (RD1/51 – 10 July 1595), by 1601 servitor to Mr Alexander Gibson, Clerk of Session (CS7/196 – 31 July 1601), burgess of Aberdeen, 22 Sept 1609 (*Misc NSC*,i). Had an illegitimate child by Katharin Sympsoune baptised 4 Nov 1599 (Edin OPR), m.(i) 11 April 1604 (Edin OPR), Katherine Nisbet, dau of George Nisbet, merchant burgess in Edinburgh (SRS – *Edin Burg Roll*) and relict of George French, merchant burgess in Edinburgh (RD1/168 – 25 Nov 1609). She d. by 1612. He m.(ii) Margaret Barclay, dau of John

Barclay, indweller in Edinburgh, d. 22 Oct 1616, m.con 14 Nov 1612 (RD1/
258 – 1 Mar 1616) [His brother was Adam Barclay of Mathers. John Barclay m.
(ii) Agnes Harlaw, m.con 11 Nov 1606. He had a natural dau Isobel Barclay, m.
John Home, tailor and burgess of Edinburgh (RD1/259 f.133; CC8/8/49 – 21
Dec 1616; CC8/8/52 – 30 May 1623)].
They had:
(i)   Agnes Mowat bap 9 Nov 1613 (Edin OPR)
(ii)   John Mowat bap 13 Sept 1616 (*ibid*) – possibly servitor to Quentin
        Kennedy, W.S. (RD1/515 – 26 Sept 1638)

3. George Mowat in Redcloak, d. July 1645 (RH15/37/95), great bailie of
    baron court of Ury, elder of the kirk in Fetteresso, m.(i) or (ii) Isobel
    Orchardtoune, 23 Mar 1623 (Fetteresso OPR). [She m.(ii) Alexander Stra-
    chan of Fallside in parish of Kinneff, m.con 27 Nov 1646 (RH15/37/94) and
    m.(iii) Alexander Barclay in Bridgeton, afterwards in Ardbirnie. He d. by 1675
    (RH15/37/152)]

4. Mr Roger Mowat, advocate in Edinburgh, prior to that servitor to Mr John
    Nicolson of Lasswade, one of the Commissaries of Edinburgh (CS7/231 – 19
    Dec 1607), burgess of Aberdeen, 11 Sept 1606 (*Misc NSC*,i), of Balquholly, m.
    12 Feb 1618 Margaret Marjoribanks, dau of Joseph Marjoribanks, merchant and
    bailie in Edinburgh (SRS – *Edin Marr*) [Her brothers were (i) Joseph Marjor-
    ibanks of Leuchie who had – Joseph, John, Andrew, Edward, George, James,
    Jonet (m. Charles Charteris, merchant burgess of Edinburgh) and Marion; (ii)
    John Marjoribanks (Misc papers, Bundle 45, no.1963 (Edinburgh City Ar-
    chives)), (iii) Mr Andrew Marjoribanks, advocate (SRS – *Fac Advoc*). His son,
    Mr Andrew Marjoribanks, merchant in Preston, m. Magdalen Kinloch, dau of
    Francis Kinloch, factor in Paris, then of Gilmerton and Margaret Adington,
    m.con 26 Dec 1673 (RD2/46 f.265)]. Mr Roger Mowat d. at beginning of
    1653.
    They had:
    (i)   Alexander Mowat bap 17 Nov 1618 (Edin OPR) – died?
    (ii)   Margaret Mowat bap 19 Mar 1620 (*ibid*), m. 4 Mar 1647 David Boswell of
            Balmuto (SRS – *Edin Marr*)
    (iii)   Isobel Mowat bap 9 Oct 1621 (Edin OPR), m. John Cockburn,
            advocate, son of Sir William Cockburn of Langton and Dame Helen
            Elphinstone (SRS – *Fac Advoc*; RD1/592 – 24 Nov 1652). She buried 21
            July 1663 (SRS – *Greyfriars Interments*)
    (iv)   George Mowat of Inglishton (See 'D' below)
    (v)   Joseph Mowat of Fallside (See 'E' below)

(vi) Janet Mowat, m.(i) David Wood tutor of Bonnyton, m.con 4 Feb 1648 (RD3/29 f.131). He d. May 1668 (CC20/4/13 – 31 Oct 1674). No issue. His heir, his nephew, Sir John Wood of Bonnyton (CS22/40 – 11 Jan 1672). She m.(ii) 2 April 1669, Captain Bryce Blair of Bogside (SRS – *Edin Marr*; RD3/29 f.131). She d. 28 April 1672 (SRS – *Greyfriars Interments*)

5. Mr Hugh Mowat, graduate of King's College in 1606 (SPC-*Fasti Aberdonenses*, 503), writer in Edinburgh (RD1/27 -21 Jan 1607), may have been solicitor martial and solicitor martial general in Denmark (T Riis -'*Should Auld Acquaintance Be Forgot*', ii,119,136).

6. Elspet Mowat, d. Nov 1614 (RD1/227 – 9 Nov 1614), first wife of Andrew Milne, younger, minister of Fetteresso, m.con 14 Jan 1611 (RD1/217 f.432). They had:
    (i) Isobel Milne, m. Robert Leslie, son of James Leslie burgess of Aberdeen, m.con 21 Mar 1629 (SC1/7/9 – 13 July 1651). He buried 13 Sept 1644 (St Nich OPR).
    They had:
    (a) Andrew Leslie bap 23 July 1630
    (b) John Leslie bap 25 June 1637
    (c) Isobel Leslie bap 3 Jan 1639
    (d) Elspet Leslie bap 26 May 1642 – buried 15 Aug 1642
    (e) Janet Leslie bap 18 Feb 1643
    (f) Anna Leslie bap 8 Oct 1644 (all St Nich OPR)
    [Only Isobel and Anna survived (SC1/7/9 – 13 July 1651)]
    (ii) Anna Milne. (*ibid*)
    [Andrew Milne, m.(ii) Katherine Erskine (A Jervise – *Epitaphs and Inscriptions*,77). He d. 12 Oct 1640, aged 58. They had: William and James (twins ?), baptised 12 Feb 1626 (Fetteresso OPR)].

7. Isobel Mowat, m. David Grahame in Arduthie and in Milne of Glenbervie, bailie of baron court of Ury in 1607. Had property in Montrose (RD1/515 – 26 Sept 1638). He d. Feb 1618 (CC20/4/7).
    They had:
    (i) Robert Grahame, eldest son (CC20/4/7), Major in Königsberg (RD1/515 – 26 Sept 1638)
    (ii) Christian Grahame (RD1/314 – 13 Nov 1621)
    (iii) Richard Grahame in Overcraigie, m. Helen Keith (RD1/316 – 14 Feb 1622). She d. 21 Dec 1624 (CC20/4/8)

(iv)   David Grahame (RD1/316 – 14 Feb 1622)

(v)   Alexander Grahame (RD1/322 – 1 July 1622)

Sons of John Mowat in Tannachie
(eldest son of James Mowat in Redcloak above)

A. Mr James Mowat of Logie, d. 5 Mar 1662 (GD248/401),interred in Ardo tomb, St Nicholas church, graduate of King's College 1619 (SPC-*Fasti Aberdonenses*, 506), governor to young gentlemen going abroad, wadsetter of Logie (RS7/6 – 3 May 1657), heir to father 22 Nov 1633 (C22/13) and heir to maternal grandfather, Thomas Gardyne, in part of lands of Milne of Tillihelt (RS5/10 f.349), m. Margaret Mowat, dau of Thomas Mowat of Ardo and Janet Ogilvy (see Mowats in Cowie and of Ardo)

They had:

(a)   Mr John Mowat bap 8 Nov 1661 (St Nich OPR), advocate in Edinburgh – of Balquholly -(See 'F' below)

(b)   Margaret Mowat bap 15 Jan 1663 (*ibid*), m. 19 Dec 1682 Alexander Orem, merchant and bailie in Aberdeen (*ibid*). He d. March 1712 CS229/ F/1/22)

       They had:

       (1) John Orem bap 7 Feb 1686 (St Nich OPR)

       (2) James Orem bap 25 Nov 1688 (*ibid*)

       (3) Alexander Orem bap 5 Jan 1690 (*ibid*)

       (4) Margaret Orem bap 11 Oct 1692 (*ibid*) – died (CS229/F1/22)

       (5) Barbara Orem bap 11 Oct 1696 (St Nich OPR) – died (CS229/F1/ 22)

B. Alexander Mowat in Redcloak, d. Dec 1685 (CC20/4/15), initially in Powbair, then in Redcloak (SC1/60/19), wadsetter of Mergie (CS150/111), tutor to his brother, Mr James Mowat above's children, m. Sibilla Mowat, dau of John Mowat in Glithno and Isobel (Elspet) Hervy (see Mowats in Cowie), m.con 1638 (SC5/1/3). She d. by 1670 (CS150/111 – Mowat v Mowat)

They had:

(a)   George Mowat bap 1641 (Fetteresso OPR) – died?

(b)   Margaret Mowat (CC20/4/15) – d. unmarried

(c)   Elizabeth Mowat, m.(i) James Mowat, brother of Magnus Mowat of Balquholly, he d. Dec 1693, according to testament dative, recorded 22 May 1693 (CC20/4/15), probably d.in 1686 or 1687.

       They had:

       (1) James Mowat – went to Maryland (CS29;23 Nov 1742)

(2) Christian Mowat, in Stonehaven in 1702 (SC5/8/17), m. William Mowat, maltman in Aberdeen, admitted burgess 2 Sept 1722, Treasurer of the burgh in 1724 (RD4/137/1 – 29 Jan 1725), a native of Banchory Devenick? (his brother, James Mowat, lived in Ruthrieston (SC1/61/67 – 14 Jan 1726)). Involved in 1715 Rising (A Munro – *Memorials of aldermen, provosts and Lord provosts of Aberdeen*). In 1747, acquired North Colnay and other property from Alexander Mitchell (RD4/186/2 – 2 Nov 1759).

They had:

(I) Elizabeth Mowat bap 4 Mar 1705 (St Nich OPR)

(II) John Mowat bap 8 July 1706 (*ibid*)

(III) Margaret Mowat bap 23 Dec 1708 (*ibid*)

(IV) William Mowat bap 10 April 1712 (*ibid*). Of Colpnay, Provost of Aberdeen 1754–55 (A Munro – *Memorials of aldermen, provosts and Lord provosts of Aberdeen*), m. Jane Osborn, she d. 17 Mar 1786 (*Aberdeen Journal*, Notes and Queries, ii). He d. at Newbridge, a few months later (*John O'Groats' Journal*, 11 June 1948)

(3) Jean Mowat, m. John Anderson merchant in Stonehaven (SC5/58/7).

They had:

(I) Helen Anderson (*ibid*)

(II) Christian Anderson, m. James Jollie, mariner in Stonehaven (*ibid*)

Elizabeth Mowat m.(ii) Andrew Strachan, sheriff clerk of Kincardineshire, before 18 Oct 1688 (RD4/125 – 20 June 1719), she his second wife, she d. by Jan 1701 (SC5/8/17 – 9 Jan 1701). He died July 1697 (CC20/4/16). [By his first wife, Margaret Stewart, he had (i) Margaret Strachan m. David MacDougall, writer in Leith; (ii) Elizabeth Strachan m. William Shepherd in Arduthie; (iii) Anna Strachan; (iv) Magdalen Strachan m. William Duthie in Drumlithie (SC5/58/7); (v) George Strachan (SC5/58/8)]

They had:

(4) Andrew Strachan (SC5/58/7), apprenticed to William Mowat, merchant in Aberdeen (see Christian Mowat above) for 5 years from Whit 1704, recorded 2 Mar 1711 (F J McDonnell – *Aberdeen Apprentices, Burgh of Aberdeen* 1700 – 1750)

(5) Helen Strachan (*ibid*)

(6) Mary Strachan (*ibid*)

(d) Marie (Marjorie) Mowat, d. by 1675 (CC20/4/16; DI 66/2), m. Andrew Moncur in Barnhill at Bervie 3 Nov 1672 (IGI), m.con 31 Oct 1672 (SC5/58/1).

They had:

(1) Robert Moncur (*ibid*)

(2) Elizabeth Moncur (DI 66/2)

C. Roger Mowat, writer in Edinburgh, Commissary Depute of Shetland, May 1666 to 1668 (CS15/410), burgess of Edinburgh, 22 Mar 1659 (SRS – *Edin Burg Roll*), buried 16 Nov 1686 (SRS – *Greyfriars Interments*), m. 6 Aug 1667 Marie Logan, dau of Mr Robert Logan of Mountlothian and Marion Logan (SRS – *Canongate Marr*). [They also had Alexander Logan who went abroad and Jean Logan m. Sir Ludovick Stewart of Minto (CS26/61 – 16 July 1681). Jean Logan died April 1687 (SRS – *Greyfriars Interments*)]. Marie Logan buried 24 June 1689 (*ibid*).

They had:

(a) Roger Mowat born pre-Oct 1668 – interred Greyfriars 14/15 Feb 1677 (CS229/M 1/3)

(b) child, interred 16 Aug 1669

(c) Bethia Mowat bap 21 Jan 1670, m. Alexander Campbell of Barvoline (GD34/714; RS3/114 f.408)

(d) John Mowat bap 21 Sept 1672, interred 14 Mar 1673

(e) Roger Mowat bap 29 Mar 1678 – a haflin, interred 27 Jan 1687

(f) Elizabeth Mowat bap 21 Nov 1680 – d. by 24 June 1689

(All above Edin OPR; SRS – *Greyfriars Interments*)

Sons of Mr Roger Mowat, advocate, (son of James Mowat of Redcloak above)

D. Sir George Mowat of Inglishton, buried 4 Mar 1666 (SRS – *Greyfriars Interments*), created a baronet of Nova Scotia, burgess of Edinburgh 11 July 1656 (SRS – *Edin Burg Roll*), m. Elizabeth Hope, dau of Sir John Hope of Craighall (d. 28 April 1654) and Margaret Murray, dau of Sir Archibald Murray of Blackbarony, 1st Bart and Margaret Maull (G. E. Cockayne – *Complete Baronage*, iii, 345(a)).[Elizabeth Hope – sister of Sir Thomas Hope of Craighall (d. 10 July 1659) and of Sir Archibald Hope of Rankeillor, Senator of College of Justice (d. 11 Oct 1706 aged 67) (OPR – Greyfriars Interments), and of Bethia Hope m. Sir John Harper of Cambusnethan (G. Brunton and D. Haig – *Senators of College of Justice*, 444)]. Elizabeth Hope d. by May 1686 (RD3/74 f.24).

They had:

(a) Thomas Mowat bap 16 June 1657 (Ceres OPR) – died

(b) Sir Roger Mowat of Inglishton, student at Leyden in 1676 (RD3/41 f.120), recorded arms as Baronet of Nova Scotia (*Register of Arms*, i,187), d. by 1683

(c) Sir William Mowat of Inglishton, heir to Sir Roger above (*Retours*,37,128), apprenticed to Charles Charteris, merchant in Edinburgh, 15 May 1678 (SRS – *Edin App Roll*), m. Antonia Willobie (RD4/107 – 1 Sept 1710). Moved to London, d. by 1690.

They had:

(1) Sir Winwood Mowat, only lawful son (DI 15/7A – 17 Sept 1708)

(d) John Mowat, student at Leyden 1685 (RD3/74 f.18)

(e) Mary Mowat, m. Captain George Hamilton (RD3/74 f.24; CS226/6017)

(f) Elizabeth Mowat, m. Robert Monteith of Randiefurd 30 April 1680 (SRS – *Lyon Office Genealogies*; *Edinburgh Marriages*). He d. 4 May 1703, his executor dative his son, Charles Monteith (CC8/8/84 – 12 Aug 1710)

E. Joseph Mowat of Fallside, in Berwickshire, d. by 1668 (CC15/5/6), burgess of Aberdeen 6 May 1646 (*Misc NSC*,ii), m.(i) Helen Hamilton, 26 Aug 1655 (Gordon OPR), dau of Sir Patrick Hamilton of Littlepreston (Prestonhall) and Elizabeth McGill, (dau of Sir James McGill of Cranston Riddell) (GD135/1519), m.con 20 Aug 1655 (GD135/2137). Her tocher of 5,000 merks had been paid by 14 Dec 1657 (Discharge – GD135/2137). She possibly d. by 19 March 1658, not named in father's will (CC8/8/71), m.(ii) Jonet Lyll, dau of William Lyll of Bassendean, m.con 1663 (Askew of Ladykirk muniments – NRAS – 007/1). She m.(ii) James Horn in Flos, parish of Westerkirk, 11 Feb 1679 (CH2/457/8) [Her sister, Margaret Lyll, married Mr Daniel Robertson, sometime minister of Hutton, servitor to the Earl of Annandale, merchant and guild brother of Edinburgh (*Fasti* ii,206). He of Fallside in 1710 (RS3/99 f.207). They had (i) William Robertson of Hillhousefield; (ii) Sophia Robertson m. John Philip, indweller in Edinburgh (*Fasti* i,206)]

They had:

(a) David Mowat bap 7 Sept 1665 (Gordon OPR) – died

(b) Elizabeth Mowat bap 4 Feb 1667, m.(i) John Kerr, merchant and burgess of Edinburgh, no issue; m.(ii) 10 July 1692 (Gordon OPR), Mr John Hay of Easthopes, secretary of the Earl of Tweeddale, High Chancellor of Scotland (RD4/72 f.127; RD2/76 f.177)

(c) William Mowat bap 5 July 1668 (*ibid*), heir to his father, Ensign in Col. Douglas's Reg.(RD2/78 f.1146), Captain of Grenadiers in regiment of Foot Guards (CC8/13/4 – 9 May 1705) d. unmarried in May 1705 (CC15/5/7).

THIS LINE DIED OUT

Son of Mr James Mowat of Logie above.

F. Mr John Mowat, advocate in Edinburgh, bap 8 Nov 1661 (St Nich OPR), d.
May 1709 in Aberdeen (CC8/8/24), of Balquholly, as creditor after death of
young William Mowat (CS29; 21 June 1705), m. Helen Mitchell 3 Oct 1689
(Edin OPR), m.con 28 Sept 1689 (CS29; Box 450), she bap 6 Mar 1670, dau of
Andrew Mitchell, provost of Aberdeen and Elizabeth Hunter (St Nich OPR).
They had:

(1)   James Mowat, apprenticed to Thomas Boyes, W.S, 24 July 1711 (Mcleod
       index, vol 15, p.116), 'furth of Scotland' 16 Sept 1715 (CS29; Box 450)

(2)   Elizabeth Mowat bap 6 May 1693 (Edin OPR), reached her majority by
       Mar 1714 (RD4/114 f.649). In London in 1726 (RD4/140/3 – 12 Nov
       1726)

(3)   child interred Greyfriars 23 Mar 1696

(4)   Margaret Mowat bap 29 July 1698

[Elizabeth and Margaret served heir to their father – 6 Jan 1726 (*Service of Heirs*).
On 27th July 1726 they granted a bond for 50,000 merks to Alexander Duff of
Hatton (RD4/140/2 – 12 Nov 1726)]

The Mowats of Balquholly

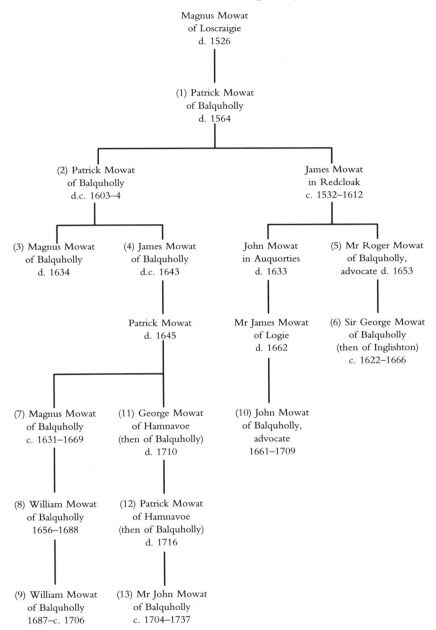

Magnus Mowat
of Loscraigie
d. 1526

(1) Patrick Mowat
of Balquholly
d. 1564

(2) Patrick Mowat
of Balquholly
d.c. 1603–4

James Mowat
in Redcloak
c. 1532–1612

(3) Magnus Mowat
of Balquholly
d. 1634

(4) James Mowat
of Balquholly
d.c. 1643

John Mowat
in Auquorties
d. 1633

(5) Mr Roger Mowat
of Balquholly,
advocate d. 1653

Patrick Mowat
d. 1645

Mr James Mowat
of Logie
d. 1662

(6) Sir George Mowat
of Balquholly
(then of Inglishton)
c. 1622–1666

(7) Magnus Mowat
of Balquholly
c. 1631–1669

(11) George Mowat
of Hamnavoe
(then of Balquholly)
d. 1710

(10) John Mowat
of Balquholly,
advocate
1661–1709

(8) William Mowat
of Balquholly
1656–1688

(12) Patrick Mowat
of Hamnavoe
(then of Balquholly)
d. 1716

(9) William Mowat
of Balquholly
1687–c. 1706

(13) Mr John Mowat
of Balquholly
c. 1704–1737

James Mowat of Fallside, W.S.
Sheriff clerk of Berwickshire[1]

A close associate of Mr Roger Mowat, advocate and his brother, Alexander Mowat, writer, was James Mowat, Writer to the Signet. He was no relation, being a native of the burgh of Lanark. He was the son of William Mowat, town clerk and burgess of Lanark and grandson of John Mowat who had also been town clerk of the burgh.[2] He had three brothers, Hugh who married Agnes Kennedy, Thomas, a merchant, whose wife was Agnes Mumphrey and Robert.[3]

He appears to have started his training as a writer in Edinburgh at the same time as Mr Roger Mowat began to train as an advocate. In 1613 he is recorded as Sheriff Depute of Nairn.[4] By 1621 he had become a Writer to the Signet. Much of his time was taken up with the legal affairs of Sir John Campbell of Cawdor who appears to have been his main client. He was required to go up north to Sir John's estate near Inverness to collect his rents and recover debts. He also journeyed down to England on several occasions on business for him. In 1621, in a letter to Sir John, he recorded that he had 'spoken with his Majesty at Woodstock' and had also attended the King at Windsor.[5] While he was away, Mr Roger Mowat acted as his factor in Edinburgh.[6]

He, like Mr Roger Mowat and his brother, Alexander Mowat, lent out money to various people, among whom were several burgesses of Edinburgh. Thomas, Bishop of the Isles, borrowed large sums from him in the 1620s. In 1608 he was granted the Gift of the 'Ladies' chapel of the Chapeltown of Meigle by the Earl of Crawford. He then sold it to Alexander Mowat, writer.[7] Four years later he was granted the gift of the escheat of Duncan Campbell of Glenlyon.[8]

In his native burgh of Lanark he owned an acre of land in the Chapellands and property in the Grusgrene.[9] From Sir John Campbell of Cawdor he acquired the wadset of Urchany and Little Budgate, part of the Cawdor lands in Nairn.[10] By 1623 his healthy financial state enabled him to purchase the lands of Fallside in the parish of Gordon in Berwickshire from Mr Alexander Seaton of Gargunnock and his wife, Margaret Levingstone.[11] He subsequently sold the property to Mr Roger Mowat who, in turn, assigned it to his second son, Joseph Mowat, shortly before he died.

James Mowat married three times. His first wife was Margaret Rollock, daughter of Mr Hercules Rollock, advocate, and Elizabeth Rollock.[12] They were married on 2nd June 1611.[13] She died on 2nd June 1621.[14] Their only daughter, Jonet, was baptised in Edinburgh on 20th June 1613.[15]

His second wife was English and he must have met her on one of his visits down south. She was Dame Anna Saltounstall, sister of Sir Richard Saltounstall of Huntweik, owner of property in Yorkshire. She had another brother, John Saltounstall, who journeyed north to visit her, shortly after their marriage.[16] The marriage was very brief, for she was soon dead, possibly dying in childbirth.

His third wife was Jean Chirnside, daughter of Sir Patrick Chirnside of East Nisbet and Dame Anna Home.[17] They were married in 1624, but appear to have had no children. James Mowat died in July 1657.[18] In July 1640 his only daughter, Jonet, had eloped with George Home, son of the deceased John Home in Kelso. George Home appears to have been chamberlain at Fallside, and after their marriage James Mowat ordered them to leave his property. Thereafter he appears to have disinherited his daughter.[19] After his death his 'only heir of line' was named as Alison Mowat who must either have been a niece or grand-niece.[20]

SOURCES

1. *RPC* iii, 475 (first series).
2. CS7/311 – 5 Dec 1616
3. B 45/4 f.1; RD1/216 f.351
4. RD1/204 f.294
5. *The Book of the thanes of Cawdor* (SPC), 247.
6. RD1/383 – 3 June 1626
7. RD1/256 – 19 Dec 1616
8. CS7/271 – 24 Jan 1612
9. RD1/287 – 11 Aug 1615
10. RS1/11 f.214
11. RS18/2 f.93
12. RD1/203 f.200
13. *Canongate Marriages* (SRS).
14. Edinburgh Commissary Testaments, CC8/8/31 – Testament of Margaret Rollok – 21 May 1622
15. Edinburgh OPR
16. RS1/11 f.214
17. RD1/336 – 4 April 1623
18. *The Register of the Society of Writers to Her Majesty's Signet* (Society of Writers to the Signet)
19. RD11/288 – 12 June 1650)
20. CS18/64 – 27 July 1675 – Mowat v Mowat

The family of John Mowat in Nether Elsick

In the early part of the seventeenth century, Nether Elsick, in the northern part of the parish of Fetteresso, belonged to Alexander Bannerman of Elsick. Tenant there in the early years of that century was John Mowat who died on 18 October 1614 (CC20/4/5 – 21 Dec 1615). He m. Agnes Reid who survived him.
They had:

1. Edward Mowat who moved to Aberdeen, m. Marjorie Menzies. They had:
   - (i) Alexander Mowat bap 31 Jan 1609
   - (ii) Thomas Mowat bap 16 April 1613
   - (iii) Magnus Mowat bap 27 April 1615
   - (iv) Paul Mowat bap 30 Aug 1618
   - (v) a daughter bap 4 Dec 1621 (St Nich OPR)
2. Magnus Mowat in Overcairnhill in 1614 (CC20/4/5), in Nether Elsick by 1616 (CC20/4/6), witness to m.con of John Mowat and Isobel Hervy (see Mowats in Cowie).

   He had:

   sons, one named John (CC20/4/5))
3. John Mowat in Powbair, possibly depute bailie of baron court of Ury.
   He had:
   - (i) Beatrix (*ibid*)
   - (ii) son, d. by Jan 1624, m. Jonet Mowat, dau of John Mowat in Powbair, son of Magnus Mowat in Cowie (see Mowats in Cowie)
4. Gilbert (George) Mowat in Nethertown of Elsick, d. 18 April 1615 (CC20/4/6 – 4 June 1616).
   He had:
   - (i) Elspet Mowat (*ibid*)
5. Isobel Mowat m. Thomas Rany in Miln of Elsick.
   They had:

   Five children, one, a daughter named Catherine (CC20/4/5; CC20/4/6))

John Mowat in Nether Elsick also had an illegitimate son, James Mowat, legitimised 14 Jan 1617, living in Fishertown of Muchalls pre 1617, thereafter in Cantlahills (*RMS* vii, 1509).

Descendants of this family are most likely those found at Rothnick, Sauchenshaw, Monquich and other farms in the vicinity of the Elsick lands.

Mowats of Hugoland, Garth and Ollaberry

(★ refers to documents listed in *Shetland Documents*, 1584–1811 – (ed.) John H Ballantyne and Brian Smith)

Andrew Mowat of Hugoland, d. by 1611 (★no.541) m.(i) Ursula Tulloch (possibly dau of William Tulloch of Skea and Barbara Thomasdochter).
They had:

1. John Mowat of Ollaberry (★no.281), then of Hugoland (*RMS* iv,2672) m. Christian Stewart, natural dau of Robert, Earl of Orkney (CS7/342 f.251; F Grant – *Zetland Family Histories*,195). He d. August 1617 (*RPC* xiv,717 (first series)). His widow continued to reside at Ollaberry, having the liferent (*ibid*). They had:

   (i) Andrew Mowat of Hugoland and Skea b. c.1596 (*ibid*), m. Grizel Pitcairne, dau of Mr James Pitcairne, minister of Northmaven and Ursula Sinclair, m.con 1611 (RD1/240 – 16 Nov 1616). He appears to have only had the liferent of the lands of Hugoland, the property belonging to the Mowats of Ollaberry (GD144/48/9 – 2 May 1664)

   (ii) John Mowat (*RPC* xiv,717 (first series))
   [and several other children]

2. Malcolm Mowat, d. by 1597 (★no.281))

3. Patrick Mowat, d. by 1597 (*ibid*)

4. Mr Gilbert Mowat of Garth, b. post Mar 1576 (*ibid*), graduate of Edinburgh University, 30 July 1601, minister of Delting in 1607, thereafter in Northmaven. He m.(i) Janet Pitcairne, dau of Mr James Pitcairne and (ii) Margaret Forbes (F Grant – *Zetland Family Histories*,195). He was buried in St Magnus kirk, Northmaven (GD144/113/22).
   He had:

   (i) Mr James Mowat of Ollaberry, m.(i) Margaret Sinclair, dau of James Sinclair of Quendale (F Grant – *Zetland Family Histories*,196). She d. March 1645 (CC17/2/5 – 14 Aug 1648).
   They had:
   (a) Mr Gilbert Mowat – died. (*ibid*)
   (b) James Mowat, heir (*ibid*), d. in Copenhagen by 1672 (*Retours, Orkney and Shetland*,106)

(c) Barbara Mowat (CC17/2/5) m. George Cheyne of Esslemont
(Nicolson papers – Memorial for Arthur Nicolson of Lochend, 1803)
[Their eldest son, John Cheyne (CS21 – 6 Dec 1679); their dau, Barbara
Cheyne m. Patrick Mowat of Hamnavoe, then Balquholly (see Mowats
of Balquholly)]

(d) Margaret Mowat (CC17/2/5 m. George Mowat of Hamnavoe (see
Mowats of Balquholly)

(e) Jonet Mowat – died (*ibid*)

Mr James Mowat of Ollaberry m.(ii) Margaret Sinclair, dau of George
Sinclair of Rapness, relict of Edward Sinclair of Gyre in Orkney (CS15/
341 – Thomas Stevenson v Mowat) [She had a son, George Sinclair of
Gyre, by her first marriage (RD3/39 f.426) and a dau, Barbara Sinclair m.
Walter Reid, advocate in Aberdeen (CS22/66 – 7 Nov 1677). She was
buried 9 Nov 1699 (SRS – *Greyfriars Interments*). They had: Margaret
Reid (CC8/8/81 – Testament of Barbara Sinclair)] Mr James Mowat of
Ollaberry d. between Sept and Dec 1666 (CS22/41 – 14 June 1673;
RD2/19 f.500)

(ii)   Thomas Mowat of Garth, of Hamnavoe in 1648 (CC17/2/5). His lands
        apprised by John Ross, merchant in Unst, 5 Aug 1664 (*RMS* xi,657)
[and several other children]

5. James Mowat of Ure, b. post-Mar 1576 (*ibid*). [He m. Agnes Pitcairn, dau of Mr
    James Pitcairne, minister of Northmaven (*no.474). They had a son, Mr
    Gilbert Mowat, client of James Mowat in Paris (RD1/528 f.508), m. Margaret
    Forbes (CC8/8/86 – 15 Nov 1714). He was secretary to the Earl of Middleton
    (*ibid*) and later governor to George, Marquis of Huntly from Whit 1662 to
    Whit 1663 (CS22/46 – 2 July 1674)]

6. Barrell/Berald Mowat of Collafirth (*no.328)

Andrew Mowat of Hugoland m.(ii) Elspet or Elsie Trunsdochter of Erisfiordt, 'an
honourable and highborn lady' from Norway, by June 1597 (*no.256).
They had:

7. Axel Mowat (*ibid*), in Heifland in Norway (CS7/344 – 8 Dec 1620), Norwe-
    gian admiral

8. Christopher Mowat (RD1/212 – 26 July 1616).

The Ollaberry estate consisted of lands in the parishes of Northmaven, Delting and
Aithsting and the whole island of Papa Stour and Papa Little. There were also small
parcels on the islands of Yell, Fetlar and Unst. (Detailed in RD4/11 f.214 and RS3/
1 f.114.)

Inventory of the contents of the house of Balquholly (presented at Edinburgh, 1st December 1699)

Three feather bedds with on[e] bolster and two coddes

Four old litle feather bedds and two bolsters and seven codds

Two pair of old shewed blankets and two pair with ribbons ten elns being in everie pair

Seven pair of old bed plaids moth eaten

Two coverings for beds on[e] shewed and ane oyther plaine green say

Four pair of Holland sheets two pair quherof verrie old being ten elns in everie pair

On[e] pair of old linnin sheets and ane oyther pair torne

Two pair of rainder linning sheets

Sex codwars

Two sait of linning courtains on[e] pair quherof torne

Three stand of old large courtains moth eaten

Twentie two elns of allasant designed for courtains

On[e] stand of chamber hangings of cloath collaired say

Two corded bedsteds with iron rods belonging to them

Fyve old timber bedsteds with timber bottims of ane old fashion for servants

Twelve carpat chairs verrie old and worne

Ane old carpet moth eaten in the midle

Twelve new carpets for chairs

Ane old short resting carpet chear

Six old frams of chairs for servants

Ane folding table in the dyneing roume

Two old fashioned tables in the hall

Four old fashioned chamber tables

Three woolen stript table cloaths for the chamber table twelv years old and moth eaten

Two sait of fyne dornick naprie

Ane oyther sait of old round naprie

Ane lyned basket

Ane pair of virginalls with the frame they stand on

Ane hour knock with the caiss quhich stood in the hall

Seven pewtar plets and eightein trinchers all old fashioned weighing sextie two
    punds

Two old iron potts on[e] quherof riven

Ane old girdle

Ane brass morter

Ane old litle frying pan

Ane litle brander

Ane pair of standing raxed with ston[e] feit about halfe a ston[e] weight of iron

Ane iron ladle

Ane litle wheell

Two washing tubbs

Ane old litle ketle of a midle syz

Ane old heckle . . . and a pair of small cards

Two litle barrells for holding of ale

Two standing barrells or bouies for ale

Ane greatt chist and two lesser chists or girnalls for meill on[e] in the sellar and two
    in the lardner

Ane litle barrell for holding of butter

Ane frame for working of carpet

Ane pair of twisters for winding of yairne

Ane old Bible wanting leaves in the beginning

Two sermone books in octavo

In addition, there were:

A hair stuff cloak lyned with scarlet plush

A black velvet coat lyned with bloom satine

A bloom collaired tubie vest lyned with cesnet

Ane pair of frenged gloves

Ane small sword

Ane carobin

Ane fouleing peice   (Total value – £360/14/8d)

(Katherine Lauder, by then living in Dundee, had left behind):

A dressing box

A trunck or coffer with K.L the initiall letters of her name on it

A small looking glass for the chamber table quhich was for her own particular use
    (Valued at £28)

(CS181/3605 – Katherine Lauder v Mr John Mowat, advocate)

Glossary

Abefoir formerly

Abulziements clothes

Aliment provision for maintenance (noun); to give support or maintenance (verb)

Apprising judgement by a court whereby the heritable rights of a debtor were sold to offset the debts owed to the appriser

Assedation lease

Bailie executive officer of a franchise court, such as a barony; a magistrate of a burgh

Barony/Baron Court a court franchised by the Crown to a landowner who could then administer justice over the people living on his lands

Bear/Beir/Bere barley

Birlaymen (Barleymen) jury of a baron court made up of tenants who assisted in setting local disputes etc; a constable

Boll measure of grain

Bouies/Bowies small barrels open at one end

Brander gridiron

Brokit threshed

Cards/Cairds combs for dressing wool

Carobin carbine, a short light musket

Cess land tax

Cessioner one to whom an assignation has been legally made

Chalder a dry measure of grain consisting of 16 bolls

Chirurgeon surgeon

Civilist one versed in civil law

Clogged/Clagged encumbered

Codds pillows

Codwars pillow cases

Cum beneficio heir by right

Cunzeit coined

Curator person either appointed by a testator or by the Court to administer the estate of a minor

Decern to give final decree of judgement

Decreet decision of a Court

Deforce to prevent an officer of the law from executing his duty, such as delivering a
    summons

Depone to give evidence

Dispone to convey

Doit a coin worth half a farthing

Dornick linen cloth made in Tournay for table use

Exhorter reader of the common prayers and Scriptures

Factory a deed in which one party appoints another to act for him in one or more
    transaction

Faughed cleaned and then left to lie fallow

Fee full right to property in heritage, as opposed to the liferent

Ferme rent

Fiar owner of a fee, used when someone else, such as a widow, had the liferent

Fold dyke turf wall

Following a young animal following its mother, e.g. a calf

Gear movable goods

Gift of the ward grant by the Crown to another person during the minority of an heir

Girnel/Girnal granary

Goods farm animals, stock etc

Grintalman man in charge of girnal or granary

Haa house manor house

Hagbut arquebus or small hand gun

Heckle steel-toothed comb for dressing hemp and flax

Holland fine linen cloth

House-head ridge of the roof of a castle

Infeft to invest in heritable property

Insicht plenishings household goods and furniture

Intaker porter

Jack a leather-lined jerkin for purpose of defence

Knock clock

Ky cow

Last of land measure of land approximately 16 to 24 acres

Letters of four forms execution against a debtor consisting of four charges, the final
    one ordering the debtor to enter prison under pain of denunciation

Letters of Horning letters obtained by a creditor directing an officer of the law to
    charge a debtor to repay a debt

Liferent for use during the person's life only

Maill money rent

Merk worth 13/4d Scots; £1 Scots being worth 1/12th of £1 Sterling

Milne a mill

Mortified left by a deceased person for a specific cause, usually charitable

Multure corn paid to the miller of a particular mill a tenant was thirled to in payment for his grinding the rest

Nolt cattle

Non-entry failure to enter formally into possession of property, e.g. by an heir

Obligation a bond

Oxgate/Oxengate a measure of land, as much as could be ploughed by one ox, about 13 acres

Pennyland/Farthingland divisions of land in those parts of Scotland once under Norse occupation

Pistolles a coin worth ten Francs

Pleugh a ploughgate consisting of 8 oxgates

Port gateway

Poynd to impound or to sell by warrant

Rainder mended, repaired

Rix dollar silver coin worth 58/- in 1645, once current in several European countries

Roup auction

Sasine object handed over as a token of possession, originally a handful of earth and stone of the property, later a document called an instrument of sasine

Say woollen cloth made by families for their own use

Seise legal term, to put in possession of

Sequels small amounts of grain given to the servants at a mill

Serge de berie strong twilled fabric

Service of Heir judicial process whereby the ownership of land belonging to a deceased person was transmitted to the heir or whereby a person's title as heir to a deceased person was established

Shewed sewed

Spulzied plundered

Standing raxed andiron

Suckeners tenants thirled to a particular mill

Surak sorrel

Tack lease

Teind tithe, 10th part of annual produce of the land

Tenement either a building consisting of several separate dwellings or a small piece of land

Terce widow's liferent of a third part of her deceased husband's estate

Testament dative confirmed inventory of movable goods of a person who died intestate, given up by an executor appointed by the court

Thirl to bind a tenant to grind his corn at a particular mill

Tocher/Tochair dowry, usually paid a year and a day after the marriage

Tome tomb
Treisting/Trysting meeting
Tutor guardian of children during their minority
Under the Signet under the Seal of the Court of Session
Utrikement outfitting
Wadset a pledge of lands in security, recorded in a sasine containing a clause of redemption
Wheell spinning wheel
Writer lawyer
Yett gate

Abbreviations

Abn	Aberdeen
ADC	Acta Dominorum Concilia, 1478–95
ADCP	Acts of the Lords of Council in Public Affairs
B	Burgh records
C	Chancery record
CC	Commissary Court records
CH	Church records
CS	Records of the Court of Session
CR	Council Register
DI	Diligence records
E	Exchequer records
Edin App	Register of Edinburgh Apprentices
Edin Burg Roll	Roll of Edinburgh Burgesses and Guild Brethren
Edin Marr Reg	Index to Marriage Register of Edinburgh
ER	Exchequer Rolls
Fac Advoc	Faculty of Advocates
Fasti	Fasti Ecclesiae Scoticanae
GRS	General Register of Sasines
HH	Home and Health Departments
IGI	International Genealogical Index complied by the Mormon church
MI	Monumental Inscription
MSC	Miscellany of the Spalding Club
NP	Notary Protocol
NRAS	National Register of Archives Surveys
NSC	New Spalding Club
OPR	Old Parish Register
PS	Register of the Privy Seal (manuscript)
RD	Register of Deeds (Books of Council and Session)
RH	Register House series
RHP	Register House Plans
RMS	Register of the Great Seal
RPC	Register of the Privy Council

RS	Register of Sasines
RSS	Register of the Privy Seal (printed)
SC	Sheriff Court
Sh Crt Recs	Sheriff Court Records (printed)
SHS	Scottish History Society
SIG	Register of Signatures
SPC	Spalding Club
SRS	Scottish Record Society
SRO	Scottish Record Office
SN&Q	Scottish Notes and Queries
St Nich	St Nicholas
TBFC	Transactions of the Banffshire Field Club
TSC	Third Spalding Club
WS	Writer to the Signet

Bibliography

Key to manuscript sources, indexes and surveys:

Scottish Record Office:

B 45   Lanark Burgh Sasines
C 2   Retours (Inquisitionum Retornatarum Abbreviato)
CC 1   Aberdeen Commissary Court
CC 3   Brechin Commissary Court
CC 4   Caithness Commissary Court
CC 8   Edinburgh Commissary Court
CC 15   Lauder Commissary Court
CC 16   Moray Commissary Court
CC 17   Orkney and Shetland Commissary Court
CC 20   St Andrews Commissary Court
CH2/153   Fetteresso Kirk Session Records
CH2/457   Gordon Kirk Session Records
CH2/699   Longside Kirk Session Records
CH2/871   Turriff Kirk Session Records
CS 7   Acts and Decreets of the Court of Session (first series)
CS 15   Warrants of Decreets (first series)
CS 18   Acts and Decreets of the Court of Session (second series)
CS 22   Acts and Decreets of the Court of Session (second series)
CS 26   Acts and Decreets of Court of Session (second series)
CS   (all others) – mostly Unextracted Processes
DI   Diligence records – Registers of Hornings and Inhibitions
E   Exchequer Records
GD1/12   Records of Incorporation of Tailors of Edinburgh
GD 16   Airlie muniments
GD 18   Clerk of Penicuik muniments
GD 30   Shairp of Houston muniments
GD 34   Hay of Haystoun muniments
GD 33   Haddo muniments
GD 44   Gordon papers

GD 96   Mey papers

GD 105   Fetteresso papers

GD 135   Stair muniments

GD 164   Rosslyn muniments

GD 172   Henderson of Fordell muniments

GD 225   Leithhall muniments

GD 226   Trinity House of Leith muniments

GD 248   Seafield muniments

GD 305   Cromartie muniments

GD 345   Grant of Monymusk muniments

HH 11   Edinburgh and Tolbooth Warding and Liberation Books

NRAS   Inventory of Erroll charters, no.0925 Askew of Ladykirk, no.0071/1

PS 1   Register of the Privy Seal

RD 1   Register of Deeds – First Series

RD 2   Register of Deeds – Second Series – Dalrymple

RD 3   Register of Deeds – Second Series – Durie

RD 4   Register of Deeds – Second Series – Mackenzie

RD 11   Warrants of Deeds

RH 6   Calendar of Charters

RH15/37   Register House Series – Rait of Hallgreen papers

RH9/7   Miscellaneous papers – marriages contracts

RS 1   General Register of Sasines, 1617–1652

RS 2   General Register of Sasines, 1652–1660

RS 3   General Register of Sasines, from 1660

RS 4–5   Aberdeenshire Register of Sasines

RS 6   Kincardineshire Register of Sasines, first series

RS 7   Kincardineshire Register of Sasines, second series

RS 8   Aberdeenshire and Kincardineshire Register of Sasines from 1661

RS 16   Banffshire Register of Sasines

RS 18   Berwickshire Register of Sasines

RS 24–27   Edinburgh Register of Sasines

RS 35   Forfar Register of Sasines

RS 37   Inverness-shire Register of Sasines

RS 45   Orkney and Shetland Register of Sasines

RS 62   General Register of Sasines Minute Book

RS 64   Aberdeen and Kincardine Sasines Minute Book

SC1/2   Aberdeen Sheriff Court Diet Books

SC1/7   Aberdeen Sheriff Court Decreets

SC1/11   Aberdeen Sheriff Court Processes

SC1/60   Aberdeen Sheriff Court Deeds

SC1/61   Aberdeen Sheriff Court Deed Warrants
SC5/1   Stonehaven Sheriff Court Act Books
SC5/8   Stonehaven Sheriff Court Processes
SC5/58   Stonehaven Sheriff Court Deeds
SC5/62   Stonehaven Sheriff Court Minute book of Deeds
SC14/50   Caithness Sheriff Court Deeds
SIG   Register of Signatures

Aberdeen City Archives:
CRL111   Aberdeen Council Letters

Edinburgh City Archives:
Miscellaneous Papers – Moses and Macleod Indexes

Shetland Archives:
D 6 E. S. Tait Collection
D 16 Irvine of Midbrake Collection
GD 144 Bruce of Symbister muniments
Unclassified:
  Nicolson papers
In Private hands:
  Gardie House Papers
SC10   Orkney and Shetland Sheriff Court
SC12   Lerwick Sheriff Court

Old Parish Registers:
Parish of Canisbay – Caithness
Parish of Ceres – Fife
Parish of Dundee – Angus
Parish of Edinburgh
Parish of Fetteresso – Kincardineshire
Parish of Gordon – Berwickshire
Parish of St Nicholas – Aberdeen
Parish of Turriff – Aberdeenshire

Printed Primary Sources:

Acts of Lords of Council in Public Affairs 1501–1554
Exchequer Rolls (to 1600)
Register of the Great Seal (to 1668)

Register of the Privy Council (to 1691)
Register of the Privy Seal (to 1584)

Abbreviated Calendars:

Retours Inquisitionum Retornatarum Abbreviato – abridgements of Retours pre
  1700 – 3 vols
Service of Heirs – post 1700

Texts and Calendars: First number refers to volume.
Scottish Burgh Records Society:

8. Extracts from the council register of the burgh of Aberdeen, 1625–1642, ed. John
  Stuart (1871)
9. Ibid, 1643–1747 (1872)

Scottish History Society, first series:

12. The court book of the barony of Urie in Kincardineshire, 1604–1747, ed.
  Douglas Barron (1892)
36. Journals of Sir John Lauder, Lord Fountainhall, 1665–1676, ed. Donald
  Crawford (1910)
47. The Wardlaw manuscript, ed. William Mackay (1905)

Third series:

5. Papers from the collection of Sir William Fraser, ed. J R N Macphail (1924)

Scottish Record Society, old series:

26. Register of interments in the Greyfriars burying-ground, Edinburgh, 1658–
  1700, ed. Henry Paton (1902)
27. The register of the marriages for the parish of Edinburgh, 1595–1700, ed. Henry
  Paton (1905)
28. The register of apprentices of the city of Edinburgh, 1583–1666, ed. F J Grant (1906)
31. Lyon Office Genealogies – F J Grant (1908)
46. Parish of Holyroodhouse or Canongate. Register of marriages, 1564–1800, ed. F
  J Grant (1915)
48. Parish registers of Canisbay (Caithness), 1652–1666, ed. Donald Beaton (1914)
59. Roll of Edinburgh burgesses and guild-brethren, 1406–1700, ed. Charles B B
  Watson (1929)
60. Register of Edinburgh apprentices, 1666–1700, ed. Charles B B Watson (1929)
76. The Faculty of Advocates in Scotland, 1532–1943, ed. Sir F J Grant (1944)
83. Register of the burgeses of the burgh of the Canongate from the 27th June 1622
  to 25th September 1733, ed. Helen Armet (1951)

New Series:

3. Scottish parish clergy at the Reformation, 1540–1574, ed. Charles H Haws (1972)

Spalding Club:

6. The Miscellany of the Spalding Club, vol ii, ed. John Stuart (1842)

11. A breiffe narration of the services done to three ladys by Gilbert Blakhal, priest of the Scots mission in France, in the Low Countries and in Scotland, ed. John Stuart (1844)

18. A genealogical deduction of the family of Rose of Kilravock, Rev Hew Rose (1848)

21. Memorialls of the trubles in Scotland and in England, AD 1624 – AD 1645 by John Spalding, ed. John Stuart, vol i (1850)

23. Fasti Aberdonenses – Selections from the records of the University and King's College of Aberdeen, 1494–1854, ed. Cosmo Innes (1854)

30. The book of the thanes of Cawdor, ed. Cosmo Innes (1859)

Uniform with but not part of the series:

 List of pollable persons within the shire of Aberdeen, 1696 (two volumes) ed. John Stuart (1844)

New Spalding Club:

6. The Miscellany of the New Spalding Club, vol i (1890)

11. Officers and graduates of the University and King's College, Aberdeen, ed. Peter J Anderson (1893)

26. The house of Gordon, ed. John M Bulloch, vol i (1903)

28. Records of the sheriff court of Aberdeenshire, ed. David Littlejohn, vol i (1904)

31. *ibid*, vol ii (1906)

32. *ibid*, vol iii (1907)

33. The house of Gordon, vol ii (1907)

34. The Miscellany of the New Spalding Club, vol ii (1908)

40. History of the Society of Advocates in Aberdeen, ed. John A Henderson (1912)

Uniform with but not part of the series:

 Charters and other writs illustrating the history of the royal burgh of Aberdeen, ed. Peter J Anderson (1890)

Third Spalding Club:

4. The Valuation of the county of Aberdeen for the year 1667, ed. A and H Tayler (1933)

9. The House of Forbes, ed. A and H Tayler (1937)

10. The Miscellany of the Third Spalding Club, vol ii (1940)

Stair Society

16. Gillon, A (ed.) – Selected Justiciary Cases 1624–50, vol i (1953)
27. Irvine-Smith, J (ed.) – Selected Justiciary Cases 1624–1650, vol ii (1972)
36. Gouldesbrough, P – Formulary of Old Scots Legal Documents (1985)

Society of Writers to the Signet

The Register of the Society of Writers to Her Majesty's Signet (1983)

Articles:

A Forgotten Family – The Mowats of Balquholly by J Malcolm Bulloch – SN&Q, first series, xii, 91–94; 103–5;

The Kennedys of Kermuckes – SN&Q, second series, iii, 174–5; third series, v, 109–11

The Genealogy of the Hays of Rannes by William Cramond – Transactions of the Banffshire Field Club, 7 Feb 1889

A Northern Diary by Wm Barclay – Transactions of the Banffshire Field Club, 4 Mar 1930

The Ogilvies of Boyne by Alistair Tayler – Transactions of the Banffshire Field Club, 15 March 1933

The Regality of Strathisla by Mr Thomas Innes of Learney – Transactions of the Banffshire Field Club, 13 May 1935

The Mowats. Some Notes towards a Family History – John O'Groats Journal, April-June, August-September 1948

Secondary Sources:

Aberdeen Journal, Notes and Queries (Aberdeen, 1888 and 1893)

Balfour Paul, Sir James (ed.) – The Scots Peerage (Edinburgh, 1914)

Ballantyne, J H and Smith, B (ed.) – Shetland Documents, 1580–1611 (Lerwick, 1994)

Bardgett, F G – Scotland Reformed (Edinburgh 1989)

Brunton G and Haig D – Senators of the College of Justice 1532–1850 (London, 1832)

Calder, James T – Sketch of the Civil and Traditional History of Caithness (Wick, 1887)

Chambers, R – Domestic Annals of Scotland (Edinburgh, 1858)

Cockayne, G E – Complete Baronage (Exeter, 1903)

Committee of the Royal Geographical Society – The Early Maps of Scotland, vol i (Edinburgh, 1973)

Cowper, A S and Ross, I – Some Caithness Burial Grounds, Parts 8 and 9 (Edinburgh, 1987)

Dalrymple of Stair, Sir James – Decisions of the Lords of Session, (Edinburgh, 1683)

Donaldson, G – Scottish Historical Documents (Edinburgh and London, 1970)

Donaldson, G and Morpeth, R S – A Dictionary of Scottish History (Edinburgh, 1977)

Fraser, Alexander, Lord Saltoun – The Frasers of Philorth (Edinburgh, 1879)

Grant, Sir F – Zetland Family Histories (Lerwick, 1907)

Hay Denys (ed.) – Letters of James V (collected by Robert Kerr Hannay) (Edinburgh, 1958)

Hay, M V – The Blairs Papers 1603–1660 (London, 1929)

Henderson, John – Caithness Family History (Edinburgh, 1884)

Hibbert, S – Description of the Shetland Islands (Edinburgh, 1818)

Jervise, A – Epitaphs and Inscriptions (Edinburgh, 1879)

Lynch, M – Scotland, A New History (London, 1991)

Lythe, S G E – The Economy of Scotland in its European Setting, 1550–1625 (Edinburgh, 1960)

McDonnell, Frances J – Roll of Apprentices, Burgh of Aberdeen, 1700–1750 (St Andrews, 1994)

MacGibbon, D and Ross, T – The Castellated and Domestic Architecture of Scotland (Edinburgh, 1899)

Mackintosh, J – History of the Valley of the Dee (Aberdeen, 1895)

McKean, C – Banff and Buchan (Edinburgh, 1990)

Marren, P – Grampian Battlefields: The Historic Battles of North East Scotland from AD 84 to 1745 (Aberdeen, 1990)

Mitchell, A – Pre 1855 Gravestone Inscriptions of Kincardineshire (Scottish Genealogy Society, (Edinburgh, 1987)

Monteith, R – An Theater of Mortality (Edinburgh, 1704)

Munro, A M – Memorials of the aldermen, provosts and Lord provosts of Aberdeen, 1272–1895 (Aberdeen, 1879)

Pennant, T – A Tour of Scotland 1769 (Edinburgh, 1776)

Pitcairn, R – Criminal Trials in Scotland 1488–1624 (Edinburgh, 1829–31)

Register of Arms, vol 2 (Lyon Office)

Scott, H (ed.) – Fasti Ecclesiae Scoticanae (Edinburgh, 1915–1929)

Scottish Notes and Queries, 3rd series (Aberdeen, 1888–1935)

Smout, T C – A History of the Scottish People, 1560–1830 (London, 1969)

Snoddy, T G – Sir John Scot Lord Scotstarvit, His Life and Times (Edinburgh, 1968)

Stevenson, D – The Origins of Freemasonry; Scotland's Century 1590–1710 (Cambridge, 1988)

Taylor, L B – Aberdeen Council Letters (Aberdeen, 1952)

Temple, Rev W – The Thanage of Fermartyn (Aberdeen, 1894)

Warden, A J – Angus or Forfarshire (Dundee, 1882)

Whyte, D – Kirkliston, a parish history (Kirkliston, 1991)

Young, Margaret D (ed.) – The Parliaments of Scotland. (Edinburgh, 1992 and 1993)

Index of Mowats

Alexander
in Brownhill 106
of Loscraigie (c. 1433) 133
of Loscraigie (c. 1495) 133
in Redcloak (d. 1685) 74–83, 90,
102, 103, 116, 131, 150
son of Charles of Knokintebir 51
son of James of Ardo 38
son of John (d. 1633) 28, 38
writer in Edinburgh ('Saunders')
(d. 1616) 17, 24–5, 31, 67,
147
Andrew
exhorter at Turriff (1563–1567) 5,
13, 105
of Swenzie (now Swiney) 25

Barbara, sister of James who died in
Copenhagen (before 1672)
68, 114, 115
Beatrix, sister of Patrick 6, 134
Bethia, daughter of Roger (d. 1686)
89, 90, 152

Charles, of Knokintebir 51
Christian
daughter of Elizabeth and James
83, 116, 117, 131, 151
daughter of Magnus 18–19, 36,
62, 136
Christian (?Christine), daughter
of Patrick, second laird 9,
135

Elizabeth
daughter of Alexander in
Redcloak 78, 82, 83, 116,
131, 150
daughter of Roger (d. 1686) 89,
152
daughter of Thomas of Ardo 40,
53, 74, 93, 119, 146
sister of Magnus (d. 1634) 11, 31,
67, 137
sister of William (d. 1688) 96
Elspet
daughter of James in Redcloak
149
daughter of Magnus 18–19, 36,
136
sister of Magnus (d. 1634) 32
wife of Thomas Mitchell 129

George
Captain, grandson of James of
Stennes 132
of Craigfintray 110
elder (c. 1670s) 132
of Hamnavoe (d. 1710) 68, 98,
112, 115, 118, 122, 123,
139
in Loscraigie (d. 1608) 134
of Mill of Colp 105, 107
in Redcloak (d. 1645) 21, 22, 27,
102, 103
Sir, of Inglishton, of Balquholly
(d. 1666) 54–8, 60, 63, 67,

Index